Comparative criticism

25

Comparative criticism

An annual journal

Lives of the Disciplines:
comparative biography

25

Edited by

E. S. SHAFFER

SCHOOL OF ADVANCED STUDY,
UNIVERSITY OF LONDON

Edinburgh University Press

© Edinburgh University Press 2004

Edinburgh University Press
22 George Square
Edinburgh EH8 9LF

Printed and bound in Great Britain by the Cromwell Press, Trowbridge, Wilts

A CIP record of this book is available from the British Library

ISBN 0 7486 2036 2
ISSN 0144 7564

CONTENTS

ILLUSTRATIONS

CONTRIBUTORS

TIMOTHY ADÈS is a translator-poet. The sonnets won a BCLA/BCLT award and appeared in *Comparative Criticism* 19. Arc has now republished his *33 Sonnets and Other Poems* by Jean Cassou Victor Hugo's *How to be a Grandfather* is published by Hearing Eye. *Homer in Cuernavaca* by Alfonso Reyes won the Premio Valle-Inclán for the Edinburgh U.P. journal, *Translation and Literature*. He is working on a large selection of the poetry of Robert Desnos. Some of his work is on the internet at www.brindin.com.

MALCOLM BOWIE is Master of Christ's College, Cambridge, and former Marshal Foch Professor of French Literature at Oxford and Fellow of All Souls. He was the initiator of the European Humanities Research Centre in Oxford and the LEGENDA series of monographs in modern languages. His many publications include *Proust Among the Stars* (1998), books on Freud and Lacan, and articles exploring interdisciplinary aspects of the arts. He is currently President of the British Comparative Literature Association.

KATHARINE CONLEY is Associate Professor of French at Dartmouth College. She is the author of *Robert Desnos, Surrealism, and the Marvelous in Everyday Life* (The University of Nebraska Press, 2003) and of *Automatic Woman: The Representation of Woman in Surrealism* (The University of Nebraska Press, 1996).

BRIAN HARRISON has been studying, teaching and researching at Oxford since 1958. After thirty-three years as a Tutorial Fellow teaching history and politics at Corpus Christi College, he became Editor of the *Oxford Dictionary of National Biography* in 2000. He has published many books and articles on nineteenth-century British social and political history, and is writing the final volume (1951-1990) in the *New Oxford History of England*.

SCOTT MANDELBROTE is Official Fellow, Tutor for Undergraduate Admissions, and Director of Studies in History at Peterhouse,

Cambridge. He is also Fellow of All Souls College, Oxford. His publications include *The Garden, the Ark, the Tower, the Temple* (with Jim Bennett, Oxford UP 1998) and *Footprints of the Lion: Isaac Newton at Work* (Cambridge UP 2001).

MIKE MOTTRAM lives in Fife, where he cultivates his own and other people's gardens.

BEATE J. PERREY is visiting professor in musicology at the École Normale Supérieure in Paris during 2003-4, after which she will take up a Senior Lectureship at the University of Liverpool. She is the author of Schumann's *Dichterliebe and Early Romantic Poetics: Fragmentation of Desire* (Cambridge UP 2002), and editor of *The Cambridge Companion to Schumann* (Cambridge UP forthcoming) and of *Schubert after Adorno*, a volume to comprise the first English translation of Adorno's 1928 essay 'Schubert' and twelve short critical commentaries. At present she is working on a book about Schubert song cycles entitled 'Schubert Constellations'.

D. VENKAT RAO teaches in the School of Critical Humanities at the Central Institute of English and Foreign Languages, Hyderabad, India. He has publications in the areas of postcolonial studies, mnemocultures, new technologies and India studies. *In Citations: Readings in Area Studies of Culture* (Delhi, 1999), was his last publication. Apart from finalizing the translation of 'The Last Brahmin', he is nearing completion of a full-length work on critical uses of song-cultures in India (with a special focus on the continuing work of a legendary cultural-political activist).

ELINOR SHAFFER is Senior Fellow, Institute of Germanic Studies, School of Advanced Study, University of London, and Director of the Research Project on the Reception of British Authors in Europe, a multi-volume series published by Continuum Books. She is the author of a number of books and articles on Coleridge and European Romanticism, and on Samuel Butler, organizer of exhibitions on Butler's painting and photography, and Editor of *Comparative Criticism*. *William Beckford and the Visual Arts* (with John Wilton-Ely) is in preparation.

RANI SHIVASHANKARA SHARMA teaches Sanskrit in a small-town school in the Southern state of Andhra Pradesh. His literary work includes short stories, poetry, and essays in Telugu. He has written experimental, 'hybrid' poetry in collaboration with Dalit (marginalized castes of India) writers. His collection, *Vooru Vada: Samkara Kavita (Village and Street: Hybrid Poetry)* is well known in this regard. Sharma has actively participated in grass-root social movements in Andhra Pradesh.

GALIN TIHANOV holds doctorates in Bulgarian literature (Sofia, 1996) and in Comparative Literature (Oxford, 1998). He is Reader in Comparative Literature and Intellectual History at the University of Lancaster. His publications include *The Master and the Slave: Lukács, Bakhtin, and the Ideas of Their Time* (Oxford UP, 2000), two books on Bulgarian literature (1994 and 1998), and numerous articles on the history of ideas and comparative literature. He is also co-editor of *Materializing Bakhtin: The Bakhtin Circle and Social Theory* (Macmillan, 2000; with Craig Brandist), of *The Bakhtin Circle: In the Master's Absence* (Manchester UP, 2003; with D. Shepherd and C. Brandist), and guest-editor of *Russian Avant-Garde Visual Culture and Photography (1910s-1930s)*, a special issue of *History of Photography* (2000).

JANET TODD is Francis Hutcheson Professor of English at the University of Glasgow and an Honorary Fellow of Lucy Cavendish College, Cambridge. She is an authority on early women writers and her most recent books are *The Secret Life of Aphra Behn* (Andre Deutsch, 1996), *Mary Wollstonecraft: A Revolutionary Life* (Columbia UP 2000), *Rebel Daughters: Ireland in Conflict* (Viking, 2003) and an edition of the letters of Mary Wollstonecraft (Columbia UP 2003). She is General Editor of the Cambridge edition of the complete works of Jane Austen and is working on a study of the early life of Mary Shelley.

CHRISTOPHER WILEY is a doctoral student and Teaching Assistant in the Department of Music at Royal Holloway, University of London, where he is preparing a thesis entitled 'Re-writing Composers' Lives: Critical Historiography and Musical Biography'. He is the author of articles in *Music & Letters* (2004), *Dictionnaire Berlioz* (2003), *Scope* (2003) and *Virginia Woolf Bulletin* (2002). He also pursues a parallel career as a performer, principally on oboe and organ.

ACKNOWLEDGEMENTS

Grateful acknowledgments are due to Editions Gallimard in respect of the copyright of Robert Desnos' *Against the Grain* translated from the French by Timothy Adès, and George Herbert, 'What breath is it mastering me': A selection of poems translated from the Latin by Mike Mottram, have been obtained by their respective translators.

Any permissions relating to the illustrations accompanying Beate Perrey's article, 'Visual musical poetry: the feeling of Pallaksch', have been obtained by the author.

Frontispiece: *Study after Velasquez's Portrait of Pope Innocent* X, Francis Bacon, 1953. Oil on canvas, 153 × 118,1 cm. © DACS London 2003

Comparative Criticism **XXV**, pp. xv–xxix.   © 2004 Edinburgh University Press
Printed in the United Kingdom

EDITOR'S INTRODUCTION

Dances of life and death: comparative biography

As Wordsworth wrote to an aspiring biographer of Coleridge three years after the latter's death, refusing his cooperation:

I cannot bear that the Public should be made Confidants of several friendships and affections almost as soon as one or both of the partners are laid in their graves. (*Letters*, III, 442)

In these days of less scrupulous regard for privacy and propriety such a sentiment will be brushed aside (and even in 1837 the biographer proceeded to publish his work). Delicacy in this instance concealed a good deal of personal culpability. A greater degree of openness may benefit as well as harm the subject of biography (for respect for privacy often went hand in hand with censoriousness). Yet many serious questions must attach to the current vogue for biography, which appears to have followed like a frenzied tarantella or dance of death on the attempts to construct a less personal literary theory that have dominated the last thirty years. Barthes' proclaimed 'death of the author' and Foucault's 'author-factor' have dropped below the critical horizon. One of the most serious questions is how the actual achievement of the subject in his particular discipline or métier (the reason for interest) can be conveyed to an audience of non-specialists. The resort to, substitution, or invention of more entertaining or intimate aspects of the life has become all too familiar, as life-story shoulders aside the text. As in a now infamous icon, Marilyn Monroe's body is attached to Virginia Woolf's head.

 Cinematic biography is of course a special offender. A recent account by a baffled scriptwriter called upon to script a film about Ted Hughes and Sylvia Plath records the 'eureka' moment of his solution: 'I suddenly realized that when they were doing the washing up, they didn't speak in verse. From that point on, wherever possible, I cut dialogue and if I couldn't cut it I made it as banal as I could.' 'It was a love story between two giants', he enthuses. (John Brownlow, 'Who's Afraid of Sylvia Plath?',

The Guardian, Aug. 22 2003). But in what sense are they giants, once shorn of their shared poetic vocation, and stripped even of words?

Biography is often considered an English concern, though as a form it had been flourishing in Italy between 1300 and 1600, the word appearing first in English only in the 1660's, when Thomas Fuller's *History of the Worthies of England* appeared, an early dictionary of national biography, including for each county leading figures and 'memorable persons' who have 'an extraordinary (not vicious) remark upon them'. (Quoted in Ian Donaldson, 'National Biography and the Arts of Memory', in *Mapping Lives*, eds Peter France and William St. Clair, OUP for the British Academy, 2002, p. 77.)

Biography has never been considered a serious form in Germany (though practiced at the popular level). Academics and writers look down on it, and much biographical detail is provided in editions of correspondence rather than in chronicles of the life. But there are positive reasons for these attitudes, and very real German contributions to biographical writing which arise from them. The *Charakteristik*, a form notable for its succinctness, is intended to extract the significance of the life work, or to understand the life as a function of the work. One of its best practitioners was the Romantic critic Friedrich Schlegel, whose 'Lessing' is a fine example (though in fact there are several good large-scale biographies of Lessing). More fictionalized works, like the brief but immensely influential portrait of an imaginary composer, Wackenroder and Tieck's *Herzensergiessungen eines kunstliebenden Klosterbruders* (1797), 'The Outpourings of an Art-loving Monk', capture the essence of the vocation; and the Romantic novella and *Künstlerroman* or novel of the artist developed this into major works now looked on as fiction. But the portrait of the vocation, or of the discipline, bore fruit in more philosophical biography as well. A major example is the *Life of Jesus*, by David Friedrich Strauss (1835), translated into English by George Eliot, in which all the sources for the life and the meaning of the life were sifted, the fruit of more than a century of Biblical criticism. Another major biography of a discipline was produced by Wilhelm Dilthey, philosopher and critic: in writing a two-volume *Life of Schleiermacher* (1870), on the Romantic writer and religious philosopher, whose lectures on hermeneutics were then little known, he founded the history of the emergent discipline of modern hermeneutics and began its application to the diverging methods of the humanities and social sciences.

But recently there has been a surge in biography as we know it even in Germany–Michael Butler (*TLS* Apr 25 2003) points out that in the last few months substantial books have appeared on Peter Handke,

Franz Kafka, Christa Wolf, Siegfried Unseld, and Leni Riefenstahl (the first, third and last then still living) as well as major reassessments of Willy Brandt and Erich Honecker; capped by a life of the major author Günther Grass: Michael Jürgs, *Bürger Grass: Biographie eines deutschen Dichters* (Bertelsmann), Citizen Grass: Biography of a German Poet. Of these eight, half are literary writers, two are well-known east German politicians, one a reputable publisher (Unseld of Suhrkamp), and one, the unclassifiable Riefenstahl, is perhaps best called a film-maker. Now despite this increase in the number and range of biographies it is not biography as such that is gaining attention but the gradual re-emergence of German experiences that for more than half a century have been buried, glossed over, lived through with gritted teeth, suppressed and forgotten with might and main, overcome, outlived, transcended. *Vergangenheitsbewältigung*, the overcoming of the past, has entered a new phase. At least three recent books, Jörg Friedrich's *Der Brand: Deutschland im Bombenkrieg 1940–1945, The Fire: Germany in the Bombing War;* Max Sebald's posthumous *The Natural History of Destruction* (2003), on the suppression of the experiences of the last days of the war; and most of all Günther Grass's latest novel itself, on the great ship disaster, the sinking of the Wilhelm Gustloff, in which a boatload of German refugees, mainly NS supporters, fleeing from Russia in 1939, went down at sea, have opened up chapters of German suffering, especially in the bombing raids at the end of World War II and their aftermath, that have long been left undescribed yet form part of the first-hand memory and experience of still living persons now overdue for biography. Sebald, in his Zurich lectures *Luftkrieg und Literatur, Air War and Literature,* takes German writers to task for not dealing directly with these sufferings, and he pillories Albert Andersch as typical of the evasions of morality and of taste that show up evasions of truth. (This essay was added to the German edition of 1997, two more, on Jean Améry – whose *At the Mind's Limits* he approved – and Peter Weiss, to the English edition, 2003.) The general charge against German-language writers is certainly not wholly justified; but we cannot discuss it adequately here.

The point for our present purposes is that the spate of biographies is only a new phase of the displacement of biography, for it is a new phase of comment on 'the German condition', on the German (not the Jewish) Holocaust ('Der Brand', the Fire), on the overcoming of collective guilt, past and present, on a new phase of memory and forgetting. This brings one up short, for 'Holocaust' has properly seemed to refer to the fate of victims of Nazism; yet the world's history, we have increasingly come to know, has many holocausts, genocides, and democides. As Blanchot has

said, 'The disaster always takes place after having taken place.' It continues
to take place; and 'cultural memory' has become one of the themes of our
time, in and out of the academy. The studies of the trauma of defeat and
loss, both historical and current, have mounted. The individual biography
as chronicle of a life becomes, or stands for, a group experience, even a lived
myth. Only victors can afford to take their own myths as straight history,
as the English do, as 'pragmatic' and 'empirical' and 'commonsense' –
because no one has forced them to eat their words. They have not had
to say 'sorry'. Only victors can assume that the trivia of their enduring
past, the even tenor of their ways, are all of consuming interest, and
only victors can continue unperturbed to pen triumphal biographies of
the great and the good, the small and the amusingly naughty. The loser
must die, or grovel, surrender, lie, forswear, betray himself and his friends
and all he and they once stood for, in order to survive; and he must
undergo trial, conviction, punishment, penance, conversion, pardon, self-
examination, and public examination in order to reinstate himself. Only
the defeated could produce a study like Albert Speer's of himself or Gitta
Serenyi's relentless interrogation of him and his own public and private
subterfuges and evasions, his twists and turns of bad faith and conscience.
The German and English cases only highlight a general truth: history
belongs to the victors. It is of some interest that whereas the home audience
of the television series on 'The Greatest Briton' voted for Churchill, the
BBC Overseas Service audience voted for Newton. A truly comparative
form of biography (in the days of European Union and of post-colonialism)
might well be expected at least to take cognizance of a supranational
standpoint, overcoming, as with other intellectual and cultural history,
the narrowly national interest.

In this volume on the 'Lives of the Disciplines: comparative biography'
we publish a rich and diverse group of papers which shed light on
the current state of biography, and suggest some unexpected ways in
which lives may render the actual achievement of a biographee in a
particular field for a general public. The discipline itself may be a new
one, definable only through the experience and the work of the individual
under scrutiny, or it may be the achievement of the biographer to make this
emerge, as Dilthey's biography of Schleiermacher served to bring modern
hermeneutics to light. Further, comparative biography of disciplines
figuring within individual lives may yield insights that no mere chronicle
of the life could.

Brian Harrison surveys the ground from the magisterial standpoint of
the New *DNB*, or as it will be known on publication the *Oxford Dictionary*

of National Biography, of which he is General Editor, in succession to
Colin Matthew, after the latter's untimely death. The old *DNB* was a
great undertaking in national biography under the editorship of Leslie
Stephen, Virginia Woolf's father, who guided it through the first massive
edition and contributed notable entries. The New *DNB*, necessarily more
massive still (incorporating the supplements published in the intervening
century as well as recent entries), maintains the obligation to render the
lives of the nation's great and good in a manner that does justice to their
accomplishments and to the nation's credit and gain. It has scrutinized
its own criteria, as Harrison shows, and made some adjustments to allow
more space for women, and to give in some instances a less 'varnished',
Victorian account of the lives of the biographees. While a number of
entries for minor figures in the Church included in the first *DNB* have
been omitted or curtailed, the 15% of entries for women they set as an
initial target has not been met. The laudable aim of representing the
contributions of foreigners, whether or not they became British subjects,
settled permanently, visited for short or long periods, carried on trade,
or simply wrote productively from afar on British phenomena (like the
Russian who first described the practicalities of holding a democratic
election) opens a potentially large and somewhat fuzzy field of new material
which comparatists will take a particularly keen interest in. The role of
obituaries in building these entries has been highlighted recently by the
publication of four volumes of *Daily Telegraph* obituaries; so popular
did they prove, that a fifth volume was selected from the others. The
will and the obligation to show the recently dead in the best light, as an
act of homage and of respect, often of personal memorial, continues to
leave its traces on official biography, which adds the need to express the
nation's long-term, historical debt to the individual. This long view – now
lengthened by another century – may lead to a more balanced judgement,
but is still concerned to locate the positive contributions of the individual
life to the communal life. The *Oxford Dictionary of National Biography* is
official biography as practised today. It serves as a norm to set others next
to, though not as a 'gold standard'.

In early life-writing and in other traditions, the exemplary life
provides the standard. The life of the eminent person is governed by
accomplishment in a particular kind, according to the ideal definition of
that office or profession: the life of the Chinese imperial official, or of the
religious figure, or of the artist. Suetonius, with Plutarch the major Roman
writer of lives of the illustrious, explicitly embraced the logical ordering
according to criteria as against the chronological telling of the events.

(See Sergei Averintsov, 'From Biography to Hagiography', in *Mapping Lives*, 20-1.) The classical *Lives of the Artists* by Pliny the Elder lays down standard elements that have continued to be observed in constructing the lives of European artists from Vasari's pioneering *Lives of the Artists* (1550) onwards. Western religious hagiography, the Catholic *Lives of the Saints* or the Protestant Foxe's *Book of Martyrs,* has similar 'patterned' characteristics reinforced by Christian interpretations of the desirable traits.

We publish here an extraordinary contemporary version of the life of the religious figure, in 'The Last Brahmin', by Rani Shivashankara Sharma, which exhibits with great clarity the traditional attributes of a Hindu sage (marked out by his high caste status) while also displaying the challenges and tensions that in today's world threaten to undermine this vocation and its values. D. Venkat Rao has translated Sharma's work from the South Indian language Telugu and introduces the narrative of the life. The form of the traditional life has undergone changes: for there is a fictional element here, the voice of the young son of the religious sage, which is a troubled and dissenting voice. The son sees with intense pain what price is paid for the spirituality and the caste claims of the sage, and he ultimately refuses to play his appointed role, either as continuator of the tradition or as the son of his father, leaving his mother to carry out the last rites and to immolate herself as tradition demands. The biography is a tragic one, in which the traditional form of authority is destroyed by new historical conditions, and the traditional form of the biography is broken in on by outside generic conventions.

The traditional, impersonal biography treated in fictional terms has itself become a genre; the German, then Swiss novelist Hermann Hesse's novel *Glasperlenspiel* (1943), The Glass Pearl Game, translated as *Magister Ludi*, raises the dedicated life to an aesthetic form; a recent book by a young Swiss-German writer, Richard Weihe, *Meer der Tusche,* Sea of Ink (itself an honorific title for the academy of artists) takes as model the life of the historical Chinese painter, Bada Shanren, born a prince at the end of the Ming dynasty who survived into the Manchu era in the seventeenth century, and relates the traditional training of the Buddhist painter in a quiet, impersonal, unembellished style; but on closer inspection the book writes the life of the paintings that have survived, displaying the individual emerging within the highly stylized paintings. In effect, the life of the man is inferred from his paintings, and the interpreted paintings (described in the act of making) render up his inferred life, rather than the life being read into the works, as so often in vulgar biography in the West. The Romantic

Charakteristik, fictions of the lives of the artist, and the biography of the discipline set the parameters of the still flourishing genre. The narrow and precarious boundary between fiction and biography is proving a fertile ground for recent writing as for criticism.

Janet Todd, in speaking of the lives of women, in particular that of Mary Wollstonecraft, author of the *Rights of Women*, the equivalent of Paine's *Rights of Man*, and several novels as well as travels, takes another tack: what if the facts of the life seem to undermine, even to contradict the significance of the works? What if this contradiction is a threat also to the biographer, to whom this significance is all-important, both in a personal sense (as a woman looking for the pioneers of liberation) and as a biographer? She pinpoints Wollstonecraft's failed attempts at suicide, apparently prompted by abandonment by her lover (and father of her child), and accompanied by a suicide note in the style of the 'deserted woman'. This contradiction, Todd argues, is not and must not be smoothed out; and indeed became the spur to the biography she wrote. Perhaps this contradiction between the life and the works has itself become a hallmark of women's biography, for so often the work has had to be born against all the odds and carried out against opposition or disapproval, which often curtailed or crippled it. The contradiction between life and work is a condition of the production of women's works in whatever discipline. If in novel-writing women were numerous and even dominated this still despised genre for a time at the end of the eighteenth century, in music (as Christopher Wiley makes clear in his study of nineteenth-century music biographies) they were firmly relegated to the role of 'muse', even when as patently gifted as Clara Schumann. Only one woman made her way into the recent account of scientists' lives and careers in *Cambridge Scientific Minds*, which Scott Mandelbrote reviews here: Mary Cartwright (b. 1900) was the first woman to take the mathematics finals at Oxford, and the first woman mathematician to be elected to the Royal Society, for her work in differential equations. Another candidate for mention is Jocelyn Bell, the discoverer of the pulsar; but she is firmly kept in her place as a research student working for Antony Hewish, author of his own chapter on 'The Discovery of the Pulsar'. Hewish shared the Nobel Prize in Physics (1974) with his former teacher, Sir Martin Ryle. The case has been compared with the exclusion of Rosalind Franklin from credit for the discovery of DNA (though Franklin was dead and so not eligible by the time of the award of the Nobel to Crick, Watson, and Maurice Wilkins, head of the laboratory at King's College London where she had done her work on the structure of DNA). Franklin now has the dubious posthumous reward of being paired forever with Wilkins in the name of a new building at the Waterloo site of King's; and recently this recognition was crowned by an article (by a woman biographer) probing her sexuality, qualifying her as a celebrity in today's sleazy-journalistic sub-biographical media underworld. This seems the ultimate irony for a scientist whose objective, technically brilliant photographs provided the evidence of the structure of DNA and represent a permanent contribution to science conceived as an impersonal advance of knowledge. For the woman writer, nevertheless, female biography may be the means of working through the perceived contradictions and achieving a resolution, as indeed was the case for the model of such biographers, Mrs Gaskell's biography of Charlotte Brontë, her finest work. For Virginia Woolf, in order to create women's biography her father's practice in the *DNB* had to be overturned, and she did it in *Orlando*, breaking the mould through the longevity and the abrupt sex changes of the protagonist. In the life of Mary Wollstonecraft, who once said she stood up like a street sign in sodden ground, on which every passer-by kicked mud, these contradictions are manifest as markers in the long struggle for equality and in the new discipline of women's history.

Galin Tihanov in his study of the great Hungarian critic György Lukács shows very clearly the impact of political pressure on the writer during the period he spent in Soviet Russia in the Thirties and Forties; yet this is not 'biographical' in a trivial sense but a phase of the European reception of Hegel, and of Lukács's already complex intellectual engagement with the major forces affecting twentieth-century thought, from his early concern with modern drama at the turn of the century and his pre-war writings on aesthetics to his conversion to Marxism after 1914, his brilliant 1923 book on the Marxian notion of 'class consciousness', his major work on the historical and realist novel in Europe from Scott to Mann, his internecine battle with the Marxist Brecht over certain modernist texts, and his post-war aesthetics. (See the translation by Stanley Mitchell of a crucial chapter 'The Heroic Age: Hebbel to Ibsen' of the most substantial and prescient book from his pre-Marxist phase, *The Evolution of European Drama*, in *Comparative Criticism* 9, 'Cultural Perceptions and Literary Values'.) Our knowledge of the relation of Lukács to Stalin and Stalinism has taken a new turn, as the lost manuscript of Lukács's defence of his 1923 work against Stalin's criticism only recently came to light in Moscow, and has been published in English as *A Defence of 'History and Class Consciousness': tailism and the dialectic* (Verso, 2000), with an Introduction by John Rees and a Postface by Slavoj Žižek. During his Soviet period he was forced to accede to Stalin's critique. Athough he died in 1971 the very name of

Lukács still carries a political charge in Hungary and elsewhere. If these controversies have sometimes been visited by personal venom yet the issues are those of the intellectual history and political context of aesthetic and literary debate in the twentieth century. It is a testimonial to Lukács's stature that the debate continues on that level.

Malcolm Bowie's fine essay on 'Proust and the Life of Italian Painting' heads a group of papers which suggest that interdisciplinary approaches offer a fruitful mode of comparative biography. Bowie's own contributions to the interdisciplinary study of the arts, as well as to Proust criticism, are well known. The essay shows forth the significance of the paintings so often referred to in *A la recherche du temps perdu* for the production of the aesthetic value of the literary text. The life of Proust is referred to only obliquely, it is a *donnée*, already known and absorbed from George Painter, Proust's main English biographer, and Jean-Yves Tadié's detailed French biography (now available in English), and from countless pieces of minor research buried in biographical notes and queries, as well as from Proust's own *recherche*. Rather it is the life of Italian painting, from Giotto to Titian, both as understood by Proust in the art-historical optic of his time, and as interwoven in the action, the sensations and the set pieces of the novel, that is delicately laid out before us. Finally, it shows how this life in the painting of the finest chapter of European painting may in some surprising ways be enlisted in the making of the modern. The comparison of the lives of the disciplines themselves, that of painting (whose Lives have a richer and more fully theorized history than the Lives of the poets) and of literary fiction, throws light on both and finally too on Proust's life and achievement.

The fruitfulness of this interdisciplinary approach is shown also in Beate Perrey's 'Visual Musical Poetry: the Feeling of Pallaksch'. She presents three artists in different media – painting, poetry, and music – who represent the crux (extremes meet) where personal experience is rejected as unbearable and where art is forced to an incomprehensible, unshareable expressiveness: Bacon the painter; Celan the poet (and before him Hölderlin); and Kurtág the composer. Again the details of their lives, now well known, indeed in Hölderlin's case the subject of detailed scrutiny in the post-war period in order to rescue him from having been usurped by Nazi celebrations of the 'pure (German) poet', are not dwelt upon – Hölderlin's retreat into a condition called for want of a better word 'madness', Celan's suicide – but only the limit case of 'silence' which they chose as the only appropriate response to their *expérience du gouffre*, experience of the abyss. Hölderlin's influence on modern translation criteria, which have stressed the importation of the recognizably foreign and the difficult, rather than the easy assimilation into current idiom, may derive in part from these experiences; see *Comparative Criticism* volume 6, the Editor's Introduction 'Translation as Metamorphosis and Cultural Transmission', and translations of Hölderlin's critical essays on Greek tragedy by Jeremy Adler in volumes 5 and 7, as well as David Constantine's translation (in Volume 20) of a passage from Hölderlin's own translations of Sophocles, considered at the time to have bent the German language beyond recognition. Celan is central in Perrey's triptych, for he chose silence, suppression with the most rigour. Again, his biography is left aside, an unspeakable life in the shadow of his escape from his mother's fate in a labour camp. Peter Szondi's famous interpretation of a poem by Celan – based on having been in his company all during the day in Berlin on which he apparently accumulated the materials of the poem – is a sophisticated summation of the outrage that biographical criticism wreaks. Yet the paradox of electing silence as the mourning garb of suffering invites intrusion and courts over-interpretation. Perrey's (proper) concern is rather with the language, with Hölderlin's and Celan's uninterpretable word 'pallaksch', the sound of self-stifled expression itself. Finally, this probing literary critical analysis serves the musical interpretation of that sound, Kurtág's song settings of this extremity of language. Francis Bacon's paintings image the force by which the human being is pressed to this extreme utterance. Perrey suggests the life of several disciplines of the arts, each complicated and refined by the interdisciplinary reference.

The Victorian biographers of the great German composers exemplify the more mundane business of constructing a canon and dressing its members in appropriate categories of experience. As Christopher Wiley indicates, these are largely hand-me-downs from the Romantics and schemata drawn from German biographies, partially acclimatized and made over for the British public; but the Master Musicians series deserves to be better known as the musical parallel to the Men of Letters series that led to the first *DNB*, in which these schemata can also be discerned.

Our review essays point to areas in which the provision of adequate biography is problematic. Scott Mandelbrote, who has written a good deal on Newton in his seventeenth-century context and is embarking on a new biography for Yale, shows the very variable modes in which scientific achievement is conveyed, even within the covers of one book, *Cambridge Scientific Minds*. While there are many good contributions (within the limits of such a survey), most of them by those with special knowledge of the fields under discussion, there has clearly been no communal thinking on how to represent scientific thought in conjunction with biography.

The second review essay centres on one singular case, which nevertheless represents the general case of the 'outsider'. The case of William Beckford is perhaps the leading example in English of how trivial and sensationalistic biographical prurience has prevented the understanding of an outstanding writer and has even prevented the publication of his works for more than two centuries. He has been treated at best as an 'English eccentric': the stress on his fabled wealth, on scandal, on his gay associations, which have been the subject on the one hand of disapproval, ostracism and censorship from his own day to this, and on the other hand of underground celebration as a cult figure, have obscured his real contributions. Author of the minor masterpiece *Vathek*, and a number of other works still too little recognized, he made major contributions to architecture and garden design, and to the commissioning, design, and collecting of paintings, furniture and silver in Britain and the Continent from 1780 to his death in 1844. There is still no edition of his works, and no edition of his correspondence even in selection, and much has remained in manuscript. Four of the five books under review do a great deal to remedy the omissions, and even augur well for a new phase of Beckford studies. But as the fourth book, a biography, illustrates, to deal with the problems presented by those who appear to be outside the norms will take still longer: both the titillating aura of the black arts, and the censorship it invites, obscure the substantial achievements. In the present, more open climate Beckford's bisexuality should no longer present a target for either prurience or censorship. Unfortunately, it appears that both still flourish, like pop-up pornography on the information highway. Today's frenzied dance of would-be biographers on every author's living grave is retribution for the premature announcement of the 'death of the author'. It does not ensure the author's true life in the work.

The BCLA-BCLT Translation Competition has been renamed the Dryden Translation Prize, after John Dryden, the Restoration laureate, a major poet and dramatist, and the most noted translator in English letters, who also wrote the seminal essay in English on translation. It will continue to be an annual open competition, inviting literary translation from any language.

This year's First Prize, for the translation of Robert Desnos' sonnet sequence *Against the Grain* went to Timothy Adès, a well-known translator, who has contributed to *Comparative Criticism* in the past, both as prize-winner and simply as an always daring and devoted interpreter – his

Dada poem from Hans Arp's 'Black on White' appeared in Volume 2, 'Text and Reader'; his translation of Jean Cassou's *Thirty-three Sonnets of the Resistance (Trente-trois sonnets composés en secret)*, written in a Vichy prison in 1941-2, published with an introduction by Louis Aragon, won first prize in 1996 and appeared in Volume 19, 'Literary Devolution: Writing in Scotland, Ireland, Wales and England'. The translation of Cassou's *Sonnets* has now been published separately by Arc Publications, which has usefully republished a number of works that had earlier appeared in *Comparative Criticism*. Here Adès returns to the poetry of the Resistance with Desnos' fine sequence, which although the circumstances of its writing must affect our perception of it yet deliberately submerges the individual author in a celebration of a nature and a nation that must and will outlive the political circumstances of its writing. Here the act of translation turns a national celebration into a universal affirmation of resistance against oppression.

The winner of the Second Prize is Mike Mottram, who has translated George Herbert's Latin poems, from which he has a selected a group to appear here. He skilfully turns the special capacities of Latin into the special capacities of English. Herbert's English poems are little masterpieces in the Metaphysical kind, and his Latin poems deserve to be as well known. We are particularly pleased now, under the aegis of the Edinburgh University Press, long interested in translation, to be able to print the originals as well as the English renderings.

The annual Competition continues as the Dryden Translation Competition and the winning entries will be published in the autumn issue of the new BCLA journal. The winning entries, including commended entries, have also been made available on the BCLA website from 2002. Inquiries about the Dryden Translation Competition should be addressed to Jean Boase-Beier, School of Languages and Linguistics, University of East Anglia, Norwich NR4 7TJ.

The award of the prizes, together with a reading by the translators from their winning entries, will take place at the triennial Conference of the BCLA.

The BCLA Conference on 'Invention' will take place at the University of Leeds 12-15 July 2004, and the readings will form the evening programme on 13 July. For information about the Conference please consult the BCLA website or write or e-mail to the Secretary of the BCLA, Penny Brown (French Department, Manchester).

The Comparative Literature Series of the LEGENDA imprint of the EHRC (European Humanities Research Centre, Oxford) continues to flourish. Two new volumes appeared last year: Adam Czerniawski's translations of the Polish Renaissance poet Kochanowski's *Treni(Laments)* (*Comparative Criticism* published Laments 5 and 14 in volume 19 from the translation of the Laments by Seamus Heaney and Stanislaw Baranczak, together with a review by George Gömöri); and Richard Serrano, *Neither a Borrower: forging traditions in French, Chinese and Arabic Poetry* (2002). Among the recent LEGENDA titles in the national European literature lists are several comparative studies: *Word and Image Across the Arts*, eds, Antonella Braida and Giuliana Pieri; *The Anatomy of Laughter*, eds, Toby Garfitt, Edith McMorran and Jane Taylor; and Will McMorran, *The Inn and the Traveller: Digressive Topographies in the Early Modern European Novel.*

Further proposals are invited. Proposals for shorter critical studies, editions, or translations as well as for theses and monographs are welcome. Please write to any member of the Publications Committee: Professor Stephen Bann (Department of the History of Art, University of Bristol, Woodland Road, Bristol BS8 1TE), Professor Peter France (Department of French, University of Edinburgh, George Square, Edinburgh EH8 9JX), or Dr Elinor Shaffer (Institute of Germanic Studies, School of Advanced Study, University of London, 29 Russell Square, London WC1B 5DP). Orders for books may be placed with Mrs Kareni Bannister, at the European Humanities Research Centre, St Hugh's College, Oxford OX2 6LE or through its website, www.ehrc.ox.ac.uk.

Our thanks and acknowledgements in this final volume of *Comparative Criticism* in the format it has appeared in since 1979 are particularly extensive. We thank the Syndics of the Cambridge University Press, the annual journal's original publishers, for its many years of support; and we thank the Edinburgh University Press and in particular Vivian Bone and her colleagues who have assisted with so much imagination and enterprise in the initiation of the new journal *Comparative Critical Studies* in Edinburgh. This present volume completes the transition to Edinburgh University Press, and paves the way for the new journal. As announced in volume 24, the new journal will absorb both BCLA journals, *Comparative Criticism* and the house journal *New Comparison*, and will appear three times a year.

Not least, our thanks are owing to Andrea Brady, the Editorial Assistant, who has ably and deftly forwarded the production of this volume, *Comparative Criticism* 25, while helping the Editorial Committee to formulate the aims of the new journal. She has also this year been awarded her Ph. D. at Cambridge, and taken up a Lectureship in English at Brunel

University. We are happy that she will continue to play a part in the new journal.

The new journal, *Comparative Critical Studies*, will continue to feature some themed issues, translation studies and translations, plenary papers from BCLA Conferences and workshops, together with an expanded reviews section. The history and present state of comparative and interdisciplinary studies in the UK will continue to be of prime concern. Association news, the annual Bibliography of Comparative Literary Studies, specialist bibliographies, and the full texts of prize-winners and commended entries in the Dryden Translation Competition, as well as further short notices of books and periodicals will appear on the BCLA website at http://www.bcla.org and a new section reserved for members.

The inaugural issue of the new journal, to appear in February 2004, will be a double issue considering the present state of comparative literature in theory and practice and containing papers originating in the Colloquium on 'The Act of Reading and After', in honour of Wolfgang Iser, held at the Institute of Germanic Studies, University of London, in November 2001. Iser was the initiator (with Hans-Robert Jauss) of the important new critical departure of Reception Aesthetics and Reception History known as 'the Constance School', which dominated the field of reading theory and practice and whose impact was immediate and its influence continuously fruitful since the publication of the English versions of Iser's *The Implied Reader* (1974) and *The Act of Reading* (1978), only two years after the German originals. The Colloquium is one of a series of conferences, workshops and seminars on Reception Studies, organized by the Research Project on the Reception of British Authors in Europe to accompany the series of volumes *European Critical Traditions: The Reception of British Authors in Europe* (Continuum Books), of which Elinor Shaffer is the General Editor.

The first issue of *Comparative Critical Studies* assesses Iser's influence in Great Britain (often underestimated) and the long-term viability of comparative reading and reception studies. It contains a major new paper by Wolfgang Iser himself, and includes articles by Martin Swales, Richard Murphy, Elinor Shaffer, David Henry Wilson (Iser's English translator), Geert Lernout, and Robert Weninger, as well as other invited papers. It was in the heady years of the 1970's that the British Comparative Literature Association was founded, at the Conference on the Theory and Practice of Comparative Literature at the University of East Anglia, Norwich, in 1975, and with this review of the impact of Iser's work it reviews also its own history and concerns, past and present.

The new journal *Comparative Critical Studies* of the British Comparative Literature Association will appear from 2004 (three issues per year, February, June, and October) from Edinburgh University Press. It will be available to members of the Association as part of their membership subscription, and as a free-standing subscription available to institutions and individuals. Contributions and proposals are welcome, and must be in the hands of the Editorial team at least six months in advance of publication deadlines (that is, eight months before publication dates), to allow for reading by specialist referees. Write to Edinburgh University Press, 22 George Square, Edinburgh EH8 9LF for information about subscriptions to the journal; to the Treasurer of the BCLA, Dr Karen Seago (London Metropolitan University), about membership inclusive of subscription; and to Dr Andrea Brady, English Department, Brunel University (andrea.brady@brunel.ac.uk) with proposals or submissions to *Comparative Critical Studies*.

Elinor Shaffer

PART I

The lives of the disciplines: comparative biography

Comparative Criticism XXV, pp. 3–26. © 2004 Edinburgh University Press
Printed in the United Kingdom

Comparative biography and the DNB

BRIAN HARRISON

People do not usually go to the *Dictionary of National Biography* [*DNB*] for comparative biography, but to look up individuals singly and then depart. When the *Oxford Dictionary of National Biography* [*Oxford DNB*] is published on-line in 2004, however, its search facilities may tempt them to venture further in. Offering readier access to several lives involved in the same episode, it may for instance encourage users towards the insights that spring from juxtaposed perceptions of a single event.[1] Yet they will know better than to use the *Dictionary* directly for prosopographical research, except in the very limited categories where its coverage is comprehensive, for its contents reflect shifting and sometimes even capricious editorial priorities. Its articles will of course be plundered for the prosopographical research of a more sophisticated kind which also draws upon many types of source, but in such cases the individual article will again be the focus of attention.

None the less, comparison lies at the *DNB*'s heart, as its second editor Sidney Lee acknowledged when in 1896 he distinguished between 'biography' and 'national biography': far more assiduously than the individual biographer, 'the national biographer has to cultivate the judicial temper... For national biography is to a large extent... a comparative study. The national biographer has not merely to record reputations: he has to adjust them. Due degree, priority, and place are to be observed among the subjects of his commemoration'. National biography diverges in method from individual biography, he continued, 'mainly... in its superior conciseness of statement; in its avoidance of the commonplace or trivial aspects of life; in its severely judicial temper; in its comparative principle'. He likened the individual biographer to 'a painter transferring a great building to canvas', whereas the national biographer 'resembles the draftsman of an architectural elevation'.[2] It was a bogus and rather pretentious distinction because every biographer, like every purchaser of biographies, makes comparative judgements of this kind. Their decision to write or purchase this biography rather than that reflects a judgement about the subject's relative importance. But whereas the biographer can inflate a subject's importance and the customer can buy whatever biography he chooses, the editor of a biographical dictionary enjoys no such freedom. What was distinctive about 'national biography' before the age of on-line publishing was its rigorous search for a match between a subject's importance and the allocation of space, and Lee when returning to the theme in 1911 rightly identified 'indulgence in rhetoric, voluble enthusiasm, emotion, loquacious sentiment' as 'for the national biographer the deadliest of sins'.[3]

The *DNB*'s first editor Leslie Stephen had to select 29,120 biographical subjects and co-subjects from a very much larger number, and then weigh up their relative importance. In launching its successor, the *Oxford DNB*, after 1992 Colin Matthew had also to take into account the 7,500 subjects in the twentieth-century supplements together with those from all periods whom Christine Nicholls included in her *Missing Persons* (1993), to which he added a further 13,500 from all periods. A sense of proportion was essential in the *DNB*'s editors. Lee said of Stephen that 'his wide reading, his catholic interests in literary effort, his tolerant spirit, his sanity of judgment, and his sense of fairness, admirably fitted him for the direction of an enterprise in which many conflicting points of view are entitled to find expression'. Lee claimed that 'both in his philosophical and especially in his literary judgments there was an equability of temper which preserved him from excesses of condemnation or eulogy'.[4] Yet there was one sphere in which Stephen lacked balance: he confessed that Lee was 'always calm and confident when I was tearing my hair over the delay of some article urgently required for the timely production of our next volume, always ready to undertake any amount of thankless drudgery'.[5] Fixed office-hours and meticulous proof-reading jarred with Stephen's temperament, his health suffered, and after nine years as editor he demitted office to Lee. Yet in the view of the Oxford University Press [OUP] Lee's balance, too, was circumscribed, though in a different respect. For in editing the first of the *DNB*'s decennial supplements – published by Smith, Elder in 1912 – the OUP thought he had so relaxed the criteria for inclusion that the second decennial supplement would need to be cut back drastically. This was the first such supplement entrusted to the OUP, and its preparation occasioned the fiercest and most public dispute in the *DNB*'s history.[6]

The formidable problems the *DNB*'s editors faced can be clarified by distinguishing between five levels of decision on priorities: on the

Dictionary's overall scope, its balance between subject areas, its selection of people to include, its allocation of word-length to each, and its priorities within the individual article. Each of these will be discussed in turn.

I

Matthew likened the *DNB*'s failure formally to specify its criteria on inclusion to the idea that British stamps needed only the Queen's head and no national label: 'the *DNB* asserted nationality but carefully avoided defining it'.[7] Its geographical scope was by present-day standards inclusive on Ireland: as a Liberal Unionist' Stephen did not envisage and would certainly not have welcomed the twentieth century's Irish north/south divide. In 1900 the *DNB* proclaimed its inclusion of 'all men and women of British or Irish race who have achieved any reasonable measure of distinction in any walk of life'. Lee felt that the principle determining admission had been 'from all points of view generously interpreted', so that 'the epithet 'national' has not been held to exclude the early settlers in America, or natives of these islands who have gained distinction in foreign countries, or persons of foreign birth who have achieved eminence in this country'.[8]

After 1919 the political boundaries of empire contracted while the population and wealth of its increasingly independent components expanded, and already by 1927 the selection committee had unanimously decided to omit Indian ruling princes and native politicians from the supplement for 1922-30. Yet H. W. C. Davis, co-editor of the previous supplement, predicted difficulties 'if a native became a Viceroy'. R. W. Chapman (Secretary to the Delegates of the OUP from 1920 to 1942) felt that 'we ought to ponder deeply before we commit ourselves to a colour-bar. It suggests the policy of George III'. In 1930 he told J. R. H. Weaver, who edited the supplement for 1922-30, that 'we at least shall have to go on including Indians on their merits, though we may be creating a difficult precedent for posterity. If Gandhi ever dies, I think we shall have to put him in'.[9] By April 1947 even the historian of empire Reginald Coupland reportedly wanted future supplements to exclude 'purely Empire figures. Now that the Dominions are separate nations, a Dictionary of National Biography published in Britain seems not to be the place for purely Dominion biographies'.[10] In October the OUP decided that for all supplements from 1941-50 onwards 'Imperial worthies outside the British Isles should not be included. Qualification for inclusion should be British Citizenship by birth in the British Isles or by naturalization, or by virtual naturalization as a general rule'.[11] This for some reason did not exclude three Canadian prime ministers and one Australian from the supplement for 1971–80. However, when in 1991 Nicholls was compiling her *Missing Persons* (1993), which supplemented all periods in the *Dictionary*, she explained that 'increasingly, nationals of former dependent British countries, now in the Commonwealth, are not included in the DNB because their countries have achieved independence. Several of these countries now have their own dictionaries of biography'.[12]

As for 'people who have spent the major part of their working lives in Britain', she thought that they could 'be considered for entry, whether or not they assumed British nationality'.[13] Here she was perpetuating the inclusive policy towards immigrants that had been predictable from a Liberal such as the *DNB*'s first editor; the original dictionary had begun with the French name Abbadie and had ended with the Dutch name Zuylestein. Globalization did not begin yesterday, and for periods when national boundaries were in flux the *DNB* inevitably included many people whom we would now see as in some sense international. It was not simply a matter of catering for the many occupations – scholars, artists, soldier-mercenaries, craftsmen – that crossed national boundaries, but of acknowledging the waves of Protestant and Jewish refugees from oppressive regimes.[14] They needed no positive discrimination: merit alone sufficed. Often with only their wits, skills, energy and alertness to cultural contrast to draw upon – refugees had every incentive to personal achievement. As for economic migrants, the *Oxford DNB* will also include several 'New Commonwealth' immigrants influential in Britain, but the group's full significance will emerge only later, given that only the deceased are included, whereas immigrants are relatively young. Matthew also aimed to include more people born abroad who spent a significant part of their lives in Britain, important non-British commentators on British life, Britons living abroad whose role outside Britain was significant, and more pre-Independence Americans. More than a tenth of the *Oxford DNB*'s subjects were born outside the British Isles.

Within the United Kingdom, the *Oxford DNB* is less centralist than the *DNB*, whose selection of subjects reflected its origin in literary London. In its medieval articles, for example, aristocrats were judged 'by their relations with the crown, largely ignoring their dealings with their fellow magnates or with the retainers without whom they were no use to the king or anyone else'. Likewise bishops were viewed 'as actual or potential civil servants, hardly ever as diocesans or pastors'.[15] The

Oxford DNB has corrected this not only within individual articles, but by supplying articles on families drawn from many localities, including sixteenth-century families in the Highlands and islands. In the seventeenth century, too, the number of 'provincial' figures has been reinforced. Volunteered suggestions from the public after 2004 and on-line linkages with local biographical databases will no doubt carry this decentralizing trend further.

The editors needed to determine time-span as well as geography. The *DNB*'s earliest entry was on Loegaire Lorc, tentatively [mis-]dated to c.590BC, but for some reason the Romans received little attention. Surprising omissions were Agricola, Constantine the Great (born at York) and Septimius Severus (who died there), yet Carausius was included even though not born in Britain. Less than a fifth of the *DNB*'s lives date from before the seventeenth century, whereas the seventeenth and eighteenth centuries each account for another fifth, and the nineteenth century for more than two fifths.[16] Lee pointed to the 'notable bound' in the sixteenth century in the numbers included, with a continued advance in the seventeenth century, a very slow increase in the eighteenth, and a resumed rapid rise in the nineteenth.[17] Apart from availability of evidence, which helps to explain the nineteenth-century boom, his explanation for these variations combined demographic with cultural factors. If the editor had successfully equalized between the centuries the chances of getting into the *Dictionary*, population and number of articles would rise together. Population increase might help to explain the sixteenth- and seventeenth-century upsurge, but not its arrest in the eighteenth. There Lee's hypothesis relied upon 'the absence of such stupendous crises in our national history as offered exceptionally extended opportunities of distinction to the sixteenth and seventeenth centuries'[18]; political, social or economic instability may accelerate a century's turnover of talent and so expose more of it. Yet even here, historiographical influences may impinge, given that the seventeenth-century revolutions specially interested the Victorians. The distinguished historians S. R. Gardiner and C. H. Firth were much involved in the *DNB*, and deductions drawn from statistical analyses of the *DNB*'s content should always bear shifting editorial policy in mind.[19] Yet the same weighting by period pervades the *Oxford DNB*, which includes new lives in all centuries. In dictionaries new and old the numbers included who died in each quarter-century rise steadily up to the end of the seventeenth century, then decline until 1750, and then rise slowly to 1775, when there begins that steep rise which persists for another century. The *DNB* then reached a plateau which the *Oxford DNB* now pushes forward throughout the twentieth century. As the twentieth century falls into perspective, the twenty-first century may well edge the nineteenth-century's steeply-rising curve further forward.

In the first decennial supplement (for 1901-11) – the last among Smith, Elder's *DNB* publications – Lee aimed to hold admission to late-Victorian levels, but in August 1917 he envisaged some future relaxation to accommodate First-World-War deaths. The Smith family gave the *DNB* to the University in 1917, and the second decennial supplement (1912-21) was the OUP's first. Lee viewed the OUP's policy on inclusion as 'a matter of urgent national, or rather imperial, concern': it was 'a national duty' to ensure that memorable lives among those killed should not oust deserving non-combatant people who would on earlier *DNB* criteria have got in.[20] A. F. Pollard, consulted by the OUP in March 1921, admitted that 'it is painful to speak' about friends killed in the war, but felt that the offspring of the famous could not be included simply because they had died, for this would have multiplied 'ten-fold our biographies of men who fell in previous wars'.[21] In the outcome, the famous wartime casualties – Julian Grenfell, Rupert Brooke, Elsie Inglis – went in, but Wilfred Owen remained a 'missing person' till 1993.

Chapman told Davis in 1919 that the OUP felt 'sadly embarrassed' by the sheer scale of Lee's supplement for 1901-11, and hoped that some minor lives could henceforth be consigned to *Who Was Who*, whose first volume (for 1897-1916) appeared in 1920.[22] Chapman also noted that the nineteenth-century peak for inclusion had been the 1870s, and that Stephen and Lee had cut down the annual rate of admission for the 1890s to 113, as compared with the average of 133 for the century as a whole. Instead of continuing this downward trend, however, Lee in the supplement for 1901-11 had (according to Chapman) pushed it up beyond 160.[23] Chapman's eagerness to reverse this trend in the forthcoming supplement for 1912-21 also reflected his private conviction that this decade was 'an age of mediocrity', but Humphrey Milford (Publisher to the University 1913-45) thought that to say this in the volume's preface would be 'too dangerous, I timidly submit'.[24]

In the outcome, the OUP applied a drastic squeeze, the average annual number of subjects in its supplements (1911-90) being only 78. This stringency was relaxed a little after the 1912-21 supplement, but later supplements never even approached Stephen's inclusiveness for most nineteenth-century decades. Furthermore, the length of articles was also squeezed. Chapman in February 1921 told Bishop Strong about the policy of publishing only short articles on well-known but (as he thought) unimportant people like Nurse Cavell: 'the trouble about Edith Cavell is that future students of the War (and visitors to Trafalgar Square) will ask Who *was* this woman and why was such a fuss made about her? We have sought to get over the difficulty – not to our complete satisfaction, but it's an imperfect world – by the plan of 20-30 line lives for notorious but essentially unimportant persons'.[25] Whereas Lee had put 1600 people in the supplement for 1901-11, Davis and Weaver put only 437 into its successor. After 1992 it became clear that the *Oxford DNB* must repair this damage, so throughout the twentieth-century decades its proportion of new lives to old exceeds that for any other century. Add to that the 1800 among the 13,500 new lives in the *Oxford DNB* who died after 31 December 1990 and before 1 January 2001, for whom there has been no supplement – and the proportion of the new dictionary's new subjects for each quarter-century is highest of all between 1975 and 2000. Yet the *Oxford DNB* will never be up-to-the-minute while it includes only the deceased; 96% of its 1800 recruits from the 1990s were born in or before 1939. Such an interval provides protection against both hasty memoirs lacking in perspective and against unduly advertising the confected and ephemeral public career – that is, notoriety as distinct from influence, whether for good or ill. Yet the *Dictionary* cannot entirely exclude the notorious, for it is revealing in all periods to know who gains notoriety and how. As the OUP acknowledged in 1921 when announcing the supplement for 1912-21, 'the Delegates have... not forgotten that notoriety however gained has a degree of permanence'.[26]

II

With geographical and chronological allocations decided, the *DNB*'s editors had to allocate space between areas of British life. Lee claimed that 'no sphere of activity has been consciously overlooked. Niches have been found for sportsmen and leaders of society who have commanded public attention. Malefactors whose crimes excite a permanent interest have received hardly less attention than benefactors', and 'great pains have been bestowed on the names of less widely acknowledged importance'.[27] The *DNB* was, says Matthew, 'dramatically eclectic' in its coverage, including categories of subject which in the 1880s had not yet interested historians: 'particularly sportspeople, murderers, journalists, actors and actresses, deviant clergymen, transvestites, fat men, old women', and giving 'a close attention to agnostics and secularists'. Stephen, he continues, 'disliked the concept of absolute worth as a criterion for inclusion, sensibly preferring utility, interest, readers' demand, variety of coverage, spice, liveliness and individuality'.[28] Bibliographic sources greatly influenced inclusion. The distinguished Tudor historian A. F. Pollard, assistant editor to Lee from 1893 to 1901, said that Lee's first question when any name came up was almost invariably 'what did he write?'.[29] Being listed as an author by the medieval antiquaries John Leland and John Bale greatly improved one's chances, just as later subjects benefited from their showing in the British Museum Library's catalogue.[30] Stephen included so many minor clergy because he thought anyone who had written ten books qualified for entry, and Victorian clerics tended to publish their sermons.[31]

The twentieth-century supplements saw significant changes in subject-balance: diminishing space for heads of state, scholars, clergy, writers, artists and the armed services, but growing allocation for politicians, businessmen, scientists and technologists. Given the *DNB*'s entrepreneurial origins and the contemporaneous world impact of British industry and commerce, the scarcity of businessmen there is at first sight surprising. But for the Victorians, private money-making carried lower status than the more disinterested outlook that they associated with public life, nor were economic historians yet marshalled on the other side. Already by 1921 Chapman was seeking help from Sir Guy Granet – Chairman of the London, Midland and Scottish Railway – in selecting business subjects that could boost the *DNB*'s coverage of this sphere.[32] Yet in 1950 Lewis Namier could still wryly note that 'there were many biographies of William Beckford Jnr., but few of William Beckford, Snr. Merchant and city-leader...it was so much easier to write about someone who has written. More difficult to find material for 'economic' persons'.[33] Prompted by the publication of F. W. Winterbotham's *The Ultra Secret* (1974), and with much help from Dick White, the supplement for 1961-70 (1981) opened up the neglected area of intelligence, and shed light on Bletchley's counter-espionage work in the Second World War. The supplement for 1971-80 went further, braving criticism for including John Lennon, the Beatle, and its successor for 1981-85 featured the glamorous actress Diana Dors ('vulgar she may have been but there was admiration for her courage and tenacity').[34] When Nicholls came to edit *Missing Persons*, she took some pride at including (among others) more businessmen, more women, people such as Gerard Manley Hopkins who had been neglected because their fame was only posthumous, and 64 engineers, a category that had earlier been neglected.[35]

By including new subjects in all periods *Missing Persons* blazed the trail for the *Oxford DNB*, and within the OUP it was seen as doing so. On women it was also in the van: the supplement for 1931-40 (1949) had leapt forward to a new plateau in the number of both women subjects and women contributors, and *Missing Persons* did the same again, women taking up an eighth of its articles and a fifth of its contributors.[36] A quarter of the new subjects in the *Oxford DNB* are female, raising the proportion in the *Dictionary* as a whole from 4% to 10%. This advance was obtained partly by looking for activities hitherto neglected where women were prominent: as political hostesses, for example, and as voluntary workers. And to redefine public life to include women's indirect influence, and to broaden coverage of cultural life to highlight performers as well as to composers and dramatists, is to marshal more female candidates for selection. As for the future, to the extent that the separation of spheres ceases to reflect gender relations and more women classify themselves as eligible for public life, their proportion in the *Dictionary* will rise. More than half the *Oxford DNB*'s 5588 female subjects died between 1901 and 2000, and women contribute nearly a quarter of the 1800 newly-added subjects who died in the 1990s. Given the continuing weight of earlier attitudes to women, however, and given the decision to include in the *Oxford DNB* all the *DNB*'s subjects, it is difficult to see how the *Oxford DNB* can or even should seek to include equal numbers of men and women.

The *Oxford DNB* sees itself as reaching across the *DNB*'s earlier supplements, which came near to becoming an extension of *Who's Who*, so as to resume Stephen's inclusive and liberal policy. A. F. Pollard even suspected that the OUP's new regime was importing an Oxford bias. Discussing in 1921 the inclusion of R. W. Raper, Fellow of Trinity, in the supplement for 1912-21, Pollard asked 'isn't Raper's inclusion due to local affection? Would a similar Cambridge don have stood a chance? *That* is a serious danger, which, I think, is also illustrated by a comparison between the young Oxford and young Cambridge victims of the war'.[37] As we have seen, the later supplements and *Missing Persons* became broader, and among the priorities of the *Oxford DNB*, impact and influence have moved up by comparison with merit as conventionally measured. The way is now left open for criminals as well as for prime ministers, for the enemies of the state as well as for its friends – for John Chilembwe, leader of the Nyasaland rising of 1915, as well as for Cecil Rhodes. To quote Matthew's plan of 1993 for the *Oxford DNB*: 'the use of the *DNB* as a sort of establishment roll-call of national pre-eminence is recent and in my view undesirable', whereas the new dictionary should 'return to the integrationalist approach of the original edition. . . We seek today to reflect in our extra entries the incorporation of areas of historical interest and significance which have developed since the 1880s'.[38]

In allocating between and within subject areas the *Oxford DNB* enlisted the help of 13 consultant editors and about 400 associate editors, not to mention the research editors working in-house. But their decisions will have no more permanence than Stephen's or Lee's, because with society's changing preoccupations come new demands on historians. Business and commerce moved up within the inter-war supplements at the same time as economic history became the vogue; recreation and cultural life advanced in the post-war supplements concomitantly with the growth of social and cultural history. Change continues, if only because for modern subjects the earliest stage in the *DNB*'s selection process is the newspaper obituary, and the balance among them reflects the changing tastes of the newspaper's readership. In the *Oxford DNB* these trends have also had retrospective impact. The late twentieth century's preoccupation with women considerably influenced its nineteenth-century priorities, and for similar reasons Anglo-American themes – merchants, slaves brought to Britain – moved up in its eighteenth-century coverage, as did the dancing masters, musicians and minor actors so integral to that century's vibrant cultural life. Again, seventeenth-century coverage of music has been amplified, especially with string players and others to set beside the organists so beloved of Victorians.[39] Two factors none the less circumscribe the editor's responsiveness to the pressures of the time. First, the *DNB* publishes articles only on the dead, whose careers usually reflect the priorities of an earlier period. But second, Matthew rightly decided to include all the *DNB*'s subjects in the *Oxford DNB* – all those lesser-ranking Victorian clergymen whom we would probably have omitted if starting afresh.

III

Who then should be included within each subject area? Publishing quarterly from 1885, beginning with A and ending with Z, Stephen and Lee were more constrained by early decisions than Matthew, whose plan was to publish the entire work only after all the articles had been written. They compiled lists of potential subjects sorted by initial letter from 'all names that had hitherto been treated in independent works of biography, in general dictionaries, in collections of lives of prominent members of various classes of the community, and in obituary notices in the leading journals and periodicals', supplemented by 'a survey of the most miscellaneous records and reports of human effort'. Stephen circulated the list for letter A in January 1883 'to persons – most of them being specialists of literary experience – who it was believed would be willing and competent to write articles'.[40] The second list, on Baalun-Beechey, appeared in the literary weekly, the *Athenaeum*, which had a good circulation and was for the Late-Victorian literary and antiquarian world what the *Times Literary Supplement* is now, but with a stronger scientific emphasis. Thereafter, until Z was reached, its readers were invited to improve the lists, periodically published. This presumably they did, because the *DNB* omitted many listed names and included many that had not been listed.[41] Lee could justifiably claim in 1900 that 'a detailed history of the enterprise is needless, for it has been conducted in the full light of day'.[42]

Less so the twentieth-century supplement regime. In 1932 Chapman told Bruce Richmond, Editor of the *Times Literary Supplement*, that an equivalent of the *Athenaeum* system was not needed because 'when it is mainly a matter of selection from the obituaries of a decade, there is no appeal to the learned'.[43] The supplements' editors up to and including E. T. Williams were advised by scientific and other specialists to whom lists were sent, and by a committee whose pleasant proceedings, to judge from surviving correspondence, combined intellectual sociability with somewhat jovially exercising the power that flows from dividing the sheep from the goats. They included representatives of the Press and a handful of Oxford scholars drawn from a broad range of the humanities. In March 1921 Bishop Strong facetiously suggested that the committee might appropriately meet in the dark room to which a cataract operation had temporarily confined him: 'there would indeed be a certain fitness – a body of conspirators meeting in the dark, like the murderers of Becket, who met in the dark at Saltwood Castle'.[44] Inviting R. C. K. Ensor to attend in December 1939, Chapman explained that J. R. H. Weaver, the Editor, 'arranges a little dinner. . . in Trinity and after dinner we fall to in his Lodgings. I hope you will join the dance'.[45]

Williams eventually dispensed with the committee, which he found unhelpful, and Nicholls (who edited or co-edited the *DNB*'s four latest supplements) rendered the list system universal. She combined scrutiny of obituaries in the national press with a trawl through *Who's Who* and wide reading, put the accumulated information into 28 categories, and compiled lists for the five or six people who advised within each category.[46] When it came to compiling *Missing Persons* (1993), she was advised by four Oxford-based historians, meeting initially in a more serious-minded variant of the earlier post-prandial committee, but gravitating later to reaching decisions with its members one-to-one. She also revived the extensive public consultation promoted by Stephen and Lee: her letters to academic journals and the quality press evoked far more suggestions than the 1086 names included.[47] Matthew carried this process further after 1992 when planning what became the *Oxford DNB*. His editorial decisions were informed by the many thousands of replies received in response to questionnaires distributed through societies, universities, and other interested groups, as well as to individuals. This information supplemented the corrections and suggestions which had long been accumulating at the Institute of Historical Research and with the editors of the later supplements. Suggestions flowed into the *Oxford DNB* from many other places too: from every level of Matthew's editorial hierarchy (from editor to consultant editors to associate editors to research editors), as well as from members of the general public. Whereas Nicholls needed only four consultant editors for *Missing Persons*, Matthew appointed twelve, in addition to his own role as consultant editor for the nineteenth- and twentieth-century areas. Nicholls even kept a file on self-proposals for entry. Presumptuous at first sight, such self-proposals were in one way sensible, for in the ideal world the *Dictionary* would without being influenced by self-proposals in its policy on inclusion, identify 'inevitable subjects' in advance of their death, and would quietly collect significant information about them.

IV

The decision on how much space to assign each selected individual is circumscribed by such factors as the subject's longevity, period of salience in any sphere, number of spheres of influence, number of items published, and number of opportunities for influence emerging during a lifetime. Nor is there any necessary correlation between a subject's importance and the length of the subject's article; as Matthew pointed out, 'there are some significant subjects about which there is not a great deal to be said: they may have had simple careers/lives, and held few offices'.[48] But here too objectivity is elusive, and the *DNB* has responded to shifts in British society. Saints and scholars, soldiers and statesmen go in and out of fashion, attitudes change on the individual's capacity for influence, and in any one generation each expert is tempted to inflate the importance of his specialism. Allocation of space was 'one of the greatest difficulties we experienced', George Smith recalled, because the specialist consulted was 'always tempted to over-estimate the importance of his own particular department... It needed the cool and balanced judgment of the editor, to adjust the relative scale of the articles, and the process was not always either easy or pleasant'.[49]

Leslie Stephen admired Thomas Carlyle, but by no means all Victorians shared Carlyle's 'idolatry of great men', as the *British Quarterly Review* described it in 1849: the aim should rather be 'to diminish the power of great men as far as possible, by endeavouring to diffuse as much greatness as may be through society at large' because such idolatry tends 'to perpetuate in humanity generally a feeling of dependence, helplessness, and despair'.[50] In their attitudes to the individual's role in history, Victorian radicals and dissenters were torn between on the one hand a self-helping individualism which emphasized how much the individual could achieve, and on the other hand a faith in reason and participation which implied achievement of a collective kind. Belief in the impact of the great man, like belief in the direct intervention of the Almighty in human affairs, were for Herbert Spencer primitive sentiments: they failed to acknowledge that 'the genesis of the great man depends on the long series of complex influences which has produced the race in which he appears, and the social state into which that race has slowly grown'.[51] Luther, Wilberforce and Grey of the Reform Bill, said Buckle, 'are only to be regarded as tools by which that work was done which the force and accumulation of preceding circumstances had determined should be done'.[52]

Debates of this kind inevitably moulded the *DNB*'s allocations of space. Stephen, despite his respect for Carlyle, had no inflated view of the individual's distinctive impact. In 1884 he pointed out that the 'most valuable articles' concerned 'secondrate people, who are not very conspicuous but precisely the kind of people for whom one searches in a biographical dictionary'.[53] As for the major literary figures, on whom he wrote such influential articles, he was so alert to the impact of social context on individual achievement that some see him as pioneering the sociology of literature.[54] 'Had I succeeded in my most ambitious dreams and surpassed all my contemporaries in my own line, what should I have done?', he asked towards the end of his life. 'I should have written a book or two which would have been admired by my own and perhaps the next generation. They would have survived... because they would have expressed a little better than other books thoughts which were fermenting in the minds of thousands... even the best thinkers become obsolete in a brief time'.[55] Even without this initial standpoint, working with the

DNB might well have inculcated such a view. In 1912 his successor noted how the *Dictionary* seemed in some sense to level its subjects, housing under its capacious roof the fiercest competing controversialists, the most bitterly warring politicians: 'Lord Kelvin now meets on the same plane in the Dictionary all the fellow-workers of smaller fame, whose early co-operation helped on the triumphant discoveries of his later life.... Achievement of whatever colour, magnitude, or epoch is measured by a single historic standard, and reduced to a common denominator'.[56]

The *DNB*'s transfer to Oxford in 1917, however, introduced the inegalitarian influence of the examination schools. 'There are really, as I see it, three classes', Chapman told Edmund Gosse in 1921: '(1) Olympians, Kitchener, Henry James, Cromer, Parry; (2) eminent persons: George Wyndham, Andrew Lang, Speaker Peel, Bywater, Redmond; (3) Minors, to be summed up in a few sentences'.[57] The circular sent to the supplement's contributors in that year distinguished between 'supermen' (4–6 pages), alphas (2 pages), betas (one page) and gammas (half a page).[58] A somewhat facetious tone pervaded the selection committee, and there were links with the *Times* obituaries department. Elsewhere, however, a very different tendency was building up among inter-war British intellectuals, strongly influenced as they often were by Freud and Marx, both of whom from different directions brought down the mighty from their pedestals. Such influences in diluted form no doubt helped to mould the outlook on biography taken by the daughter of the first editor: Virginia Woolf. Discussing biography in 1939, she asked 'whether the lives of great men only should be recorded. Is not anyone who has lived a life, and left a record of that life, worthy of biography – the failures as well as the successes, the humble as well as the illustrious? And what is greatness? And what smallness?'. The biographer, she felt, 'must revise our standards of merit and set up new heroes for our admiration'.[59] From Bloomsbury's inter-war reaction against chauvinism and hero-worship to the sixties' revival of women's biography and pursuit of 'oral history', the journey was short.

By the 1990s fashions were changing again. The careers of General de Gaulle and Thatcher, and the way the cold war had ended, reminded scholars how forcibly individuals can mould events, though the fashion did not go so far as to revive the earlier distinction between 'men' and 'great men'. A more important change in the 1990s lay in the perceived relationship between greatness and fame. Whereas Woolf's generation had questioned conventional notions of heroism and had proposed new candidates for commemoration, the 1990s increasingly blurred the distinction between fame and notoriety, and to its media the earlier notions of privacy and reticence seemed merely quaint. Media figures and sports personalities were prominent among the hundred 'Great Britons' advertised on BBC television in 2002, and the chances of inclusion for more traditional types of 'great Briton' were greatly enhanced if they too had featured on the screen: Henry II because of 'The Lion in Winter', and Edward I because of 'Braveheart'.[60] As Daniel Johnson pointed out, 'the contemporary notion of 'celebrity' seems to have left people genuinely confused about what greatness is. Many perhaps suppose that to be great is the same as to be famous'.[61] In such circumstances Millicent Garrett Fawcett, for example – rationalistic leader for decades of the non-militant suffrage movement – had little chance of worsting her histrionic rival, Emmeline Pankhurst, leader of the much smaller and more ephemeral but relatively flamboyant militant movement. 'The difficulty of this job', wrote Ray Strachey, writing Fawcett's life in 1930, 'is that nothing sensational remained so in her atmosphere. It was all level and quiet and eminently reasonable'. Reviewing the book in the following year, Vera Brittain exclaimed that 'the reader longs almost with desperation for... Dame Millicent to burst the bonds of her habitual commonsense and moderation, and exhibit unreasonable passion on any subject whatsoever'.[62]

In scaling down the longest entries in the *Oxford DNB*, Matthew's impulse was more practical than ideological. The *DNB*'s really long articles, he noted, reflected three situations long gone: the monarch's biography was no longer seen as a vehicle for chronicling events during a reign, the OUP did not need to offset the *DNB*'s costs by creating lives long enough to sell separately as books (as Lee had done with Shakespeare and Queen Victoria), and scholarly biographies now existed of those on whom the *DNB* had lavished space.[63] Furthermore Matthew, like his predecessors, could in allocating space be seduced into treating a well-written and perceptive article less austerely than an article that was ill-written and pedestrian.

V

The editors enjoyed less control over priorities within the individual article than in the four types of decision so far discussed, if only because most articles were written by outside contributors. Because the user needs to find the desired article quickly, first paragraphs in *DNB* and *Oxford DNB* articles are relatively formulaic. Nor can the biographer's approach be capricious, whimsical or glancing: each article must focus firmly on the subject, and must provide standard types of information where available. The life must also be well rounded and quickly intelligible, which usually means a chronological framework. Within these limits, however, contributors enjoy considerable discretion; freedom makes for creativity and stylishness, and each generation has its own biographical priorities. As Woolf pointed out, biographers 'are subject to changes of opinion... What was thought a sin is now known, by the light of facts won for us by the psychologists, to be perhaps a misfortune; perhaps a curiosity, perhaps neither one nor the other, but a trifling foible of no great importance one way or the other. The accent on sex has changed within living memory'.[64]

Unanimity is lacking even about which periods in a person's life are important. Havelock Ellis, studying British genius in the 1890s, wrote 'An Open Letter to Biographers' complaining that 'you do not... tell me a fair portion of the things I desire to know... You do tell me a great many things that I have no desire to know'. Ellis's eugenic and psychological ideas convinced him that 'the fate of all of us is in large measure sealed at the moment we leave the womb', so he sought full details on the hero's conception, birth and early upbringing. After the age of thirty 'what is there further left to tell? The rest is but the liberation of a mighty spring, the slow running down of energy. The man recedes to give place to his deeds'. Biographers in the *DNB* and elsewhere, he complained, burdened him with superfluous late-life details such as honours received; 'in any volume of it, I can turn from 'biography' to 'biography' which contains not one line of genuine biography to the page; instead you have given us slices of mis-placed history'.[65] To an earlier and more religious age, on the other hand, it was the deathbed scene that seemed most important. A later generation sees the twenty-third chapter of *The Life of Edward Baines by his Son* (1851) as a period piece with its ample detail on failing health, last public appearance, offspring assembling, hymns at the deathbed, parting words, public funeral, burial and funeral sermon. It will echo Baines's faint deathbed whisper that 'this is almost more than I can sustain'[66] – but for entirely secular reasons, so greatly have values subsequently changed. Medieval biographers ventured even further, with speculations about the fate of the subject's soul.[67]

Even more crucial is the decision on how much space is assigned to the key problems posed by, or to the climacteric within, the individual life. The *DNB* has no space for the 'life and times' approach to biography. Distinguishing clearly in 1911 between 'history' and 'biography', Lee saw 'the circumstance of politics' as 'the scenery of the statesman's bio-graphy', whereas it was 'the art of the biographer sternly to subordinate his scenery to his actors'. So for him, 'biography is not a peg for anything save the character and exploits of a man whose career answers the tests of biographic fitness'[68] – though his *DNB* article on Queen Victoria does not practise what he preached. Nor did the *DNB* ever espouse J. G. Lockhart's motto, 'he shall be his own biographer', as 'the theme of the work'.[69] Yet lack of space is not necessarily a biographical drawback: it sharpens the focus and highlights the priorities. The biographer of a wartime hero, for instance, focuses upon the roots of physical courage, just as the literary biographer highlights 'the mysterious and magical process of creation'.[70] With space so limited, the author must explain, however briefly, why the subject deserves inclusion at all, as well as the length allocated. Contrast the book-length biographer, free to sail without a compass to obscure destinations on a sea of wordage.

The shrewd biographer identifies some key puzzle or central episode and then sets about resolving or analysing it. 'In each life I tackle...', Humphrey Carpenter told Lyndall Gordon, 'there is some hidden story or fact, some clue, which when you get hold of it begins to unravel the whole thing'.[71] Robert Rhodes James did not need to apologize for focusing, in his *Churchill. A Study in Failure. 1900-1939* (1970), on Churchill's career during the years before his great moment, for that moment is thrown into relief by what went before, but no *DNB* article on Churchill could proceed in this way. The *DNB*'s biographer of Hartington, by contrast, would be entirely justified (as was Bernard Holland) in weighting his two-volume biography towards the years 1884-6 when Hartington's influence on British politics was at its height, given that 'a biographer's aim should be to make character stand out; character most appears in times of greatest stress, and the years 1884, 1885, and 1886 were the critical period of Lord Hartington's political career'.[72] Giving equal weight to all years in a career can itself be distorting: was it wise of Harry Thompson, in his thorough and fair-minded biography of the actor Peter Cook, to cover Cook's declining years so fully? The miserable descent into drink and failing powers should not of course be concealed, but Cook's great comic moment was the early 1960s, whereas the aftermath adds little but the repetition and lack of individual distinctiveness that resembles pornography.

This is not to say that context is not required: a good *DNB* article provides it at two levels: the social and the individual. The *Dictionary* must of course avoid repetitious social context and confine itself in each article to the specially relevant aspects of context. With Mark Pattison, for example, who announces at the start of his autobiography that 'I have really no history but a mental history',[73] it is the history of ideas that is central to the relevant context, since no thinker, not even the most abstract of philosophers, operates in a social void. Nobody knew this better than Stephen, predictably excellent in his biography on the intellectual climate that moulded Henry Fawcett. Noel Annan thought Stephen 'one of the first Englishmen to argue that the character and demands of the reading public influenced literary expression. He explained changes in taste by unravelling social relationships, and liberated the history of literature by suggesting that it was more than a search for influences and movements. No one before him in England had made it quite so evident how intimately literature was bound up with the customs, manners, money-sense and the unspoken assumptions of different classes in society'. For John Gross, Stephen 'pioneered the sociological study of literature in England', with his lectures on 'English literature and society in the eighteenth century' sketching out at the very end of his life how the sociology of literature should be written.[74] Here, as so often, the *Oxford DNB* seeks to follow where Stephen led.

Political institutions provide the politician's context, and Skidelsky's biography of Mosley illustrates the harm done by their absence, for without explaining how Britain's two-party system operated in the 1930s, the biographer cannot account for Mosley's defeat by the far less charismatic Baldwin and Neville Chamberlain.[75] Conversely, essential background was provided by the ninth chapter of John Wilson's *CB. A Life of Sir Henry Campbell-Bannerman* (1973) – on the 'vanished world' of the Edwardian European spa which the Liberal prime minister inhabited, for the reader in the 1970s could no longer provide it for himself. Nor does the importance of context end with the subject's death; the *Oxford DNB*'s article on King Arthur, for example, inevitably consists of little else than 'after-life'. Indeed, the *Oxford DNB* will carry the *DNB*'s alertness to social context still further by including about 400 prosopographical group articles – on family businesses, schools of artists, aristocratic networks, the Tolpuddle martyrs, the Salem witches and their accusers, for example. Such articles acknowledge that a life is often not best understood in isolation.

Individual as distinct from social context renders relevant Sidney Lee's distinction in 1912 between a 'life' and a 'character'. The *DNB*, he said, must focus on the life, with no 'expansive canvas' for the character: contributors must often instead 'rely for the suggestion of distinctive personality on apt arranging and presentment of facts and dates. . . A few summary touches must suffice'.[76] Lee's view reflects a conviction that activity is the central biographical preoccupation, and it did not ultimately prevail. 'We can no longer maintain that life consists in actions only or in works', wrote Virginia Woolf. 'It consists in personality'.[77] In seeking to portray character, the skilful biographer will seek to capture the importance of silences and intervals – necessarily for earlier subjects where the evidence is lacking, but deliberately for later subjects. 'A great part of the discipline of life arises simply from its slowness', wrote T. H. Green. 'The long years of patient waiting and silent labour, the struggle with listlessness and pain, the loss of time by illness, the hope deferred, the doubt that lays hold on delay – these are the tests of that pertinacity in man which is but a step below heroism'.[78] Since no biographer aims to bore the reader, the reality must somehow be conveyed without inducing the mood.

So lives in the *DNB*'s later supplements were more fully-rounded, with the public aspect complemented where possible by the private, and with the entrepreneur pursued beyond the factory gates. The supplement for 1961-70 opened up references to homosexuality,[79] and its co-editor Nicholls encouraged contributors to provide 'some little sentence or two that was more light-hearted, explaining some foible or characteristic of the person, describing them personally'[80] – a welcome advance upon Sidney Lee's austere downgrading of 'the commonplace or trivial aspects of life'. The new openness was not always readily grasped: Woodrow Wyatt, writing on George Wigg, wondered in 1987 whether to mention the discrediting kerb-crawling episode and decided against.[81] None the less, the key OUP document marshalling in 1990 the arguments for a completely revised *DNB* pointed out that 'sexuality, illegitimacy, suicide, alcoholism, and mental illness are no longer taboo'. This shift introduced inconsistencies into the *Dictionary* as a whole. Where the *DNB*'s Victorian contributors had ventured to mention sexual conduct, they sometimes did so awkwardly or even uncomprehendingly. More importantly, significant sexual conduct was omitted from some articles – the *DNB* article on Oscar Wilde (1901) ignored his homosexuality, for example – but not in others, as witness the articles on E. M. Forster and Joe Orton (both 1981).[82] In the *Oxford DNB* there will be less reticence in one further area: wealth at death.

Personal presence, difficult to capture, was not ignored by the *DNB*. Arguing in 1856 for a national portrait gallery, Earl Stanhope cited in support Carlyle's view: 'often have I found a portrait superior in real instruction to half-a-dozen written biographies, as biographies are written...I have found that the portrait was as a small lighted candle by which the biographies could for the first time be read, and some human interpretation be made of them'.[83] Leslie Stephen echoed Carlyle:

he told Thomas Hardy when planning the *DNB* that he aimed to mention his subjects' personal appearance whenever possible: 'a few words on the look of a man as he walked and talked, so far as it could be gathered from portraits and traditions, was worth a page of conjecture on his qualities'.[84] The *Oxford DNB* will carry this awareness further when, in collaboration with the National Portrait Gallery, it illustrates a fifth of its 50,000 subjects with a likeness – though a likeness, particularly before the advent of photography, may be closer to aspiration than to actuality.

Edmund Gosse described biography as 'the faithful portrait of a soul in its adventures through life' – a view that Stephen seems to have shared. In 1893 Stephen claimed that the biographer should aim at 'the construction of an autobiography'. The biographer to breathe life into a biography 'must put us into direct communication with the man himself; not tell us simply where he was or what he was seen to do, but put him at one end of a literary telephone and the reader at the other'; the biographer was, he said, 'merely the conducting wire'.[85] It is a vivid metaphor and more an aspiration than an agenda. Perhaps success comes only to the biographer who has directly observed the subject. Only close personal observation could have produced the eighth chapter of F. D. Maurice's two-volume biography by his son Frederick, with its enlivening detail on home life, habits and mannerisms. Likewise the 23rd chapter ('Attlee at home') of Kenneth Harris's *Attlee*, gains much from Harris's conversations with Attlee's children. There are, however, arguments for both proximity and distance in a biographer. The biographer who consults the subject's contemporaries at once experiences the tension between on the one hand knowing too little, and on the other hand deriving so much from family, friends and colleagues that feelings of personal obligation distort judgement. Stephen's biography of the Liberal politician Henry Fawcett illustrates the dilemma: the sections on Fawcett's early life when he and Stephen were friends outshine its later and political sections, and yet with friendship came the watchful attentions of a fond widow.[86]

Perhaps most taxing of all for the biographer is capturing the flavour of a person's conversation, though in the ninth chapter of his *Macaulay. The Shaping of the Historian* John Clive made a valiant attempt at it.[87] Reassuringly, Stephen himself, when reading his successor's memoir of George Smith, saw biographical imperfection as inevitable. 'There is, of course, always something a little disappointing in a biography of a man whom one has known intimately. It is impossible for any body to describe conversation and manner and all the things and shades of things that make up one's picture'. Yet, making due allowance, Stephen felt that 'the life was as good as was possible under the circumstances. It gives clearly and impartially all that is really wanted and can be told, and I do not see how it could be materially improved'.[88] After all, as a remark of Stephen's quoted by Matthew illustrates, all the *DNB*'s editors have known well enough that in publishing biographies 'even a very defective performance is immensely superior to none at all'.[89]

NOTES

1 A point I owe to Dr. May. I gratefully acknowledge here the comments on an earlier draft generously provided by the *Oxford DNB*'s research director Dr. Elizabeth Baigent, its project director Robert Faber, and by the following members of the *Oxford DNB*'s fine team of research editors: Drs Philip Carter, Mark Curthoys, Matthew Kilburn, Vivienne Larminie, Alex May, Annette Peach, Jane Potter and Henry Summerson. Mr Alan Bell generously and meticulously commented upon the draft at a late stage. For a chronology of significant events in the history of *DNB* and *Oxford DNB*, see R. Faber and B. Harrison 'The *Dictionary of National Biography*: a Publishing History' in Robin Myers, Michael Harris and Giles Mandelbrote (eds.) *Lives in Print. Biography and the Book Trade from the Middle Ages to the 21st Century* (2002), p. 190.

2 S. Lee 'National Biography', *Cornhill Magazine*, Mar 1896, pp. 266-8.

3 S. Lee *Principles of Biography. The Leslie Stephen Lecture Delivered in the Senate House, Cambridge on 13 May 1911* (Cambridge 1911), p. 51.

4 *DNB 1901-11* Vol. 3, pp. 402, 404.

5 L. Stephen *Some Early Impressions* (1924), p. 160.

6 Faber and Harrison 'The *Dictionary of National Biography*', pp. 174-7.

7 H. C. G. Matthew 'Dictionaries of National Biography', in Iain McCalman (ed.) *National Biographies and National Identity. A Critical Approach to Theory and Editorial Practice* (Humanities Research Centre, Australian National University, Canberra, 1996), p. 4.

8 'Statistical Account' prefaced to *DNB* Vol. 63 (1900), p. x.

9 OUP Archive PB/ED/12916/OP1722: Davis to Chapman 6 Dec 1927; Chapman to Milford 7 Dec 1927 (copy), Chapman to Weaver 6 June 1930.

10 OUP Archive PB/ED/12920/OP1723: minutes of a meeting at the Press, dated 10 Apr 1947 of the Provost of Oriel (G. N. Clark) and others as reported by G. N. Clark.

11 OUP Archive: PB/ED/12919/OP1723: A. L. P. Norrington's (23 Oct 1947) note of meeting at the Press on 21 Oct.

12 OUP Archive: files on the 1986-90 supplement: C. S. Nicholls 'Notes on the DNB for 17 September 1991 Meeting' dated 17 Sept 1991.

13 C. S. Nicholls 'Notes on the DNB for 17 September 1991 Meeting'.

14 For more on this see the valuable contributions by Drs. Larminie and May to the New DNB's *Newsletter* No. 6 (June 2001), pp. 3-4.

15 I owe these points to Dr. Summerson.

16 'Statistical Account', p. xii.

17 'Statistical Account', p. lxix.

18 'Statistical Account', p. lxix.

19 This paragraph owes much to Dr. Larminie's comments, though she is in no way to be blamed for the use I have made of them.

20 OUP Archive: *The Dictionary of National Biography. A Statement Addressed by Sir Sidney Lee to the Contributors* (8-page pamphlet, 31 Aug 1917), p. 4.

21 University of London Library, A. F. Pollard papers: Pollard to his parents, 27 Mar 1921.

22 OUP Archive PB/ED/12909/OP1720: Chapman to Davis, 1 Apr 1919.

23 P. Sutcliffe *The Oxford University Press. An Informal History* (Oxford 1978), p. 216.

24 OUP Archive PB/ED/12909/OP1720: Chapman to Milford, 26 Apr 1927 (copy); Milford to Chapman, 3 May 1927.

25 OUP Archive PB/ED/12909/OP1720: Chapman to Bishop Strong of Ripon, 25 Feb 1921.

26 OUP Archive PB/ED/12909/OP1720: draft undated typescript 'Notice to Contributors'; this quotation does not appear in the one-page printed version dated Oct 1921 in the same file.

27 'Statistical Account', p. x.

28 H. C. G. Matthew *Leslie Stephen and the New Dictionary of National Biography* (Cambridge 1997), p. 13; see also p. 18.

29 A. F. Pollard 'Sir Sidney Lee and the Dictionary of National Biography', *Bulletin of the Institute of Historical Research*, June 1926, p. 10.

30 H. Summerson 'Problems of Medieval Biography: Revising the *DNB*', *Medieval Prosopography* Vol. 17 No. 2 (Autumn 1996), pp. 201-2.

31 Nicholls interview with Michael De-la-Noy in *Time and Tide*, Summer 1991, p. 11.

32 OUP Archive PB/ED/12909/OP1720: Chapman to Granet, 11 Mar 1921 (copy).

33 OUP Archive PB/ED/12895/OP1718: typescript headed 'D. N. B. Discussion, 26 January, 1950', p. 1.

34 *DNB 1981-1985* (1990), p. 120.

35 *Time and Tide*, Summer 1991, p. 10.

36 G. Fenwick *Women and the 'Dictionary of National Biography'. A Guide to DNB volumes 1885-1985 and 'Missing Persons'* (Aldershot 1994), pp. 18-19; Preface to *Missing Persons*, p. vii.

37 OUP Archive PB/ED/12909/OP1720: Pollard to H. W. C. Davis, 29 Mar 1921.

38 C. Matthew, 'Editor's Report, April 1993', p. 16.

39 I owe this point to Dr. Larminie.

40 'Statistical Account', p. vii.

41 Fenwick in *Victorian Periodicals Review*, Vol. 23 No. 4 (Winter 1990), p. 184.

42 'Statistical Account', p. v.

43 OUP Archive PB/ED/12913/OP1721: Chapman to B. L. Richmond, 30 Dec 1932 (copy).

44 OUP Archive PB/ED/12908/OP1720: Thomas Strong to Chapman, 26 Mar 1921.

45 OUP Archive PB/ED/12916/OP1722: Chapman to Ensor, 1 Dec 1939.

46 OUP Archive (uncat): C. S. Nicholls 'Notes on the DNB for 17 September 1991 Meeting'.

47 Preface to *Missing Persons*, p. v.

48 'Editor's Report, April 1993', p. 13.

49 National Library of Scotland, MS 23192: typescript 'Autobiography' of George Smith, f. 227 (Chapter 26, p. 9); f. 228 (p. 10).

50 *British Quarterly Review*, Vol. 10 (1849), p. 36.

51 H. Spencer *The Study of Sociology* (1873), p. 35, cf. pp. 32, 34.

52 G. St. Aubyn *A Victorian Eminence. The Life and Works of Henry Thomas Buckle* (1958), p. 168.

53 National Library of Scotland, Stephen/Smith Correspondence, MS 23175, f. 119: Stephen to Smith, 22 Sept 1884.

54 N. Annan *Leslie Stephen. The Godless Victorian* (1984), p. 317.

55 *Sir Leslie Stephen's Mausoleum Book* (Oxford 1977), p. 95.

56 S. Lee 'At a Journey's End' *Nineteenth Century*, Dec 1912, p. 1160.

57 OUP Archive PB/ED/12909/OP1720: Chapman to Gosse, 10 Mar 1921 (copy).

58 OUP Archive PB/ED/12909/OP1720: documents accompanying the draft and final version of the 1921 circular.

59 'The Art of Biography' (first published 1939) in her *Collected Essays* IV (1967), p. 226.

60 Michael Gove in *The Times*, 22 Aug 2002, p. 11.

61 *Daily Telegraph*, 22 Aug 2002, p. 24

62 Ray Strachey MSS: Ray Strachey to her mother, 5 Feb 1930, consulted when in the care of Ray's daughter, Barbara Halpern. Vera Brittain in *Week-End Review*, 18 July 1931, p. 86.

63 'Editor's Report, April 1993', p. 12.

64 'The Art of Biography', p. 226.

65 Quotations from H. Ellis 'An Open Letter to Biographers' in his *View and Reviews. A Selection of Uncollected Articles 1884-1932. First Series: 1884-1919* (1932), pp. 87, 92, 88.

66 *The Life of Edward Baines. Late M.P. for the Borough of Leeds. By his Son Edward Baines* (1851), p. 352.

67 H. Summerson 'Problems of Medieval Biography', p. 205.

68 S. Lee *Principles of Biography*, p. 30.

69 epigraph to the first volume of R. S. Churchill's official life, *Winston S. Churchill. Volume I. Youth 1874-1900* (London 1966); see also p. xx.

70 L. Edel *Literary Biography. The Alexander Lectures 1955-56* (1957), p. 3.

71 interview in John Batchelor (ed) *The Art of Literary Biography* (Oxford 1995), p. 268.

72 B. Holland *The Life of Spencer Compton. Eighth Duke of Devonshire* (1911) II, p. 184.

73 M. Pattison *Memoirs of an Oxford Don* (1885, ed. V. H. H. Green, 1988), p. 1.

74 Annan *Leslie Stephen*, p. 317; J. Gross *The Rise and Fall of the Man of Letters. Aspects of English Literary Life since 1800* (1969, Penguin ed. 1973), pp. 99-100.

75 As noted by Alan Beattie in his review in *Political Quarterly*, 1976, p. 106.

76 S. Lee 'At a Journey's End', p. 1159.

77 'The Art of Biography' in her *Collected Essays* IV, p. 230.

78 T. H. Green, 'The Value and Influence of Works of Fiction' in his *Works* (ed. Nettleship, 1888), III, p. 36.

79 *DNB 1961-70* (1981), p. vi.

80 C. Nicholls, tape-recorded interview with the author on 11 Dec 2000. I am most grateful to Dr. Nicholls for this interview and its precursor on 5 Dec 2000, and for allowing me to quote from it.

81 W. Wyatt *Journals* I (1998, Ed. S. Curtis, paperback ed. 1999), p. 300 (25 Feb 1987).

82 OUP Archives: N. W. Wilson's report, 'A Second Edition of *The Dictionary of National Biography*', Nov 1990, p. 11.

83 *House of Lords Debates*, 4 Mar 1856, c. 1772.

84 As reported by T. Hardy in his introductory note to J. J. Foster's *Wessex Worthies* (1920) in M. Millgate (ed) *Thomas Hardy's Public Voice* (Oxford 2001), p. 409. I owe this reference to Sir Keith Thomas.

85 Gosse quoted by R. R. James 'The Strange Art of Political Biography' in *Essays by Divers Hands*, Vol. 34 (1967) p. 124. Stephen in *National Review*, Oct 1893, pp. 178, 180.

86 For his problems see L. Stephen *Selected Letters* (ed. J. W. Bicknell, 1996) II, pp. 320-1, 326, 328, 331, 334.

87 *Macaulay. The Shaping of the Historian* (1973), pp. 240-6.

88 National Library of Scotland, Stephen/Smith Correspondence, MS 23175, f. 69: Stephen to Mrs. Smith, 3 July 1901

89 as quoted from Stephen's article on 'National Biography' in the *National Review*, Mar 1896 by Colin Matthew at the conclusion to his article on 'Dictionaries of National Biography', p. 18.

Comparative Criticism **XXV**, pp. 27–56. © 2004 Edinburgh University Press
Printed in the United Kingdom

Ends of Learning: Tradition and the Problem of Inheritance

WITH EXCERPTS FROM *THE LAST BRAHMIN*
BY RĀNI SHIVASHANKARA SHARMA
TRANSLATED FROM THE TELUGU
WITH AN INTRODUCTION
BY D. VENKAT RAO

INTRODUCTION

For over two millennia Sanskrit language provided the sources of reflection and ritual on the Indian subcontinent. The Sanskrit heritage has left an indelible mark on all the major Indian languages. Although the Indian languages ('vernaculars') either emerged or consolidated themselves in the second millennium, they have no reflective traditions independent of Sanskrit (the Prakrit heritage cannot be easily opposed to the Sanskrit one). The Sanskrit heritage retained its hegemony in creative and reflective realms in pre-colonial India.

Traditionally Pandits are the makers and movers of the Sanskrit heritage. The word *pandita* derives from the feminine noun *panda* which connotes 'waking up, realization, intellect and intelligence.' The tradition of associating Pandit with learning and scholarship goes back to pre-Paninian (before 500 BC) period.[1] Although Pandits are largely from the Brahmin community, the word is also used to refer to Buddhist, Jain and (occasionally) Muslim savants. The Sanskrit tradition is synonymous with the Brahman tradition.[2] Although the word refers to a specific caste or community, originally it has a more general significance: '[B]rahman refers originally to a 'formulation' (*Formulierung*), the capturing in words of a significant and non-self-evident truth.'[3] These form-giving abilities are believed to endow the 'Brahmán' with the power to perform in the cosmic realm as well.

27

The 'formulations' in the ṚgVeda, the oldest available verbal corpus, are considered in the Brahmin tradition as the 'compilations' (*Samhitas*) of such significant and 'non-objective' truths. In a way the Sanskrit tradition is little more than a relentless and unending effort to articulate the 'truths' of these compilations. The extant verbal corpus is incomplete, fragmentary and it contains only remnants. The tradition is acutely aware of this incompleteness, the fact of the 'lost Veda'.

The fragment and the incomplete have become the irreducible sources of reflection, speculation and performance in the tradition. But nowhere in the tradition, even to this day, have these millennial reflective and performative energies been devoted to an archaeological venture to search for the lost, to fulfil the incomplete. Unavailability has become the interminable condition of ritual and thought in the tradition. Consequently, the Sanskrit heritage is a palimpsest of heteronymic tissues spacing themselves across the diversity of Indian languages and cultural soils and in the process undergoing inevitable transformations. It is a heritage with neither a central archive nor a jussive custodian of the heritage. The Pandit is not an archon guarding excavations. The dehiscence of this heritage remains immeasurable: it is still spreading its pollen.

For millennia the survival of the Sanskrit heritage depended on a non-tangible and non-filial pedagogical bond between the teacher and the pupil. What is central to the survival of the heritage is the *sikṣa* – the discipline of rigorous learning. It is a learning gained through intimacy – from the face of the teacher (*gurumukhatah*). Learning emerges from a bond formed by the teacher on one side and the taught on the other – face-to-face. If the linking cord is knowledge – then the imparting is achieved through verbal discourse (*pravacana*). This pedagogical bonding between the *ācārya* and the *antevāsin*, as an old Upaniṣad specifies, is the basis of all learning.[4] Whatever may be the vicissitudes of continuities and discontinuities, ruptures and repetitions in the tradition – all these departures moved on this essential pedagogical bond.

Colonialism disrupted this heritage precisely by rupturing the pedagogical bond between the teacher and the pupil. Colonialism advanced an alternative pedagogical ideal. That's why colonialism is analyzed as an epistemic violence in post-colonial critiques. More than economic depredations and political subjugation, colonialism's decisive and long-lasting impact can be noticed in the epistemic disruption of the survival base of the Sanskrit tradition. Colonial response to the Sanskrit tradition and Pandits grew out of a culture of suspicion.

William Jones decided to learn Sanskrit himself, for instance, as he became suspicious of the native informants (Pandits and Maulvis) on the Hindu Law (and Muslim Law) in his court; he feared they were totally untrustworthy.[5] The univocal judgements of 'Orientalism' (in Edward Said's use of the term) on the 'lacks' of the Sanskrit tradition (lack of history, religion, morality) are too well known to be rehearsed here.

Because of popular mindsets about Islam's alleged destruction of Indian heritage, it is important to point out that the Sanskrit tradition continued to function, despite adversities, creatively and critically during the Mughal period. It is possible to name the noteworthy Pandits and poets of the tradition like Jagannatha, who continued their work in Sanskrit during this period. Further, the support of Islamic rulers to the traditional Institutional Orders of Shankaracharya[6] in the eighteenth century is acknowledged by the Chiefs of these orders. Isn't it intriguing that one seldom comes across Pandits of repute functioning within Sanskrit tradition during the nineteenth century?

The Orientalist 'discovery' of Sanskrit and India was described as a 'second Renaissance' for Europe. This 'Oriental Renaissance' ushered in an alternative to the Sanskrit tradition. The alternative, strategic but decisive, evolved from two fundamental objectives – knowledge production and educational reforms. But the agents of both these tasks were now the European Orientalists. Consequently, the Sanskrit tradition received a decisive blow as it became bereft of the two sources of its life – critical and creative reflection and performance, and the millennial pedagogical bond between the teacher and the taught. Orientalism initiated a 'new' mode of knowledge production and a 'new' method of teaching – through newly developed institutions. The language of this new knowledge was no longer Sanskrit (or Prakrit) but European; and its creators and teachers were no longer the traditional Pandits and Acharyas – but (European) Orientalists. No wonder the Sanskrit tradition in the nineteenth century (and subsequently) is replete with the names of Jones, Wilson, Max Müller, Mcdonnel, Keilhorn, Caland, Keith and a host of others – and no longer with a Sastry and a Sharma. In other words, the Sanskrit tradition began to be claimed by a new set of inheritors. The Sanskrit tradition was metamorphosed into Indology. Even to this day Indology is quintessentially a European discipline of thought ('The specter [of Orientalism] seems to be still haunting us.'[7]] Its objective: professional knowledge production; its method: European philological, historical and anthropological paradigms of the human sciences.

Indology's two centuries' long signature can be said to leave a critical mark on the Sanskrit tradition – but it cannot be said to have exhausted this millennial tradition. This is for two specific reasons: (i) Indology is essentially a communication network among Indologists. Its transactions with the tradition would only consolidate the 'inside' of this field. Indology has a place for those 'new Pandits'[8] who are created by the field itself; and it cannot contain those of the tradition who are indifferent to the field – except, of course, as ethnographic objects. (ii) Unencumbered by the Indological weight, even unaware of it, survivors of the Sanskrit tradition carry on in the 'received' ways of the past. The European Indological humanities have little role to play in the living on of this tradition.

It is from this surviving realm of the tradition that a voice emerges in these early years of the twenty-first century. It recounts a tale of survival – survival in difficult and adversarial conditions. It's a tale of learning, scholarship and the rigours of a pedagogical bonding. It's a *fiction* of the tradition's self-representation. It's indeed a fiction as the narrative, even as it deals with historical figures, is woven with shifting frames of continuity and discontinuity. As the principle of discontinuity is the irreducible condition of representation, the recounted 'self' of the tradition ('*Brahmaṇa ātmakathā*') can only be the effect of a critical mediation. This is a narrative about the pain of discontinuity. This narrative is enigmatically titled in English as *The Last Brahmin*.

The narrative of *The Last Brahmin* offers a literary reflection on a series of 'philosophical' notions and their consequences that are deeply internalized in Indian languages. The series consists of pairs like caste/religion, karma/debt, expansion (*vyāpti*)/contamination, agent (*karta*)/self/creation (*sṛṣṭi*), history/time, continuity/rupture, tradition/modernity and destiny/duty. The series can be traced back to the Sanskrit tradition. *The Last Brahmin* thematizes this series entirely in the context of the rigour of disciplinary learning and the lifeline of pedagogical bonding. This critical unraveling of the tradition sets it apart from the Indological disciplinary frames on the one hand and the partisanal Hindu ideological forces on the other. Going against the entire field of Orientalist knowledge on India, *The Last Brahmin* insists on the difference and distinction between the Brahmin Sanskrit tradition and the so-called Hinduism. At the center of these philosophical-historical themes is the problematic filial bonding of paternity – and this bond amplifies the tragic poignancy of this postcolonial narrative of mourning.

Could there be a people without religion? Can there be cultural heritages with neither textual nor anthropomorphic center points? Can the question of agency be understood in non-theological and non-humanist terms? The work called *The Last Brahmin* written in the South Indian language of Telugu (spoken by more than 70 million people), begins to address these questions.

The Last Brahmin is a philosophical, intellectual (auto)biography of a Sanskrit Pandit. Written by a schoolteacher of Sanskrit, this work embodies an effort to grapple with the enigma of the Brahman tradition, its pervasive spread across periods, movements, forms and examines its implications and stakes. The work emphasizes the enormity of tasks involved in finding an alternative to it. *The Last Brahmin* is a philosophical *critique* of the Brahman tradition.

The enigma of the tradition is dramatized through a scene of disinheritance in the book. The Veda Pandit, Mahamahopadhyāya Rāni Narasimha Sāstry, is on his deathbed at the age of 80 (in 2001). He has two sons. The Pandit declares that none of these sons is eligible to perform his funeral rites. He disinherits them. The sons are disowned as ritual heirs because the first one is a 'Hindu convert' and the second one, a non-believer. As he cannot filiate himself with the customs and ceremonies of the tradition, the non-believing son is disallowed to perform the rites. But what's wrong with the Hindu son? The Pandit declares that a Brahmin is not a Hindu; that there is no place for the term Hindu in the canonical Vedic tradition and Vaidic heritage. He pronounces that Brahmins are a people free of (or outside) religion. *The Last Brahmin* brings to crisis the term and concept of Hindu(ism), and unravels its historical and strident aspirations from the vantage of the Brahman tradition. *The Last Brahmin* dramatizes the philosophical and historical issues of cultural practice in the form of filial disinheritance.

But how do these people outside religion respond to or fare with traditions of monotheistic religions like Islam and Christianity? *The Last Brahmin* shows that through a measured and responsive distance and rigorous self-conservation the Brahman tradition faced these religions in its historical encounters with them. A substantial section of the book is devoted to identifying significant differences in the responses of these religions toward the Brahman tradition. Once again, these responses are also gathered in the book from the acknowledged custodians of the Brahman tradition – the Chiefs of Shankara Mathas (of Sringeri and Kanchi, in particular). Historical records and responses of the Shankara Orders show that the 'non-interfering' policy of Christianity was more devastating and insidious than the apparently violent and disturbing acts of Islam in the historical encounters of the Brahman tradition with these religions.

Christianity's suasive modes of grace, kindness and benevolence efface singularities in its aspiration to build a 'world empire', argues *The Last Brahmin*. One central current of the book is to persistently reiterate that the life and marrow of the aggressive-benevolent Hinduism, on the ascendant now, is derived in form and method from the empire-building aspirations of Christianity. (This aspect of *The Last Brahmin* comes close to what a contemporary philosopher termed the 'globalatinization' of Christianity.) *The Last Brahmin* compels a rethinking and reexamination of the interfaces of religion with people before or outside religion and their respective responsiveness to the singularities of the other.

While drawing on the resources of the tradition, *The Last Brahmin* orchestrates two kinds of contestation of the tradition. If a certain heritage of the Brahman tradition receives the Shankara Orders as the custodians of the tradition, the critique traces another formidable vein that challenges the legitimacy of Ādi Shankara as the representative of the ancient order. *The Last Brahmin* amplifies an internal critique of the tradition which exposes Āadi Shankara's complicity with Buddhism and unravels Shankara's Advaita as a disguised Buddhism (from which it was said to save the tradition). If Ādi Shankara's status is challenged on the one hand in the book, we find *The Last Brahmin* questioning the real-politik indulgences of the current head of the Shankara Order – Jayendra Saraswati, on the other. The latter's Hinduism, his endorsement of reconversions into Hinduism and his embracing the cause of Ayodhya receive critical scrutiny in the book.

The most crucial and vibrant current of *The Last Brahmin* is the thematic of singularities. Running through the entire work, this thematic manifests itself in the form of Varṇa/caste-specific singularities and their centrality in the 'Indic episteme'. Often reduced to a certain 'homo-hierarchicus', this emphasis on singularities becomes a part of the Brahman tradition's enigma. *The Last Brahmin* demonstrates how this apparently hierarchical and casteist 'ideology' conceals within itself a ferocious commitment to singularities and a relentless practice of the principle of difference. Unraveling a number of contemporary social movements like the Dalit, the eradication-of-caste movement and the proselytizing practice of Christianity and its inverse affirmation in the Hindu (re)conversions, *The Last Brahmin* bares their intolerance of singularities, their effacement of the other. The process of effacement is shown to occur through the programmed contaminations of name, 'colour-clan' and culture (*nāma, varṇa and samskritika sankara*). *The Last Brahmin* demands a patient meditation on the imperatives of singularity – and invites an inquiry into the (re)sources of Varṇa-caste on the basis of this emphasis.

Contamination is another salient thematic of *The Last Brahmin*. Notwithstanding the hegemonic Brahman tradition's desire and effort to safeguard its singularity unscathed, the writer illustrates with vigour how this tradition was always already exposed to contamination – how the much-dreaded Varṇa-*sankara* has gone on all along. Yet this contamination at the core of the tradition has never disturbed the dual structure of 'high' and 'low', the hegemonic-white and the subjugated-black domains, says the writer. The force of contamination only maintained this division with its opposed elements. *The Last Brahmin* insists on comprehending this paradoxical structure of complicity and outlines the immense task of displacing the structure. Such a task, *The Last Brahmin* states, can only be achieved by a protracted, collective labour of several generations.

If Varṇa-caste is an 'intimate enemy' and the force of enabling violence filiated to the Brahmin tradition, there is another, largely unacknowledged undercurrent in this tradition. *The Last Brahmin* describes it as the 'ancient tragic saga'. This is the unrecounted and effaced accounts of the woman figure in the tradition. *The Last Brahmin* evokes this account in the figures of his mother and sisters. Yet the writer confesses that he cannot tell this ancient saga directly. It can only be put together in the shadow of the overarching paternal Brahmin tradition. There is no story of her own to be recounted, let alone in her own voice. Mental illness, says the writer, is the only wealth that women in his house have inherited from this venerated Brahmin tradition. The widow remains a very poignant figure in this saga. *The Last Brahmin* mourns the 'loss' of the mother (and sister) in the shadow of the father.

Written by the disinherited non-believing son of the Veda Pandit, *The Last Brahmin* mixes genres of (auto)biography, narrative, discursive analysis, dialogic utterance, exegetic prose, and Sanskrit verse forms (mantra, sutra and sloka etc). Rāni Shivashankara Sharma is an accomplished writer in Telugu. The book exemplifies its critique through an elaborate account of how the Brahmin tradition circulates and determines the work of two radical modern writers in Telugu (Chalam and Sri Sri), and many other literary figures of the contemporary Telugu literary-political scene.

Published by an emergent enterprise – New Syllabus publications –
The Last Brahmin has already sold several hundreds of copies and has
now come out in the second edition. The book is distributed through
the sole channel of the Publisher's circulating salesmanship. Hence its
unavailability in the commercial book market. (This is entirely due to the
Publisher's dismal financial situation to meet all the commercial cuts). Yet
The Last Brahmin has already gained the attention of a serious readership
and provoked several groups of people in Andhra.

The Last Brahmin is perhaps one of the very few works to have
emerged as a critique of the tradition from 'within'. The academic field
of Indology has developed a formidable edifice of ethnographic, historical
and literary-anthropological work on the Brahmin tradition in the last
two centuries. But almost all of this work is only a Euro-American
representation of the Brahmin tradition. Only in recent times does one
come across 'experiential', (auto)biographical accounts of the singularities
of caste (but these too have largely provoked anthropological curiosity).
Written in the world of professionalized knowledge production where
the field of Indology has decisive claims over the representation of the
Sanskrit [Brahmin] tradition, *The Last Brahmin* is untouched by the 'new
inheritors', the 'new Pandits' of the field.

While engaging with the question of singularity as the central enigma
of the Brahmin tradition, *The Last Brahmin* delineates its epic and tragic
dimensions. *The Last Brahmin* narrativizes the pain and the necessity of
disinheritance, the necessity of discontinuity with what one is born into,
with that which gifts one one's being.

A work like *The Last Brahmin* would be inconceivable with training or
exposure only to English or European languages. It is impossible to think
of a work like *The Last Brahmin* without the millennial resources of Indian
languages in their singular receptions of the Brahmin tradition and the
Sanskrit language. *The Last Brahmin* could be a harbinger for what could
possibly emerge from the undecidable futures of Indian languages.

The author Rani Shivashankara Sharma teches Sanskrit in a school in a
remote town in the Southern State of Andhra Pradesh. He has published
several short stories and poems.

The Last Brahmin by Rāni Shivashankara Sharma
Edited by Aruna and Sauda (Hyderabad: New Syllabus, May 2002)

The Last Brahmin

RĀNI SHIVASHANKARA SHARMA

Father

    In the eons past,
        Among the infinite births
        And endless forms

    You were never in this very form.

Father

    In the eons to come,
        Among the endless births
        And infinite forms

    You will not appear in this very form.

I

On seeing my father, Kāmeshwara Somayāji's eyes were tear-filled. His voice broke.

My father, Rāni Narasimha Sāstry, is now eighty. His body has become 'watery', his health deteriorating badly. It is not his illness that brought tears to Kāmeshwara Somyāji. Kāmeshwara Somayāji is the custodian and caretaker of our family rites and rituals. Every year Kāmeshwara Somayāji himself would perform the oblations (*apakarmalu*) and the sacred annual death rites of our grandfather, the renowned Veda Pandit, Rāni Subbiaha Deekshitulu. He alone performed the paternal death-rites for our uncle, the Veda Pandit, Subrahmanyāvadhāni, and thus made it possible for him to gain his proper destiny. He personified for me the world of rituals and rites. Among his sons no one inherited the status of being a custodian of these rites. This vocation would end with him in his family genealogy. What brought tears to Somayājulu, who is like the doorway to the ancestral universe, are not some worldly issues. Neither was it due to our father's illness, nor his physical suffering. . . .

Renowned as an unchallenged Pandit of the 'science' (*sāstra*) of Vedanta in the entire country, my father lived a life of discipline based on rituals, and stood out as an exemplar amidst other exceptional Brahmins wedded to the ancient and eternal *dharma*. Yet for such a father of mine there was no son fit enough to officiate at the obsequies after his death and rescue him from the fiery hell. Somayājulu was sorrow-filled at the prospect of this void gaping in my father's life.

My father, endowed with titles and honorifics like Mahāmahopadhyāya and Mahā Veda Pandita, has two sons. As he converted into a Hindu, the older son degenerated. The younger one became a non-believer. Where was the luck then with these two sons? With doors unopened to the noble worlds after death, tormented by hunger and thirst, where was the destiny's path for this venerable soul? Whence the despairing grief of Somyājulu.

My father once said to me: your brother is a Hindu and you are a non-believer. I alone am still clinging on to this Veda and the tradition of the sages. Grief pervaded his words.

Kāshyāntu Maraṇānmuktihi . . .

They say that dying in Kāshi can relieve one from the cycle of life and death. Married couples that have no sons to perform their death rites, offer ritual balls of rice in advance at Gaya. This is like performing a death-rite for a living person (*ghataśrāddha*). Some people go to Kāshi and end their lives in the Ganges. Such people have no rebirth, my mother used to say. Perhaps Kāshi is the only destination for your father and me, she said. 'If you can not render the death-rites, when either of us dies, you should not come to visit us,' said my mother, with tears in her eyes.

'Regret and atone, *ore* Saayi, and wear your sacred thread,' mortified Kameshwara Somayajulu pleaded with me.

I didn't say a word. He looked at me as though I were a criminal . . .

When he learnt about this, my father, I believe, said to Kāmeshwara Somayājulu: 'He might repent, alright. But would belief engender in his heart? Would he believe in the eternal dharma of the sages?'

Indeed so. That is impossible. To re-claim and render the ancient tradition of the sages with its basis in the 'colour-clan' regulative code [*varna* dharma] would never happen. I am an ideologue who believes in the eradication of caste, and a non-believer to boot. I am the one who has declared a permanent enmity with the culture of my father.

In the Palanadu region of Andhra Pradesh, anyone who sees me walking on the bank of the Karempudi canal and talking to myself aloud would surely think I am a madman.

I think mental ill health is an inheritance from one's line of birth and family-clan. 'I am mad. You too are mad. Isn't it so?' queried my elder brother once, ruminating from his deep interior. Two of my sisters are also mentally unbalanced. Perhaps this mental ill health is the only wealth that the ancient world had saved for us. This might be a disease – but the very malady has kept us from turning into sheep. I have observed among some of my relatives this trait of talking to themselves. The tendency to float in soliloquies is most prominent in me. My writings emerge from these interior monologues, in the language of my self. 'I am a deranged Brahmin (a Brahmin psychic) in an epoch of transition,' I had announced a long time ago.

Death is of quintessential significance to the Brahmin. Our culture and our language are all entwined with death.

I had asked my father once: 'Father, if there is no difference between the individual and universal soul-life, doesn't the individual fuse with the universal, once its bodily sustenance ceases? That is, isn't death itself a release from worldly entanglements.' 'Not at all,' said my father. 'Even when the physical body is defunct, the soul-life remains as a phallic body, a subtle body. Therefore even after death, joy and sorrow, heaven and hell continue to persist. Until one gains 'knowledge' of the singular soul-self [*atmajnāna*] and is relieved from worldly entanglements, there's no escape from the bonds of the body. This subtle body too is prone to hunger and thirst. Hence the necessity of annual death rites and ritual rice-ball oblations.'

The state after death is a privileged one among Brahmins.

Janmadukham jarā dukham jāyadukham

Birth is a lamentable sorrow, old age sorrowful and marriage grief-ridden. . . .

Life is pervasive of grief and sorrow. Life is just a passage to a state after death. It has no value beyond that. The real journey for the being begins only after death. Gaining the right path or evil direction, lofty-venerable or blighted-base world, noble or shameful birth can happen only after death. Life is only a preparation for the journey after death. Life is just a shadow of death. Unless we grasp this thought-reality, we cannot make sense of Kāmeshwara Somayājulu's tears. Like an apparition of death, the soul of the Vedic dharma, Somayājulu hovered about in our desolate home, quickening despondencies of a bygone age. I experienced fear and despair of death, felt lost in a desert. Indeed, in the shadow of this ruined home, I alone have remained as the witness to my paternal soul-self and to the being's anguish; I alone am the heir to this.

If I am to put it in the language of my Hindu-convert elder brother, I have remained a wasted fellow: a degraded vestige, bearing the agonizing burden of an ancient age.

Now, in this infinite universe who would show the soul-self of paternal ancestors their path after death? Who would offer them food and water?

Somayajulu's grief has engulfed me as well.

Two kinds of specters and demons rule our home: lack of the need to do any work, excepting recitations of the Veda; and loneliness due to the lack of the need to meet any one. Against these specters and demons that kill the desire to live, I have declared war. I gathered myself to avoid being touched by Somayājulu's grief.

II

The Karempudi canal said to me: 'In your mother's life fulfilling even very simple wishes was difficult. She had asked for a radio, remember,' the canal reminded me.

True. My mother longed to spend time listening to music, plays and skits on the radio. She was very fond of stories and 'fine arts'. But my father would never allow any modern implement into the house. With all the lakhs of [rupees worth] property, we couldn't buy even a chair until now.

I was not yet born at that time. My mother used to tell me stories, serially, about what had happened before my birth. . . .'On the banks of that [Karempudi] canal I lived my life in the company of monkeys. People rarely moved about in that area. When your father went to the city for conferences or on some other work, I passed my time with children in fear and dread. Except monkeys that ran away with vegetables, there were no companions for support,' said my mother, remembering that period of her youth. Whether it flowed with laughter or inundated us with a roar, memories of the canal have permeated me through my mother's life. The canal breezes touch even the school where I teach.

Now I live near the Karempudi canal. I spend my time conversing with the canal. . . .

More than my father's learning, what remained inscribed in me was his attitude toward my mother. He used to beat my mother. Similarly, when I recall my elder brother, what I remember, more than his unparalleled learning is his habit of trivializing the non-literate. . . . He resented once that my mother didn't even know how to read the almanac.

Fear nested in me regarding my father and brother, ever since I was a child. I was born a decade and half after my elder brother's birth. By the time I was conscious of myself, my elder brother was a married man. Our worlds were very different. Only after I was a grown-up, could I begin talking to my brother. Our education, mine, my elder sisters' was nothing, just nominal. I did not go to school until I was fourteen. If any one suggested that some attention should be paid to my sisters' and my education, my father would say: 'Be it as it is, we can't change it. Let it be, we cannot change it' – that was my father's favourite syntax. Those who are incapable of learning won't get it however much you may rub it into them; and from the capable, education is not going to escape. All this has to do with our previous actions and deeds: this was the conclusion of his reasoning.

The President of India has recognized my father as a consummate scholar of Vedanta in India and felicitated him. Under the aegis of the Ministry of Human Resource Development of India, the Central Sanskrit Samsthan awarded the Mahāmahopadhyāya title and commended him.

On the banks of the river Godavari in Andhra Pradesh, in the Narendrapuram community, in Kondayya's house, which was in the lane next to a Shiva temple, my father was born eighty years ago. He was born on

16th August 1920. The renowned Vedic scholar, Rāni Subbiah Deekshitulu was my father's parent. Non-literate Subadhramma was his mother. In the Narendrapuram Agrahara there are plenty of Vedic scholars.

My father had studied Vedanta at the celebrated Mylapore Sanskrit College in Chennapatnam in those days. He gained mastery over *Tarka* (conjectural/confutational logic), *Vyākaraṇa* ('grammar'), *Mimānsa* (hermeneutic/exegetical studies) and Alamkāra (Poetics/Rhetoric). He gave talks all over the country. He provided food and shelter to a large number of Brahmin pupils and imparted them education. He was opposed to the modern world. His determined opinion was that there is little that we can learn from modern technology and its buzz. A certain reflexivity would gleam in his face. It made the most ancient world proximate.... He would imagine that all the ancients like Sri Krishna, Shankaracharya and Sri Harsha were moving past and across the doorstep, talking. Thus he would teach.

He would lecture in reflective excitement as if he were himself confronting the Buddhists and the Charvakas. He is an incomparable scholar in explicating Sri Harsha's *Khandanakhandakādya*. In word and deed, and from the recesses of his heart he practiced the codes of dharma prescribed for his caste (*varṇadharma*).... He never taught non-Brahmins. Until now no non-Brahmin pupil ever stepped across our threshold. He never concerned himself with women's hardships and comforts. None of the women of our house could escape some form of derangement at sometime or other.

My father, who followed only the caste norms/dharma, spurned the so-called Hindu norm as disguised Christianity. For the sake of Hinduism, my elder brother insisted on reforming caste norms, the essence of the *Gita* and even the Vedas as well. They are real antipodes to each other, my father and my elder brother. Both of them are incomparable scholars in their chosen fields....

What fascinated me more than my father's everlasting Brahmin dharma, and my elder brother's Hindu norm, was my mother's life. In those very days my desire to write my mother's life story as an epic poem on palm leaves was born. I even gathered a few palm leaves. Someone said that people used a stylus to write on the leaves. Not knowing what a stylus was and where one could get it, I was in distress. My mother's life is an ancient tragedy. I wished to articulate it in the most antique mode. I was twelve years old then. Already by then my ties (my essential bonding) with my father had snapped.

It suddenly occurred to me one evening that, hidden in this Brahmin of ancient and eternal norms, was a rebel who could root out the caste prejudice of India in its entirety.

Strolling by the Karempudi canal, like an infant who has just learnt to utter words, I pronounced these words aloud repeatedly, as I walked on. . . . I suddenly realized that all I had thought of as progressive themes, and personal thoughts that would do good to exploited castes, were erroneous. Above all, I could comprehend that the struggle for the elimination of caste was suicidal for the exploited.

I repeated once again that – hidden in this Brahmin of eternal dharma was a rebel who could extirpate caste discrimination in India completely.

Do I realise what I am talking about, I asked myself, looking at my reflection in the canal water. Am I compromising with my permanent enemy? No! After all these days I am able to understand and make sense of my enemy. With this new insight I could understand what a blunder the movement for caste-eradication was. On the contrary, the reflective insight revealed to me that the so-called caste institution must gain equal strength; that the so-called caste-elimination [move] was a slogan of the ideologues of Hinduism; that the Hindu [concept] was nothing more than disguised Christianity and the real enemy of the oppressed castes. . . .

Only my mother's sorrows and joys have held me and influenced me since my childhood. . . . Yet neither she nor women like her find a place in this book. It seemed to me that the debate concerning caste and religion entirely revolves around men. That it is a man's world. Only through the mediation of a male will a female have a place in it. Therefore I can talk about my mother only against the backdrop of my father's life. Only against my father's eternal dharma can I write about my elder brother's Hinduism.

My father would oppose buying any modern household objects. It was his personal reflections rather than lack of money that was the cause for not buying modern implements. . . . My elder brother's aspiration was to reform what my father practiced as the ancient Indian dharma – that [which] is changeless, perpetual and unaffected by time – and synthesize it with modernized Hindu religion. . . . My elder brother believes that the ancient Brahmin dharma was not able to spread beyond the caste orthodoxy of my father and the likes of him. Consequently, the ancient norm decays and dies out, thinks my elder brother. My brother also knows that to constrict the ancient norms to only the Brahmin clan is really suicidal. If this ancient Brahmin norm is to survive, then its expansion is necessary. If it is to grow, then it has to spread from the Brahmin caste norm to other groups. Its dispersal into other clans implies transgression of the caste norm. Transcending the caste system means infiltrating Brahmin thought-schemes into the other castes. This way the Brahmin caste culture becomes the underlying support for all other castes... This way the supremacy of the Brahmin norms will remain eternally...

[My father's] unequivocal faith is that in his ancient and eternal norm there is nothing that needs change or can be changed. He would disregard normatives and anti-normatives that modify on the basis of time and place. Sāstra alone is the testimony [for him].

Whereas my Hindu convert brother's explanation... is as follows: That several issues such as according privileges of learning... to the Sudras and women can be reexamined. If the so-called cultural conventions do not compromise over time, those conventions atrophy. Both the cultural conventions and their custodians have to bow their heads before several issues such as: Vedic study, untouchability, women's education, child-marriages, (re)marriage of the aged, and voyages beyond one's country. One cannot do anything except pity those who, even after recognizing the historical truth, refuse to accede to it. Time does not wait. This is my elder brother's Hindu logical track....

My Father continued to clarify and emphasize that expansion and propagation are not obligations of the ancient and everlasting norm. A few years later my brother became the chief of a Hindu religious order....

My brother Tattvavidānandaswāmy travels in America and Europe and like Swami Vivekananda offers discourses on the Vedanta.

My father never explicates the Upaniṣads and commentaries and imparts them to those who have no Sanskrit. He cannot accept that anyone who has no sound grasp of Sanskrit can comprehend the thought of the Vedanta. In fact, Sanskrit is the language of rites and rituals. That language and its utterance create the ambience of a Brahminic tradition. That language is nobody's mother tongue. It is the language of gods. Brahmins believe that it has divine force in it. Brahmins have specified and decided who should hear the Vedas and to whom they should be imparted. That's why I have heard that the Vedic scholars used to shy away when anyone approached them to record their recitations of the Vedic hymns. My brother's Vedic teacher, Punnalu, even spurned them. This issue emphasizes the reality that Brahmins of the tradition were without the desire for expansion. Similarly, aspiring after reputation and fame is not a part of their tradition. The renowned Vedic scholar Punnalu was to be seen most of the time on the front-yard platform at Madhyapeta in Modekurru reciting Vedic hymns. He died while reciting these hymns. The domain that spread his glory was that front-yard platform of his house. What is the source of this mode of simple living? No one can modify anybody's caste: it is the gift of life. That is gained by one's beneficial or evil deeds in previous births. For the traditional Brahmin, the reputation he gains in the society is only what is endowed by birth. No one can obliterate it. . . .

When a Brahmin deviates from his caste-norm, he is be reduced to a Brahmin scum. He would not become a non-Brahmin (or a-Brahmin). Whereas the Sudra can never become a Brahmin.

My father elucidated the subtleties of this dharma on the basis of the authoritative texts of Shankaracharya, which bore testimony to the fact that he never intended to make these commentaries seek popular acclaim. He only made visible the most essential form of Shankaracharya's expositions. He was unconcerned with the glory or ignominy his elucidations would bring to Shankara's Vedanta. . . .

These days the Chief of this Order, Jayendra Saraswathi, has been discoursing on mundane or vulgar issues like Hinduism, the construction of Rama temple at Ayodhya, and founding schools on behalf of the Order. Previously neither Chandrashekharendra Saraswatiswāmi nor his predecessors ever got involved in such common issues. I have heard this discussed in intimate conversations among some traditional scholars.

'Now times have changed. Many Sudras also are becoming renouncers. Women have embraced renunciation and are giving discourses on Vedanta. There is no use talking about testimony and command,' said my father.

I remembered what my father said once: 'Even the rivers too are losing their sanctity and purity.' The despair in those words haunted me for a long time.

III

Recently a friend of mine . . . asked me – 'Aren't Brahmins Hindus?' . . .

Why do you presume that Brahmins could be Hindus? – I asked him in reply. In response my friend said – 'All the Hindus may not be Brahmins alright, but I think all Brahmins *are* Hindus.'

My friend belongs to the lower-order of the Sudra caste (*atiśudras*). Therefore, I thought, he may not know that there can be Brahmins with no religion. Later on I learnt that even the friends of Brahmins known to me have no knowledge of these Brahmins professing no religion whatever. I thought this could be because of the distinct modes of living of Brahmins, spread across each and every region as boughs and branches.... [and they] are immeasurably vast. Among us there are numerous things pertaining to one branch of Brahmins of which another branch knows nothing at all. Among these branches one group treats another as untouchables....

Therefore the word Brahmin is not a *sarvanāmam* (common noun)....

There is no end to this world-destructive night, said my father.

Every night was like the world-destroying night. It had been a long time since sleep had come to him. He was like the golden mountain, Meru, covered by pitch-dark clouds. He didn't sleep properly at night. He would call someone or other frequently – to inquire what time of the night or day it was.... 'I have experienced all that which must be gone through. Even from society I received fitting honours. Now the time of my departure has come,' said my father....

Why should we lead this grief-ridden, sorrow-filled life, Ramarao asked my father a long time ago. Ramarao was a teacher from the shepherd community. I often recall my father's response. 'When there isn't another birth, you can die. Therefore you can't help living on,' said my father....

My father internalized Shankara's Discourse on Illusion in every atom of his self. In his living and in his speech, and in every other way of his, my father tried to practise the Discourse of Illusion. Once he was suffering from severe illness.

— 'Look at this', he said in agony, 'everything [is] illusion. The body-as-the-soul [*dehātma*] is illusion. I have always said that the body in itself is the being, which is an illusion and should be given up. I have continuously said that one should realize the everlasting and undisturbed [tranquil] being. But when it happened to come to me I am not able to face my bodily torments with Shankara's Advaita.'...

There is no one who could claim that my father was a practical person. Many of our relatives have called him an idiot; they said he was a useless fellow.... My elder brother couldn't swallow my father's credo of Brahminism. I too couldn't stomach it.... 'The Hindu race will gain nothing from this idiocy,' said my elder brother. My brother is a Hindu. As a communist I found nothing to contradict in what my brother said. Then I said: 'Our father's is an ancient but now vanishing credo of Brahminism. It is a very constricted credo with nothing progressive about it. Society will gain nothing from it – nor does he. He is an utter fool. He is a blind man who wishes to stop the tide with his knee.' This was my personal view then.

Yet my father's truth alone has shone from that day to this like the bright sun.... If you don't talk about caste, it's as if you have discussed nothing at all, he said ... Implicit in this statement was: 'know thyself is the truth: know your caste [*svadharma*]. Without the knowledge of caste and caste dharma, there's no emancipation/transcendence'. In essence and truth all are equal. But in the day-to-day dealings of the universe, caste must be seen as the unforgettable reality, my father said. Moving and renting with his luminous sword of dharma and svadharma through the dark clouds like Hinduism, humanism, universal equality that covered his skies, he lived his life.

'Father, the Puri Shankaracharya says that all those who converted to Christianity would be taken back into Hinduism after their repentance,' I said to my father, sitting at his feet, 'That's all politics,' he said unhesitatingly. He reinforced the same: 'Politics, that's all.' ...

'What time is it?' yelled my father. I started up from my ruminations. When everyone is asleep, in the silence of time, unable to sleep nor capable of being awake, my father keeps on asking for the time repeatedly. 'When will it be the dawn', my father would wait in anticipation. ...

'Father, do the followers of the ancient order accept the word Hinduism (Hindu religion)?'

He was quiet for a while. Later he said:

'On the banks of the sacred and serene Krishna river, at a convention of the Pandits, the propriety and impropriety of the term Hindu came up for discussion. Then the noble and venerable savant, Dogre Visweswarasastry, through an etymological (*upapattulato*) analysis stated that the terms Hinduism and Hindu were used first by foreigners, that these words are not related to Indian [Bharatiya] culture. However, grammarians concur that even phonic improprieties also have verbal existence. Therefore, when something is absent in the discourse but prevalent in popular usage, the learned must remain indifferent toward such phonic improprieties. When the followers of the ancient order who practise the caste dharma are called Hindus, one should receive it with similar indifference; that's all, concluded Visweswarasastry. My health won't allow me to elaborate beyond this,' said my father. Thus, when the practitioners of the ancient order are called Hindus, they just remain unconcerned but would not reckon themselves at all as Hindus.

Let's return once again to my friend's question: Aren't Brahmins Hindus? Among all the issues discussed so far nowhere was religion mentioned. Now, some say that anyone called a human must have some religion. Not just a few but a lot of them say so. This is so because everyone who had school education believes that anyone who has a caste would also have a religion. They believe that the way air and light are a part of nature, caste and religion are also a part of man: such people are in majority.

But I was born in a house without a religion. We do not know what religion is. Ours is the ancient order of the Aadi Shankaracharya.

Neither my mother nor my father, when I was young or even when I was grown up, ever talked to me about the term Hindu. Nowhere among the celebrated five *Kavyas* such as *Raghuvaṃsa, Kumāra Sambhava* or the Vedantic collections like the *Bhagavad Gita* and Upaniṣads that my father elucidated and imparted to me, did we ever come across the word Hindu. Neither during his discussions nor in casual conversations did my father ever even utter the word Hindu. He only said, 'we are Brahmins' . . . Even in my Sanskrit studies . . . did I ever face the word Hindu? Even among the chants I said in my childhood (*Namakachamaka-s*) or during the twilight rituals, or in the prayers of Shankara, or in the *Totakāṣṭakam*, I have never seen the word Hindu appear. My father treats the term 'Hindu' as a degenerate or deviant Sanskrit or foreign Islamic word (*apabhraṃsa mlecha*). There is no connection of any kind at all between our Brahmin family of the ancient order and Hinduism or Hindu religion. . . .

Historically Brahmins have no relation or connection with the so-called Hinduism. But this fact has fallen into such oblivion that the view that Brahmins (alone) are seen as representatives of Hinduism has crept into the world. That's why my Sudra friend was startled to ask: how come? Brahmins are not Hindus? I realized that even to this day a Brahmin, who follows the ancient order without belonging to the Hindu religion, is alive and this Brahmin happened to be my own father . . .

In the ancient order of the Brahmin traditions there is no word that can be seen equivalent to the term religion in the Christian language. This is because that ancient order is not a religion. It is a caste or it is 'colour-clan' – that's all. Only with another caste does it have a relation of actual knowledge (*prameyamu*) – that relation could be of friendship or enmity. They are the followers of a particular caste. Their obdurate concerns and regulative bonds are all only with another caste. And the normative is, everyone must follow his respective caste norm; disregarding it would be a genuine flaw. . . .

According to the caste norm, the Brahmins have a prerogative over the Vedas. If the other castes were to turn toward the Vedas, it would amount to a transgression of the caste norms. There are severe punitive measures against that. But how to deal with religions which have no relation to the caste system? How to live together with them? How to decide what is above and what is below (in relation to them)? All these issues are not at all available in the ancient and everlasting order. In fact the followers of the ancient norm do not know what modes of response to adopt towards Islam, Christianity or even Hinduism. If members of the first two religions study the Vedas, they do not know the way to fault them. Their own concern has always been following their own dharma. In the process of such practice, their response to Islam or Christianity was in accordance with the latter's attitude towards their Order. . . .

The followers of the ancient order were always well inclined toward Islam. This is because Muslims never bothered themselves to encroach upon what were considered to be the foundational pillars of the ancient norm – the Shankara institutional Orders. The Islamic rulers who reigned in India had an enormous regard for the Orders of Shankara. . . .

There is no [concept of the] temple in the ancient order.

The so-called temples are not the creations of Brahmins of the ancient order. They are the creations of the Kshatriyas. The ancient order has no relation with either the creation or the destruction of temples. For the kings who followed Buddhism early on, Buddhist monasteries provided wealth and sustained them. . . .

My mother and my father never went to a temple together. My father never asked me to go to a temple. Precisely because *that* [convention] was absent in the ancient tradition. The temple's role is very minimal in the lives of Brahmins of the ancient order. We belong to the Vaidica branch. We never function as temple priests. We do all our 'prayers' and ritual chants at home – and never in the temple. . . .

The devotional path that involves visiting temples and rendering collective prayers is non-Vaidic [thought-practice]. It is reckoned as an inferior and vulgar method. . . . .

A Brahmin's entire bodily and spiritual life is interlaced with home – and not with a temple. In fact even on special occasions like a wedding or thread-ceremony, there is no convention of visiting a temple. . . . it is impossible to have a single place of worship for all Brahmins. Indeed the temple never became crucial in the lives of Brahmins . . . A Brahmin of the ancient order sits at home and renders his daily Vaidica ceremonial rites. . . . That's why for a traditional Brahmin, the priest is no spiritual teacher . . .

In the ancient tradition there is no culture of writing. The ancient order has no relation to the writing culture. Those that lack script are the Vedas. For them sound alone is the reliable authority. Sound itself is the Veda.

Vedas are those that haven't been written; they are untouched by humans. They are not touched by the almighty. Without origin from the beginning, when the Vedas were in the form of sound, unperceived by the senses – ancient sages in their meditative penance viewed them. In order to manifest the Vedas that exist in sonic form into the form of sound, the human body alone can be the cause, but writing can never achieve the same. Script is combined with sound. It can only be an instrument (symbol) to sound, and can never be complete (or total on its own). Therefore, script can never be a vehicle for the Veda. Vedas are heard. They must be heard and learnt with the sense of hearing. In the proximity or presence of the master (guru), sitting at the feet of the master, hearing from the master's lips repeatedly and reiterated in impeccable melody (tune); missing the tune or the accent is the greatest evil; it destroys meaning. Therefore whoever wishes to learn the Veda must take refuge with a master. All these are the tenets of faith in the ancient order. . . .

The Veda is learning without the book, it's a study without meaning, and an education without letters. 'He knows just a fragment': my father used to say about our brother, Agnihotrudu. The fragment meant the Veda. In the colloquial 'the four pieces' meant the four Vedas. The pieces here are not letters. In [our] society even the unlettered-ness (illiteracy) of the Brahmins is respected. The illiteracy continues to receive honour. The reason for this peculiarity is entirely due to the dominant social position that Brahmins have – and not because of the learning acquired through hearing (the Śrutis). In learning them no one will gain social privilege. Social privilege is gained only through social prestige . . .

My father is a living representative of a bygone age. He lived his life swimming against the current of modern times. He lived to prove that time past would seep into time present, and that eventually we only live the past through the sorrows of the time past. In his verbal commentaries on the Puranas, in the language of reflective discourse and in the course of his life he disseminated this very truth . . .

Karma [act/deed] or some other invisible norm shapes the world. We lead our lives instrumentally, swept aside in accordance with this norm. In this, our involvement is none, but if it's there – it is so for the namesake. He offered himself as a ceremonial sacrificial beast to an ancient world. An ideology of Karma, of an apriori norm, converted my father into an indifferent being . . . It is true that in this indifference and unconcern, my sisters and I found freedom – but behind that freedom lurks an invisible demon. From the ancient, prehistoric caves a dark form would penetrate into all aspects of [our] life. That was that norm. Life is sorrowful, death, disease-ridden . . . Demons and evil forces would come up . . .

My mother's name is Rāni Sita Mahalakshmi. 'Anyone with the name of Sita will only have troubles and suffering,' my mother once said. My mother's is the colour that comes from the smoke and soot of firewood. The continuous smoke that comes from the damp firewood is of a certain colour. That spiraling smoke spread across the kitchen walls lasts for generations. Only recently, until I dared to buy a gas-stove, she cooked meals only on firewood. By then she was past seventy. . . . .

My mother's helpless and sorrowful agony in the wilderness continued from her childhood till this day. My elder sister, Bulli, said to me once, ten years ago: 'The entire life of mother's and Papatta's has moved in suffering; at least, you must pay attention to them.' My sister Bulli who said those words herself suffered enormous sorrow. In the end, she succumbed to psychic illness. . . .

Brahmin women are not the twice-born. There can be no thread ceremony for them. Women, like the Sudras, have no right to recite Veda mantras; this is the case even if they are Brahmin women. . . . .

I have learnt English in order to understand Jiddu Krishnamurthy's existentialist position and other philosophical theories. But I have started to read newspapers only at the age of twenty five. . . . While I was unemployed and stayed home 'emptily' (*khaaleega* – also 'freely'), once I cornered my mother and asked her: 'Why didn't you send me to a school?' . . . She said, 'Son! My entire life was spent in cooking and in the kitchen. Further, diseases and sickness [at home], ghosts and witches – not just one thing to talk about – my whole life has passed in painful ordeals. Now, your father never bothered about the children's studies. If only the girls' education had been taken care of, would their lives have been like this?' There were tears in her eyes. I feel now how erroneous it was on my part to question my mother with this logic of education for survival. I feel repentant.

They lived that way. They knew only that kind of living. Life is not a bazaar of profits and losses and bargaining and haggling. Knowledge has very little importance in life. Several things like mutual human relations and affinities make the life move. A stern or ferocious discipline and a modern rationalism would have killed my experience and spontaneous response. Under the burden of knowledge I would have been crushed to death. Distanced from knowledge, having become totally useless, I have stood as an heir to this ancient tragedy and women's tears. Dipping a pen into their sorrow-filled innocent world, I have been able to inaugurate a Puranic world. . . .

For eons we have lived under a patriarchal regime, and still live under the control of his gaze. Women live turning inward (*antarmukhamga*). They grasp what lurks in the interior of things, events and men. . . .

IV

My journey throughout the subsequent period took place amidst people with rooted/sedimented opinions. Until then I ran mainly into people who treated piously only those thoughts that were available in books. My peripeteia began in a progressive, forward-looking atmosphere where all my apprehensions were considered idiotic. I began to understand that those who consider attacking Brahmins as progressive do not know about Brahmins. I discovered that even those who adore Brahmins secretly also know little about Brahmins.

Brahmins do not produce food. Not just food, they do not produce any object or thing. They do not set foot on agricultural land.

They do not pound grain. They just do not know those chores. They chant some mantras. Without doing any work, they eat. . . . Abusing Brahmins, insulting, attempting to belittle them on the basis of empirical examples – all these are the instruments discovered so far in anti-Brahmin onslaughts. As long as these continue, the life of Brahmins will last or continue. These are the deeds committed by an ignoramus . . . Even if thousands of years pass, this skirmish would remain immortal. No change will come with that. . . . There is something else that needs to be done.

When we ask ourselves – 'How could Brahmins remain for thousands of years, without undertaking any work, on the pinnacle of society?' – it is difficult to answer this question. It is easy to reproach the Brahmins who sit on top and eat without doing any work. Therefore it was an easy job for the rationalists to abuse the Brahmins, which would thrill the ignoramus. They are convinced that they are engaged in progressive work. Just persisting in such a task would constitute an anti-Brahmin struggle.

This will go on as long as there is no awareness/knowledge about Brahmins. Unless one tries to know what the being-of-Brahmin is, one does not know whether one is imitating or opposing Brahmins.

Brahmins are the masters of reflection in India, who have created a hegemonic web of thought. They are enjoying the fruit of such creation comfortably. Perhaps for a long time to come they would continue to enjoy these consequences. In order to create the web of thought infinite labour and an abyss of time are required. None of this is visible to the eye. Its [such creation's] results would also remain endless. The reformers who can only recognize the production of visible chain of objects – when the web of thought created by Brahmins is invisible – are able to insult Brahmins as those who do not work. With this, one can never escape the web of thought generated by Brahmins.

This is the secret. No other caste does the amount of work that Brahmins do. There are no more labouring lives than theirs. More severely difficult to achieve than the creation of the chain of objects, they [Brahmins] have generated the web of thought. The regard for it would remain for a long time. This cannot be destroyed by abuses and insults. Those who wish to confront it must know history. They should know the norms of history's movement. They should know about the transformations of the human. They should know the culture. They should know the foundational factors for the generation of the web of thought. After learning this, one should be capable of generating an alternative web of thought. For such an enormous task an entire human collective must dedicate their entire lives for generations. Every second their focus should be on this task. Even this too, they should have the force and capacity to continue for a very long time. Vanquishing *Manusmriti* does not mean lighting a matchstick to that book. This only betrays the impulsive opinions of the agitators. It can do nothing to the culture of *Manusmriti*.

The labour of Brahmins is invisible to the eye. If it is to be fought, that is possible only with invisible labour . . .

[T]he basis for my discussions of caste and cultural issues from the beginning is my father alone. The central concern of this chapter is to demonstrate, from my father's horizon of reflection that the caste-eradication argument is the agenda of Hindu ideologues, that it is a part of the agenda of a universal Christian state. . . .

We are aware that the caste-system continued with exploiting and exploited castes . . . That is, the triumphant remaining at the top and the vanquished subjugated at the bottom has already happened.

Generally, from a broad overview, there are only two camps: the triumphant and the vanquished. From a specific and minutely closer perspective, depending on the superior or inferior victory of the triumphant, there are gradations [steps] within the camp of the victorious. Depending on the severity or the triviality of the defeat, there are gradations even within the vanquished camps. If there is victory and defeat that means a war has already taken place. That is, in a major war, in accordance with the intensity and triviality of the defeat, according to the measure of their suppression, the vanquished have been stratified and constricted in their families and homes. [Those who defied the home have become peripatetics]. These shelters are called caste. Caste means home/shelter. Belonging to various castes meant being a part of domiciles of various residences/families. Those who belong to these castes are all dark coloured people. Those who named these as castes are the triumphant, white-coloured, people. There are no castes for the white-coloured people. That does not mean they have no residences/families. Unlike the black ones, these have domiciles without peculiar limits and binds or hurdles. These are the virtuous castes. . . .

How long the war went on between them, for how many generations it continued, and in what form the war occurred is extremely difficult [to know]. Although their states and destinies are already determined on the basis of victory and defeat, war [was] continued by the ones on the top to consolidate their state and the ones below to defeat the top ones. . . . That such a war between the blacks and whites in India had taken place in the RgVedic period is mentioned in the RgVeda. The Aryans who gained hegemony then were white people; the defeated ones were the black people.

Gradually these blacks and whites began to contaminate each other. With the fear that miscegenation would take place, that the white colour would flow into the castes-people and they would change into [*Varna*] colour people (they would enter the places of the victorious), the tri-colour people imposed the most heinous violence to prevent miscegenation. Anyone who is involved in miscegenation, whether colour people or caste-people – there was no escape from punishments . . . Violence on one hand, contamination on the other, continued to happen for thousands of years. Varna [colour] and caste continued to contaminate each other. Although this has gone on for thousands of years, this has not reached its completion even to this day . . .

This is the history of India's ancient and eternal caste dharma.

In [all] this, there is no mention of religion.

In this continuously moving dharmic norm, my father is the ancient-eternal representative of the Brahmin caste-clan. He has no religion. He declared miscegenation as transgression of caste dharma. With that the sacred purity of Brahmin clans gets contaminated . . .

Hinduism is the modern religion born to the ancient eternal Brahmin nature-norms and Christianity. This is the [result of] contamination of the ancient dharma. Hindu religion is the disguised ancient dharma and proxy Christianity. Hinduism was born only after the Christian colonial rule was established in India. . . .

My father declareded the Hindu ideologues' effort to form a unit of good health with Christian notions of sin and confession, forgiving sin, christening, religious expansion, its spread – antagonistic to the ancient norms. He called it proxy Christianity. He declared in the meetings of Pandits that this is unacceptable . . .

The defeated castes, with abject feelings about their state, frightened of recognizing reality, are infringing on the dharmic norms. They are indulging in contaminating caste. Each of those castes that has experienced feelings of existential abjection, these vanquished castes, are making their caste names entirely secretive. They are becoming pariahs to their own castes. They feel that to live with their defeated caste norms itself is an evil act. Without letting even their own caste collectives know, they are weaving in secret ways conspiratorial schemes to gain the state of the Hindu Brahmin. This is the inferior path.

Acknowledging god's creation, without succumbing to existential abjection, bearing their defeated caste names and then proceeding to fight to win and enter the kingdom and become the warrior: this alone is the norm of the ancient order. This is the superior path.

For the defeated castes' access to political power this appropriate path of the normed war of the ancient order is a disciplined one. For this, a ceaselessly assiduous resolution is required: consolidation and unification are needed. This is a protracted, long-term, activity. It cannot have instant results; this is an unattractive struggle. It is difficult to attract the debased and others into this path. One should be prepared to lose. Our contemporaries do not know much about this ancient normative order.

Now the lowly path that preaches Hinduism is trickery and charlatanism. It has instant results. Feelings of abjection, cowardice and slave mentality are its raw material. Sanskritizing caste names and persons' names has now become a convention. . . . . The people who enter this path are of two kinds: one – the Hindu Brahmins who seek domination over the defeated castes; two–continuing to depreciate their own defeated castes, those who crave to gain exemplary positions under Brahmin leadership . . .

Thus the ideologue of caste annihilation depended on the Hindu Brahmin. The Hindu Brahmin has depended on Christianity. Both the ideology of caste annihilation and Hinduism lack any original formulations of sustenance. Their feet have never been on the ground. . . .

But my father never paid attention to Hinduist agitations such as the one to build Rama temple in Ayodhya. He never talked about such issues in any open meeting. He assumed them to be the worldly acts of the ignoramus – and never showed any interest in them. He was more concerned about the rarely conducted fire ceremonies and Vaidica ritual performances. My father frequently remembers the very few Brahmins who have conducted the fire ceremonies. . . .

Hindu religion is a modernized one. It is determined to destroy the dharmic norms. It has made the elimination of castes its objective. Brutally severing the duties and prohibitions [constraints] of the Brahmins of the ancient order, it is determined to spread across the defeated castes the language of the Brahmins, their reflections, and their records of testimonial authority, their culture, customs and transactions as the most privileged ones. Transgressing the norm – those who have covered their defeated caste names; those who have hidden their real situation/state in the society; those who are trying to conceal their actual situation through contaminations of colour, name and culture; those who are the target of historical existential abjection – consoling all these, Hinduism is determined to pander to Brahmanism for their health.

V

My father let out his last breath in our own house in our Narendrapura Agrahara.

By then it was eleven days since this book was completed. When the publishers were told about my father's death, this conclusion was added as a supplement.

My father refused to be admitted to a hospital.

'The time of my departure has arrived. Now I must go away,' he said.

On the November 8th in the year 2001 my father performed his morning oblations. Our Rāniannaiah, and my mother holding his waist lifted him with great difficulty from the cot; and sat him reclined on the front-yard platform. His mouth did not open. In that state, moving his lips, he performed the morning oblations.

After the oblations, he chanted the verses celebrating the conquest of death (mrutuynjaya). His was a state when the body did not cooperate. My mother said that it was the chanting of the immortality verses, and that he has been reciting it for the last month. That chant would make the approach of death easy, said our brother-in-law. That day by the second twilight my father closed his eyes. Before his death, he gestured with his hand to be brought down from the cot.

Dying on the bed is prohibited. He was already prepared for the journey.

My father called my mother nearer to him. 'I have lived according to the discipline of the dharma. After my death in accordance with the Śāstra, you get your head shaven. Do not listen to anybody's counsel,' he said. She put her hand in his.

My father's elemental, earthly, body is in the courtyard. Several people, my father's disciples and Pandits came.

Even with the sons, it looks there are none, says our guru, Sripada Goaplakrishna Ghanāpāthi. The custodian of our clan-genealogy [*vamsha brahma*], Kāmeshwara Somayājulu called me and said: 'the son's birth would be properly meaningful only when he performs the mother's and father's fire ceremonies in accordance with the duties and prescriptions as laid down in the Śāstra. You are an atheist. Your father said that you should not perform the rites. You have no prerogative. You are ineligible now. On the deathbed your father insisted that the parental funeral rites be performed by the eldest son of your paternal uncle. But, after all, how can the son not remain the son and the father not be the father? You alone would be eligible for the funeral rites. I will administer your parental rites and adorn you with the sacred thread. At least in order to provide a virtuous path for that venerable Pandit, do not decline my counsel. That is the prescribed norm for you [*vidyukta dharma*],' said Somayajulu.

But in his counsel, I sensed the command: 'follow your father's orders'.

Our elder paternal uncle's eldest son, Rāniannaiha, performed our father's funeral rites. He is the unlettered person who never stepped out of the ancient norms.

My uncle's son, Konda, who works as a chemist in Hyderabad, brought me a message from our elder-brother, Tattavavidānada Saraswati Swāmi. It asked me to perform the paternal/ancestral rites, and our mother not to shave her head.

I told my mother about my elder brother's message regarding the tonsure. 'When the elder paternal uncle, Abbayi died, aunt Doddamma did not tonsure,' I reminded my mother. Mother did not agree.

'He was a great Pandit for the entire country. Therefore, it is not proper on my part to sidestep the dharma,' she said.

NOTES

1 Ashok Aklujkar, '*Paṇḍita* and Pandits in History,' in *The Pandit: Traditional Scholarship in India*, edited by Axel Michaels (Delhi: Manohar, 2001), pp. 17–19.

2 D.H.H. Ingaals, 'The Brahman Tradition,' in *Traditional India: Structure and Change*. Edited by Milton Singer (Philadelphia: American Folklore Society, 1959) pp. 3–9.

3 S.W. Jamison and M. Witzel, 'Vedic Hinduism,' 1992, http://www.peple.fas. harvard.edu/~witzel/mwbib.htm p. 66.

4 The Taittiriya verse runs: *athādhividyam | āchāryah poorva roopam | antevāsyuttararoopam | vidyāh sandhihi | pravachanam sandhānam | ityādhividyam ||* from the *Taittiriya Upanishad*, translated from the Sanskrit by Alladi Mahadeva Sastry (Madras: Samata Books, 1980), p. 38.

5 Kate Teltscher, *India Inscribed: European and British Writing on India 1600-1800* (Delhi: Oxford University Press, 1995), pp. 195–196.

6 Ādi Shankaracharya of the 8th century was a legendary commentator/interpreter of the ancient Sanskrit tradition.

7 Bimal Krishna Matilal, 'On Dogmas of Orientalism,' in *Mind, Language, and World: the Collected Essays of Bimal Krishna Matilal*, edited by Jonardon Ganeri (Delhi: Oxford University Press, 2002), p. 373.

8 Madhav Deshpande, 'Pandit and Professor: Transformations in the Nineteenth century Maharashtra,' in Axel Michaels, op.cit., pp. 119–153.

Comparative Criticism XXV, pp. 57–66. © 2004 Edinburgh University Press
Printed in the United Kingdom

Suicide and biography

JANET TODD

*I write you now on my knees; imploring you to send my child and the maid
with —, to Paris, to be consigned to the care of Madame —, rue —, section
de —. Should they be removed, — can give their direction.*

Let the maid have all my clothes, without distinction.

*Pray pay the cook her wages, and do not mention the confession which I
forced from her–a little sooner or later is of no consequence. Nothing but my
extreme stupidity could have rendered me blind so long. Yet, whilst you assured
me that you had no attachment, I thought we might still have lived together.*

*I shall make no comments on your conduct; or any appeal to the world.
Let my wrongs sleep with me! Soon, very soon, shall I be at peace. When you
receive this, my burning head will be cold.*

*I would encounter a thousand deaths, rather than a night like the last. Your
treatment has thrown my mind into a state of chaos; yet I am serene. I go to
find comfort, and my only fear is, that my poor body will be insulted by an
endeavour to recal my hated existence. But I shall plunge into the Thames
where there is the least chance of my being snatched from the death I seek.*

*God bless you! May you never know by experience what you have made me
endure. Should your sensibility ever awake, remorse will find its way to your
heart; and, in the midst of business and sensual pleasure, I shall appear before
you, the victim of your deviation from rectitude.*

[Mary] [1]

This is the suicide note that Mary Wollstonecraft wrote in October 1795
before she set out to drown herself in the Thames once she had proof of
her lover's infidelity. What useful or tactful criticism or comment can be
made on it?

Years ago, in the 1980s, I wrote a critical article on Wollstonecraft and
suicide. It was in the literary-historical vein and consequently placed the
event in a cultural context. I noted that, despite her frequently declared
rationalism, Wollstonecraft's writings in general suggest how much she

57

struggled with deeply ingrained notions of seductive irrationality; her written presentation of her own suicide displayed a similar struggle.

Before she went to France in 1792 during the violent phase of the French Revolution she accepted that suicide was morally wrong, as most British people instinctively did. In her early melancholic life before the writing of the two *Vindications* she constantly declared she longed for her own death but never thought to anticipate this 'rest', believing there was divine sanction against it. She even went so far as to dislike death represented on stage, with its histrionic (and, it is implied, false) rhetoric recording improper passion.

I then commented on the French Revolution's decriminalising of suicide and on the classical panache with which several defeated revolutionaries exited from life before the guillotine could strike them. I suggested that Wollstonecraft, in her early adult life a pious Christian, was profoundly affected by the ideas of the Revolution and might have had a sense of heroic suicide when she set out to drown herself in the Thames after her return from France. Certainly she retrospectively regarded her (failed) act as both sensible and justified. She claimed that her attempt to kill herself had been 'rational': she would not 'allow that to be a frantic attempt, which was one of the calmest acts of reason'. When, after her death, conservative commentators learned of her suicide attempt, they also placed it within a revolutionary context, accusing her of debauched French principles; her action and its context helped make her an unfit person to lecture to the nation's women in the way she had presumptuously tried to do in her *Vindication of the Rights of Woman*.

Also relevant to any contemplation of Wollstonecraft's suicide attempts, I thought, were the attitudes towards suicide of the enlightened philosophers of the time, notably David Hume, who saw suicide as a native liberty, a right when other duties had been fulfilled. Suicide could be entirely rational and justifiable if it hurt no one and concluded irremediable misery. Jean-Jacques Rousseau allowed an extended dialogue on suicide within his infamous novel *La Nouvelle Héloïse*; he did not clearly advocate it but he did allow it some cogent and persuasive arguments. William Godwin, Wollstonecraft's husband for a few months before she died, believed the act should be considered in utilitarian terms: how much did it benefit the self and others? If it seemed on balance to decrease pain it could be allowed. Beyond philosophy was the deep power of fiction, especially in the romantic suicide of Goethe's Werther, who supposedly caused a rash of copycat real-life suicides of both sexes. Elsewhere in life and literature suicide was gendered. The eighteenth century enjoyed spectacles of female death in, for example, sentimental drama such as Calista in Nicholas Rowe's *Fair Penitent* or Edmund Burke imagining the fallen queen Marie Antoinette 'with the dignity of a Roman matron' saving herself from disgrace with the 'sharp antidote' hidden in her bosom, a chaste and virtuous Cleopatra. All these examples and arguments formed part of the cultural context in which Mary Wollstonecraft purposed to kill herself, I believed.

When I wrote the biography *Mary Wollstonecraft: a Revolutionary Life* (2000), however, this cultural context of suicide seemed less pressing than the personal one. After Wollstonecraft arrived in revolutionary France in late 1792 she fell passionately in love with Gilbert Imlay. What followed was, as far as we know, her first sexual affair. Imlay deserted her and their infant child Fanny, and it was in the wake of the ensuing misery that she tried twice to kill herself, the second time with more determination. This was the occasion on which she wrote the suicide note with which I began this paper. It remained problematic. While the suicide itself seemed more private and personal in the biography than it had in a critical piece, the note still floated in its cultural-literary context and could not entirely shed its artifice.

A suicide note is a strange document. As a letter addressed to a particular person, it is an agent intended to intervene in another's life and has a public quality. But it is also written privately in such an extremity that it seems tactless and uncivil to discuss it. If it appears false, it may be because huge emotions often express themselves in clichés. A suicide note cannot, through its generic needs, be emotion recollected in tranquillity; it has to be emotion enacted and expressed in the nearest words.

As a later reader of the note, however, not the proper recipient, we are in the position of any reader of fiction. Inevitably we find ourselves responding to literariness as well as biographical emotion. Wollstonecraft's note uses common metaphor and cannot avoid a fictional tradition of female suicides.

When she wrote the suicide note quoted above, Wollstonecraft was already a writer of several death letters. In Paris, when she anticipated a natural death, she had described her expected exit from life and the arrangements she had made for the care of her daughter; in London, before leaving for Sweden she had tried to poison herself and may well have written a note to go with her actions. In Scandinavia, she again dramatised herself in the elegiac, monitory mode of the suicide. She often wrote to Imlay as if for the last time, hinting at suicide and addressing him in the stern authoritarian tones of the dying. But these earlier letters were merely rehearsals. In October 1795 she was more determined and sure of what she was about to do than on any previous occasion. Yet, even now, when she came to write this ultimately more final letter, the sentimental models bore in on her.

Reading the suicide note away from the emotions biography raises, it is impossible to avoid thinking of Rowe's Calista when Wollstonecraft hopes that her dead self will have the power her living one had lost – much as Werther also had wished.[2] Werther had luxuriated in imagining his dead body viewed by his beloved – 'when you read this . . . the cool grave will already cover the stiff remains of the restless, unhappy man'. He died, he declared, for his Charlotte, sparing her no pain, hinting at haunting, and gaining exquisite comfort from her projected tears and tremblings – and from his own posthumous power.

Despite its literary overtones, however, Wollstonecraft's note in its overall effect is neither romantically passive nor yearningly religious, but instead stern, moral and rational. The fictional characters imagine the man repentant over the prostrate corpse, but Wollstonecraft visualises herself appearing to the recumbent man in the middle of his pleasures, rather like God in Belshazzar's Feast, so awakening him to sorrow. The body, which is so richly imagined in fiction, is in Wollstonecraft's note only present in the quite rational need for it to be disposed of and concealed. It should fall into the deepest water and not be dredged up to be gazed on by men. The romantic extremes in fiction, which are also the extremes of emotion, are present in the note–chaos and serenity, burning and cold, peace and remorse–but Wollstonecraft wishes them overcome by calmness and reason. The effeminate and frightened image is foisted not on herself but on the cause of her despair: the faithless lover, Gilbert Imlay. Interestingly, after a lifetime of religious anxiety and faith, she here in this extremity shows no fear of an afterlife. In short, I argued in my critical piece, while drawing on the line of literary suicides, Wollstonecraft avoided indulging entirely in the romantic, forsaken-woman language which she occasionally used in her other letters to Imlay.

Wollstonecraft always felt herself the product of defective mothering and, though she wished to be a good mother and was affectionate and caring with her daughter, she had little experience to call on, only principle. Indeed, she insisted in *A Vindication of the Rights of Woman* that parenting skills and parental affection were not innate but had to be learned through practice and then cultivated. In the face of her despair over Imlay, any cultural belief in motherhood or biological fondness for Fanny was too weak to withstand the overwhelming dependency she felt on a man and her definition of herself in terms of this one person. In spite of her resolve in London and Scandinavia to be a mother as well as lover and sometimes to exist for her child, in contemplating Imlay's great rejection she felt she could abrogate her own maternal responsibilities–accepting that his defectiveness as father and lover excused her own.

In the biography Wollstonecraft's second suicide attempt by drowning had to loom large. It was delivered primarily through Godwin's account in his memoir of his wife, *Memoirs of the Author of A Vindication of the Rights of Woman* (1798). Apparently Wollstonecraft planned to go to Battersea Bridge but considered it too public. So she rented a rowing-boat to take her to Putney. It was dark and raining violently. To make her clothes heavy with water, she walked up and down about half an hour. She paid the halfpenny toll to get on to the wooden bridge, climbed to the top, and jumped. She did not sink at once and she pressed her clothes round her closely to weigh her body down.

In the cold river unconsciousness took a long time coming and the pain of drowning proved greater than anticipated–quite different from the ease of Werther, who simply slid into the 'broad embrace of death'. Wollstonecraft struggled for some time, then when she managed to force herself into sinking suffered intensely as she gasped into oblivion and her lungs filled with water. Unconscious, she floated down the Thames, until pulled out of the river by fishermen. She was taken to an inn where she was revived.

Along with Godwin's account, there was another version of these events in the newspaper. *The Times* described the incident, without knowing the infamous name of the 'elegantly dressed' would-be suicide. Its reporter found the attempt rather trivial, influenced perhaps by the Humane Society which had been established by the Thames and Serpentine Lake to save sufferers from the sin or crime of self-murder. They saved a good number of 'desponding ladies':

On Saturday fortnight a Lady elegantly dressed, took a boat from one of the stairs in the Strand, and ordered the waterman to row to Putney where landing, she paid him 6s. and immediately going upon Putney Bridge, threw herself from the frame of the central arch into the Thames: fortunately she was picked up by a fishing-boat, and being carried to an inn at Fulham, was soon restored by the skill of one of the medical persons belonging to the Humane Society. She told her place of abode, and added, that the cause of this, which was the second act of desperation she had attempted on her life, was the brutal behaviour of her husband. In about two hours afterwards, her coach came, with her maid, and a proper change of apparel, when she was conveyed home, perfectly recovered.[3]

If this is Wollstonecraft, her brush with death made her conventional and the account renders it difficult to write of her deed entirely in the heroic terms she seems to want in her suicide note and letters. In this version her suicide attempt seemed less rational and the effect closer to that recorded unkindly by the writer in the *Gentleman's Magazine* when s/he contemplated Wollstonecraft's act, 'From a mind of such *boasted* strength we naturally expect fortitude; but, in this instance, she was weak as the weakest girl.'[4]

It is inadvisable to sympathise with this response: Mary Wollstonecraft is now canonised as the mother of feminism with immense cultural status and, in addition, as twenty-first century people we are exhorted to refuse to attach any blame or pass judgement on an emotional act, especially an extreme female one. Yet, if repelled by the *Gentleman's Magazine,* I have nonetheless found myself divided and disturbed by the deed and not entirely controlled in response by the rhetoric of the suicide note. I realised it was because of the deserted Fanny. I knew I wanted to write about Fanny in detail and discover as much as I could about the events of her short life.

II

After contemplating several acts of abandonment of Fanny through suicide and welcome illness, Wollstonecraft unintentionally abandoned her three-year-old child when she died of complications following the birth of her second daughter Mary (later Shelley). Left parentless (her father had long given up any interest, financial or emotional, in his child) Fanny was adopted by Wollstonecraft's husband of a few months, William Godwin. When she was eleven, according to Godwin's diary he had a serious talk with her, probably the moment when he informed her of what she may already have known, that she was not his child. Perhaps this led to an increase in the diffidence and pliancy that visitors noticed in her by now, despite the fact that her mother's description in her letters is of a boisterous, spirited child. The second Mrs Godwin complained that she sacrificed her nerves to her adopted children, Mary and Fanny, and no doubt took her feelings out on the least defended of the girls. Godwin appreciated Fanny's good nature and eagerness to please, and praised her domestic help; on one occasion he wanted her to stay behind with him as a kind of housekeeper when the rest of the family went away. Yet he made a distinction between his natural and adopted daughters: 'My own daughter is considerably superior in capacity to the one her mother had before. . . . My own daughter is, I believe, very pretty.' He noted only Fanny's 'faculty of memory'.

It is unlikely that Fanny early on in childhood read the 'Letters to Imlay', which her stepfather Godwin printed in her mother's *Posthumous Works* the year after Wollstonecraft's death, when Fanny was only four; among these letters was Wollstonecraft's suicide note. There is, however, much evidence that Fanny and her half-sister Mary in their teens read *Letters from Sweden*, which describes their mother's melancholy at her betrayal by her lover; by the time she was twenty-one it is inconceivable that Fanny had not read the *Memoirs* and the 'Letters to Imlay' in *Posthumous Works*. So, as an adult, she must have known that her mother had written a suicide letter and tried with determination to kill herself, abandoning the child who would so soon be abandoned by her mother's natural death. Fanny would see that principle and indeed maternal affection had not been strong enough to keep her mother with her child. As my attention switched to Fanny, I realised that the pathos of this abandoning was influencing my attitude to Wollstonecraft's suicide attempt. For inevitably, I had always already known the fate of the daughter who had been left at home while her mother went out to die.

So, to fast forward to October 1816 when Fanny was twenty-two. On 12 October *The Cambrian* of Swansea reported the 'melancholy discovery' at the Mackworth Arms of a 'most respectable looking female'. It printed her note:

I have long determined that the best thing I could do was to put an end to the existence of a being whose birth was unfortunate, and whose life has only been a series of pain to those persons who have hurt their health in endeavouring to promote her welfare. Perhaps to hear of my death will give you pain, but you will soon have the blessing of forgetting that such a creature ever existed as

The note did not peter out; rather the name that followed had been deliberately torn off.

Fanny Imlay had read her mother's note and knew she had not intended to die without a last dramatising appeal and a justification of her life and final act to people she was intending to leave. Mary Wollstonecraft needed to influence the living when she was dead and to call, if in a more minor form than one might expect, on the literary tradition of heroic or pathetic suicide. Imlay needed to be reminded of the noble and suffering predecessors of his lover and the note clearly made a bid for power through death. But whom could Fanny Imlay address or blame for the unhappiness of her life? And, even if she had had anyone living or dead in mind, she had the knowledge which her mother had not: that the great series of Wollstonecraft's letters, including the suicide note, had in the end no effect whatsoever on the man to whom they were addressed. Imlay was not haunted and not sufficiently affected to heed the appeal and try to become what Wollstonecraft wanted him to be: Fanny's father had not come back for his lover or his daughter. The letters had of course appealed to Godwin, who saw them as similar to Werther's powerful letters, and he had fallen in love with the author. But the rest of the nation had been less impressed and Wollstonecraft's infamous posthumous reputation had much to do with their unwise publication.

Perhaps here in part is the cause of the plainness and austerity of Fanny Imlay's note. She was a literary young woman and her letters reveal a keen interest in poetry; she could certainly have written in literary mode if she had wished. She chose not to. Unlike her mother, she probably quoted life rather than literature – one can almost hear the stepmother speaking some of the words – and she avoided Mary Wollstonecraft's threatening posture towards anyone: 'in the midst of business and sensual pleasure, I shall appear before you.' Unlike her mother, she succeeded at suicide.

And here I found it impossible to take any distance from the letter or the act that followed. It was bad enough with Mary Wollstonecraft but at least her note, as I have argued, had some artifice and in the end was not required to do its work since its writer did not die but instead lived to love again, rather soon after in fact. Fanny Imlay did succeed where her mother failed and she died without the celebrity her mother had found. She had not written the works that so insistently tied writing to life as those of Mary Wollstonecraft had done. And no one had softened the starkness of suicide by providing a sympathetic account of the last moments.

While I try to write about Fanny Imlay, then, I find the suicide intruding into the life. It is, after all, the suicide of a daughter, more over-determined, more hopelessly sad even than a mother's, a death occurring before achievement and even before much life had been lived. How are this note and this death to be treated?

So far I have not progressed much beyond sadness and pity. I found myself very quickly deflected from considering the causes of her suicide and the tone of her note into contemplating the question of who tore off the name. It was said to have been done by servants, but why should they? Possibly Fanny herself tore it off, feeling her own lack of legitimate identity–after all what name could she decently claim? But it does not feel like Fanny or servants to me. Also, I felt indignant at the treatment of the body. Wollstonecraft's admittedly living body was carefully taken to the house of friends and, when she did die two years later, she was given an organised and proper funeral and a headstone with her name on it. It should not matter what happens to a dead body in an atheist world but there are proprieties which the living should observe.

Although her father, sister and Percy Bysshe Shelley all knew that it was Fanny Imlay's body lying in the Swansea inn and all read the note printed in the newspaper, none came forward to claim it. Instead they let Fanny be buried anonymously in a pauper's grave. Godwin made their position clear. He had already received a letter from Fanny hinting at suicide. At that point he had set off after her but stopped when he received a copy of the *Cambrian* and read the report of the anonymous suicide and the discovery of a body with a Swiss gold watch and stays initialled MW. Frantic to avoid any association of his family with further scandal, Godwin told Shelley not to undertake any pursuit either. On 13 October he wrote to Shelley:

> I did indeed expect it.
> ... My advice and earnest prayer is that you would avoid anything that leads to publicity. Go not to Swansea; disturb not the silent dead; do nothing to destroy the obscurity she so much desired that now rests upon the event. It was, as I said, her last wish; it was the motive that led her from London to Bristol and from Bristol to Swansea.
> ... Think what is the situation of my wife and myself, now deprived of all our children but the youngest [their son William]; so do not expose us to those idle questions, which to the mind in anguish is one of the severest of all trials. We are at this moment in doubt whether, during the first shock, we shall not say she is gone to Ireland to her aunt, a thing that had been in contemplation. Do not take from us the power to exercise our own discretion. You shall hear again to-morrow. What I have most of all in horror is the public papers ...
> We have so conducted ourselves that not one person in our home has the smallest apprehension of the truth. Our feelings are less tumultuous than deep. God only know what they may become.

It is a remarkable closing of ranks over a dead woman's body. There is no mention of the note except in the assumption that obscurity was Fanny's 'last wish'.

Does a suicide alter the whole course of a biography, the knowledge that the subject wanted to leave the life that is being recorded? Should the successful suicide of Fanny Imlay be treated any differently from the failed ones of Mary Wollstonecraft? How does a biographer keep herself and her emotions out of the text and, if she does and should, why write?

NOTES

1 *Collected Letters of Mary Wollstonecraft*, ed. Janet Todd (Penguin 2003), Letter 205.

2 When Wollstonecraft actually contemplated Goethe's *Young Werther* in reviewing an adaptation, she both identified with the hero and lamented 'the wanderings of his distempered mind, the sad perversion of those talents which might have rendered him a useful and respectable being. . . . The sensations of the moment are confounded with the convictions of reason; and the distinction is only perceived by the consequences' (*Works of Mary Wollstonecraft*, ed. Janet Todd and Marilyn Butler (London: Pickering & Chatto, 1989), 7, 71).

3 24 October, 1795. Joseph Farington lived near Wollstonecraft before she left for Scandinavia. He mentions various rumours about her in his diary. He gave the following account of her suicide:'[S]he took a Boat and was rowed to Putney, where going on shore & to the Bridge, she threw herself into the water. Her cloaths buoyed her up and she floated, & was taken senseless abt. 200 yards from the Bridge, and by proper applications restored to life. Her mind is now calm; she is separated from Imlay, and visits her friends as usual, & does not object to mention her attempt.' See *The Farington Diary*, ed. James Grieg (London 1923), July 13, 1793-August 24, 1802.

4 *Gentleman's Magazine*, May 1798, LXVIII,1, p. 368.

Comparative Criticism XXV, pp. 67–95. © 2004 Edinburgh University Press
Printed in the United Kingdom

Revising Hegel's *Phenomenology* on the left: Lukács, Kojève, Hyppolite

GALIN TIHANOV

The Young Hegel, probably the most seminal work Lukács wrote in the 1930s, never became a canonical text; it was seen by official Eastern-European Marxism as too free and libertarian in its pronouncements, while Western Marxists and Hegel scholars believed it to be somewhat ideologically skewed and prejudiced, notwithstanding all its brilliance. Here I explore the genesis, the intellectual context, the originality and limitations of Lukács's work and his interpretation of Hegel's *Phenomenology*. I adopt a comparative approach by placing Lukács in the broad context of French appropriations of Hegel from the late 1920s to the mid-1940s, concentrating especially on Kojève and, less extensively, on Hyppolite. I also trace the relevant traditions of German interpretations of Hegel to which Lukács responded. At the same time I am concerned to understand Lukács's work as growing out of his intellectual and political biography and the specific options available to him in the 1930s in the Soviet Union. This is the subject of the final section. One of the implications of my analysis is that although Lukács, on the one hand, and Kojève and Hyppolite on the other, undertook their interpretations of Hegel at roughly the same time, their positions within and commitments to the Left were of a rather different nature, and this determined in no small measure the potential of their work to impact upon the wider philosophical scene.

That Lukács's book has not been given sufficient scholarly attention can be inferred from the fact that, despite the fact that the main tenets of the book are well known by now, research on Lukács's career has so far failed to establish incontrovertibly the precise stages through which the work on the text proceeded. We know from Lukács's preface to the second edition ([East] Berlin, 1954) that the book was completed late in the autumn of 1938;[1] and *Record of a Life* gives the second half of the 1930s as the time when the book was being written.[2] Lukács, however, does not mention the fact that the text – as yet unpublished and consequently open to, and indeed inviting, modifications of various degrees of substantiality – was defended as a doctoral dissertation (*doktor nauk*) under the title 'The Young Hegel' [Molodoi Gegel'] at the Institute of Philosophy of the Soviet Academy of Sciences during Lukács's second long (1933-1945) stay in Moscow. How far the text of the thesis overlapped with that of the book is an important question that has never been studied.[3] László Sziklai was the first to reveal that the defence took place on 29 December 1942, with Lukács obtaining his doctoral certificate on 28 August 1943.[4] The viva committee was chaired by P. F. Iudin (1899-1968), an important figure in the Soviet philosophical establishment, well-disposed towards, and very supportive of, Lukács, and included, among others, philosopher M. M. Rozental' (1906-1975), who was the deputy editor-in-chief of *Literaturnyi kritik*, a journal Lukács was closely affiliated with, and the editor, with Iudin, of the influential and norm-setting *Concise Philosophical Dictionary* [Kratkii filosofskii slovar'], which at the time of Stalin's death in 1953 had undergone three editions. Thus the outcome of Lukács's public defence appears to have been largely predetermined by the favourable distribution of power and influence on the committee. It is also significant to keep in mind the fact that Lukács's defence took place very (perhaps even too) soon after he joined the staff of the Institute of Philosophy of the Soviet Academy of Sciences. Barely four months had elapsed since his appointment at the Institute (August 1942[5]), and this timing does suggest that the whole event was carefully orchestrated, thus issuing in a public defence without a real scholarly discussion.

The pre-history of Lukács's Hegel book goes back as far as the early 1930s,[6] although Lukács's orientation towards Hegelianism, and then towards Marxism, occurred in the latter half of the 1910s,[7] with his first text on Hegel published as early as 1922. Ever since, Hegel occupied a central position in Lukács's philosophical investigations.[8] Remarkably, his *oeuvre* on Hegel from the 1930s onwards runs in close parallel to his re-interpretation of Goethe, another of Lukács's life-long intellectual preoccupations.[9] Even though Lukács clearly overrated the philosophical proximity between Goethe and Hegel and glossed over Goethe's scepticism towards Hegel's dialectic,[10] both Hegel and Goethe enjoyed his zealous protection from the assaults of the Nazi German press,[11] for they both symbolised to him in equal measure the 'supremacy of reason',[12] the triumph of universal values and of classical rationality. Thus Lukács subscribed to what Karl Rosenkranz, the author of the first authoritative biography of Hegel, described with reference to Hegel and

Goethe as the 'dogma' of 'elucidating the poet's poetry with the help of the philosopher and ascertaining the philosopher's philosophy with the help of the poet'.[13]

Yet Lukács's somewhat indiscriminative embrace of Hegel and Goethe as champions of the dialectical method should not obscure his enormous contribution to raising the awareness of the Left in the 1930s of the organic link between Hegel and Marx. Lukács, together with Karl Korsch, is the single most important thinker of the first half of the century to argue the indissoluble bond between Marxism and Hegel's philosophy or, putting it even more precisely, the impossibility to think Marx without Hegel. For that reason Korsch's 1923 book *Marxism and Philosophy* (where in the conclusion Korsch praised Lukács's book of the same year *History and Class Consciousness*) was considered by the Party orthodoxy in the 1920s (and beyond) a serious ideological deviation (as was Lukács's 1923 book). The careful student of Lukács's texts cannot avoid the impression that while an uncontested political affiliation was driving him towards a full embrace of Marx, a lasting sense of measure, historical continuity and the unrestricted sway of reason was propelling him towards an appreciation of Hegel as the philosopher *par excellence*, whose thought, regardless of all delusions and limitations, posits the true scale and depth of Marxism as an intellectual platform.[14]

THE POLEMICAL FIELD: LUKÁCS, DILTHEY AND JEAN WAHL

The Nazi distortions of Hegel's philosophy are not the only target of Lukács's criticism. In *The Young Hegel*, where the polemical pathos gives way to a more constructive tone of interpretation, the intermittent, yet nevertheless strong outbursts of discontent are clearly channelled against a philosophy-of-life (*Lebensphilosophie*) interpretation of Hegel, with all attendant nuances of Romantic intuitivism or theological metaphysics and what Lukács abrogates as an existentialist reading of Hegel.

Characteristically, Lukács's polemics against the philosophy-of-life interpretations of Hegel focus on much the same names as his reinterpretation of Goethe. A case in point is the questioning of the authority and the appropriateness of Dilthey's account of Hegel's philosophy. In 1922, Lukács was still willing to see in Dilthey's book on the young Hegel not only Dilthey's 'rejection' of the dialectical method and his failure to grasp it but also – despite this – 'a valuable contribution to the history of its genesis'.[15] In the late 1930s, things were already different. He was less tolerant to Dilthey and ready to assert his own viewpoint at the cost of disregarding the complexity of Dilthey's approach.[16] The extent to which Lukács thought of his own book as an act of intellectual and political rivalry can be derived from the almost complete identity of the titles of the two respective books: Lukács's *Der Junge Hegel* and Dilthey's *Die Jugendgeschichte Hegels*. What is even more, Lukács discusses basically the same texts as Dilthey. Since most of Hegel's texts prior to 1805/1806 were works built up through fragments, their qualification as the germs of an unequivocal philosophical and political trend would suggest the imposition of a disturbingly 'strong' interpretation which refuses to take into account their tentative nature. One has to admit that Lukács should be charged with this sin more than Dilthey. In a way, Lukács violates the rules of fair play by seeking to endorse his view of the young Hegel as a proto-Marxist by resorting to *The Phenomenology of Spirit*. Unlike him, Dilthey deliberately excludes this work from his interpretative purview: his book pays attention to a genuinely juvenile Hegel, whose thought is still in the process of fermentation rather than in a state approaching systematic completeness.

Besides Dilthey, another major source of dissatisfaction for Lukács is Jean Wahl's important book *Le malheur de la conscience dans la philosophie de Hegel* (1929). Relegated to a footnote (YH, 525, n. 72), the objection against Wahl underrates the significance of his argument.[17] Lukács accuses Wahl of taking sides with Kierkegaard in 'placing the Unhappy Consciousness at the very centre of the *Phenomenology*' (YH, 536). It is vital to note the substitution that occurs in Lukács's text. While Wahl speaks of the 'unhappiness of the consciousness' in Hegel's philosophy, Lukács interprets this narrowly as an exclusive concentration on the Unhappy Consciousness as it appears in the *Phenomenology*. He discards the fact that in Wahl's book only a relatively short fragment is directly concerned with the explication of the *Phenomenology*.[18] Wahl attempts a grand-scale reading of Hegel designed to lodge him in the history of European thought after the Enlightenment. He abundantly and willingly records his own debt to Dilthey, who understands Hegel's early philosophy as the anticipation of several central motifs reappearing later in Wahl: 'Separation, pain, labour <···> are moments of each human condition, for they belong to the very process of life. Herein the frightful seriousness finds an expression with which Hegel opposes the beatific phantasies of the Enlightenment.'[19] There is no state ever to be attained without 'pain and labour'. The path of humanity winds through the thorny fields of loss and deprivation, out of which the new self-conscious and reconciled human being is bound to emerge.

In elaborating Dilthey's idea, Wahl places particular emphasis on the threads of continuity which bind Hegel and the German Romantics. A case in point is the interpretation of the connections between Hegel and Hölderlin. Although they appear closely interwoven in Lukács's book as well, there they emerge as irreversibly, if painfully, estranged from one another. This alienation ought to be measured by the extent to which Hegel abandoned his early enthusiasm for the French Revolution, while Hölderlin remained a loyal and heroic Jacobin (YH, 87–88; 202). If Hölderlin strikes his audience as a deeply tragic poet and thinker, certainly more tragic than Hegel, then for Lukács the explanation lies in Hölderlin's lasting and uncompromised belief in the ideals of the revolution, which could not but collapse in the face of subsequent historical developments. Wahl offers an altogether different interpretation. Just as for Dilthey,[20] for Wahl Hegel's proximity to Hölderlin is deemed stronger than any divergence. Like Hölderlin, the young Hegel accepts the unhappiness of human existence which manifests itself in the increasing separation between the Spirit and the objective world. Wahl reshapes this unhappiness into a fundamental human condition. In his account, both Hölderlin and Hegel understand unhappiness as a grave existential trepidation. However, Hegel, even more than Hölderlin, believes that the state of despair will be dissolved in a final point of reconciliation. Moreover, like the Romantics and Hölderlin himself, Hegel views this change as a continuous process in which unhappiness is gradually transformed into a hard-won 'serenity in suffering' (33–34). Drawing on Schlegel's principle of irony (23–24), Wahl, in what remains an exclusively theological and existentialist interpretation of the young Hegel, claims for his philosophy the role of a powerful and wonder-working converter of unhappiness into beatitude. The tone, though strongly reminiscent of Dilthey's, conveys an essentially optimistic vision: 'the motif of division, sin, torment … little by little is transformed into that of reconciliation and beatitude' (29). The odyssey of consciousness in Hegel, Wahl concludes, unites the Romantic idea of an 'infinite anguish' with the Enlightenment project of a 'happy totality': 'Hegel knows that this totality is not to be attained save through struggle and suffering' (29). Thus, in Wahl's interpretation Hegel stands out for a synthesis between primordial human woe and the ultimate salvation of man in the activity of the Spirit. This synthesis knits together the Romantic motif of grief and the Enlightenment belief in a final happy resolution. Thus Wahl's analysis proves to be underwritten by the grand and reassuring movement from affliction to beatitude. Under a Kierkegaardian veil of world-historical irony, it asserts the power of dialectical reversal. It is this power, along with the awareness that such transitions depend on the 'low' energies of pain, suffering and initial submission, that becomes so attractive for an entire generation of Marxist-minded interpreters of Hegel in the 1930s and 1940s. Lukács's case, despite his cursory criticism of and slighting attitude to Wahl's book, is hardly an exception in this respect.

Wahl's sway has been especially noticeable in France, where it provided one of the starting points for the work of Alexandre Kojève[21] and Jean Hyppolite.[22] Kojève/Kozhevnikov, a Russian émigré in Paris, gave a series of commentary classes on Hegel's *Phenomenology* at the Sorbonne from 1933 to 1939, but they only appeared in 1947, when Raymond Queneau edited them for publication. A year earlier Hyppolite's *Genesis and Structure of Hegel's Phenomenology of Spirit* appeared, following the publication of his translation of the *Phenomenology* (1939-1941).[23] Lukács claims that his acquaintance with these studies took place in the years between the first (1948) and the second (1954) editions of his own book, and one can produce no particular reason why his statement should not be trusted. We have to be more cautious, however, not to take at face value his judgement of Kojève's and Hyppolite's work. All he has to say about Hyppolite in the preface to the 1954 edition of *The Young Hegel* is an off-handed dismissal of his fundamental study (YH, xi). As our analysis will demonstrate in the following section, Lukács's abrogating qualification of these studies as a reading of Hegel in an 'existential, irrationalist sense' is less of a misjudgement and more of a carefully pondered tactic to make his own Marxist interpretation of Hegel look unprecedented and unique.

Having outlined the main polemical fields of Lukács's book, we can now better appreciate its central ideas in the context of the concurrent Left interpretations of Hegel.

THE EPISTEMOLOGY OF REVERSAL AND THE ORIGINS OF DIALECTICS

From the wealth of philosophical arguments advanced in *The Young Hegel*, I focus here on three central moments: the dialectics of goal and instrument and that of master and slave, and the problem of *Bildung*. While analysing these crucial aspects of Lukács's interpretation of Hegel I shall also comment critically on his efforts to trace the sources of Hegel's dialectic back to Hobbes and Mandeville, for it is in these attempts that

Lukács's suggestive epistemology of reversal comes to the fore. I shall then proceed to explore in more depth Lukács's reinterpretation of the *Phenomenology* as a *Bildungsroman* and Kojève's 'theatrical' interpretation of the master-slave relation. Finally, in a brief section I touch upon the consequent problem of language in Hyppolite's reading of Hegel.

Hegel portrays the history of humanity through a range of metaphors suggesting the power of adaptation, of growth through education, and of a final reconciliation with reality. We can find strong support for this view in Hegel's later *Logic*, at the point where the relation between human needs and the instruments for their attainment is discussed. Hegel appeals to a careful 'education' of human desires, and urges the reader to recognise that the goals of labour, as far as it is a process designed to satisfy practical human needs, are finite. 'To that extent', Hegel argues,

the *means* is *higher* than the *finite* ends of *external* usefulness: the *plough* is more honourable than those immediate enjoyments which are procured by it, and serve as ends. The *instrument* is preserved while the immediate enjoyments pass away and are forgotten. In his tools man possesses power over external nature, even though, as regards his ends, nature dominates him.[24]

What is of special importance to us in Hegel's argument is not merely his pathos of rational discrimination between that which is truly durable and that which is passing, momentary, and confined to an ephemeral and insecure state of delight. The really significant element in Hegel's conclusion is the rhetoric of reversal and the attendant recognition of disguise. The tool, initially considered by common sense to be secondary, subsidiary and, therefore, of only too limited a weight, emerges as genuinely indispensable, vital and superior to human needs. The centrality of the means is, however, not immediately given: it is the outcome of a successful removal of the mask concealing the true meaning of the instrument. This cognitive turn, resulting in the exchange of the starting positions occupied by the goal and the means, rests on the insight of reason. Similarly, it takes the analytical skills of the historian before one can realise how in the process of gratifying their private ambitions and passions people act and work in favour of society as a whole. In the *Elements of the Philosophy of Right*, Hegel referred to this process from the point of view of philosophy of history as the 'cunning of reason', a term which Lukács interpreted as an emphasis on the fact that human history and practice are the outcome of deliberate aspirations which nevertheless end up producing something different from what men initially desired (YH, 354).[25]

This sense of reversal and surprise, of laying bare the obvious for the purpose of gaining access to truth, of 'outmanoeuvring' the immediate expectations of experience in favour of a deeper recognition of the design of history is nowhere exhibited in a stronger and more fascinating fashion than in Hegel's analysis of the master–slave relationship and of unhappy consciousness in the *Phenomenology*. The attention Lukács gives to this problem is not comparable with the dedicated scrutiny undertaken by Wahl, Kojève, or even Hyppolite, who place it at the centre of their discussions of Hegel. The significance assigned to the problem of mastership and slavery in Lukács's *The Young Hegel* is more in line, despite all substantial differences, with Marcuse's analysis in *Hegel's Ontology and the Theory of Historicity* (1932), where the posing of the master–slave problem is discussed as an important but in no way crucial episode in Hegel's attempts to reach a full mediation between individual self-consciousnesses.[26] This clearly suggests that my own reading of *The Young Hegel* is motivated by a critical choice: it brings to the fore motifs and tendencies which might otherwise remain dormant and sidelined in the bulk of Lukács's observations.

Lukács traces the origins of the master–slave problem in the *Phenomenology* back to Hobbes. He speaks, however, rather generally about this connection. All Lukács has to say is that Hegel's point of departure is Hobbes's doctrine of the *bellum omnium contra omnes* in the natural condition of man (YH, 326).[27] But he does not go any further in the clarification of Hegel's sources. Hegel argues that man becomes a slave as the result of his refusal to fight to the death for his freedom and recognition as a human being. Insisting on the preservation of his own life in the encounter with a stronger rival, man loses his freedom. This argument is indeed strongly reminiscent of Part Two, Chapter XX in *Leviathan*, where Hobbes discusses the two principal ways of gaining domination over another person. According to Hobbes, domination arises through generation or through conquest.[28] The latter is the situation in which slavery ensues: the victor preserves the life of the conquered, but becomes his lord. Hobbes even throws in an entertaining philological puzzle to endorse his argument: is 'servant' to be derived from *servire* or, perhaps for better reasons, from *servare*, in the sense that the one whose life is preserved inevitably has to sink to serfdom?[29] Whatever the solution to this etymological riddle, it cannot obscure Hegel's indebtedness to, but also his surmounting of, Hobbes. If for Hobbes the conditions of lordship and bondage are part of the status quo of society and therefore can be changed only through the application of external force, Hegel views them in a radically different way. For him, master and slave are bound together in an internal dialectic of often invisible transitions and reversals.

According to Lukács, the other source of Hegel's dialectical method in the *Phenomenology* is Mandeville, whose 'spontaneous dialectic' allegedly depicts the turning of private vices into public benefits (YH, 355). The similarity between Mandeville's 'spontaneous dialectic' of vices and benefits and Hegel's dialectic in the *Phenomenology* is, however, too superficial to be able to serve as more than a curious intimation. While Mandeville's narrative could indeed be read as a convincing example of the 'cunning of reason' à la Hegel, in which private vices function as an important stimulus of production and consumption beneficial to the entire society, Lukács refuses to acknowledge the fact that in Mandeville's *Fable of the Bees* there is no question of a dialectical change affecting the essence of vice: vices do not become virtues even when they facilitate public well-being 'by the dexterous management of a skilful politician'.[30] Mandeville's conservative logic of the balance between vices and benefits is perhaps best exemplified by his ideas of how morality should be sustained among women: 'there is a necessity of sacrificing one part of womankind to preserve the other . . . From whence I think I may justly conclude . . . that chastity may be supported by incontinence, and the best of virtues want the assistance of the worst of vices'.[31] In Mandeville, vices never alter their moral content; they remain vices throughout. The outward analogies (the behaviour of 'winners' and 'losers' in gambling[32]) do not contribute to a better arguing of the opposite case. After all, what is at stake in Mandeville's work is not the transformation of vices into virtues, but only the *use* of vices in a public economy sustained by incessant consumption, however immoral its sources might be.

Lukács's endeavour to find predecessors of Hegel's dialectic in Hobbes and Mandeville is ultimately frustrated by his own analysis of the dialectic of master and slave in the *Phenomenology*, where he claims for Hegel an unprecedented originality in approach, thus largely refusing to recognise the roots of Hegel's opposition of master and servant in earlier philosophy, more specifically in Aristotle's *Nicomachean Ethics* and *Politics*, in Leibniz,[33] and in Rousseau.[34] Haunted throughout his interpretation of Hegel – as was Hegel himself – by the problem of objectification, Lukács insists that Hegel's innovation rests on the decision to consider the relations between master and servant in their mediation through the 'world of things' (YH, 326). The master, Hegel argues, 'relates himself to the thing mediately through the bondsman',[35] and thus manages to attain a pure negation of the thing in the act of enjoyment. The servant, too, as far as he is 'a self-consciousness in the broad sense', strives to 'cancel' things, yet his negativity towards them is limited by the fact that he has to work on them.

But as we have seen in the brief discussion of goals and instruments in the *Science of Logic*, such acts of enjoyment are not meant to last. The attainment of ends and the quenching of desire in mastery over nature is shown to be a short-lived and false victory, whereas the real achievement proves to be the tool, which is initially thought of as something humble and dependent. A similar logic underlies the chronologically earlier section on lordship and bondage in the *Phenomenology*. Here, too, one is introduced into a performance marked by an unexpected reversal. The servant gradually emerges as the more important member of the pair; he turns out to embody the truly indispensable path of human consciousness towards emancipation. 'Desire has reserved to itself', Hegel warns, 'the pure negating of the object and thereby unalloyed feeling of self. This satisfaction, however, just for that reason is itself only a state of evanescence, for it lacks objectivity or subsistence' (PhM, 238). Labour, on the other hand, is seen by Hegel as 'desire restrained and checked, evanescence delayed and postponed'. Labour has the advantage in that it shapes and fashions the thing. In Hegel's parlance, 'the negative relation to the object passes into the *form* of the object, into something that is permanent and remains' (PhM, 238). It is precisely the servant who is capable of shaping the object, because it is only for him that the object has independence. Thus, in labour, the servant's consciousness experiences a favourable transition from complete dependence to permanence and growing independence:

In the master, the bondsman feels self-existence to be something external, an objective fact; in fear self-existence is present within himself; in fashioning the thing, self-existence comes to be felt explicitly as his own proper being, and he attains the consciousness that he himself exists in its own right and on its own account (*an und für sich*) (PhM, 239).

Lukács draws from this transition a conclusion that refashions Hegel's own. The 'dialectics of work', Lukács claims, urges Hegel to place the consciousness of the servant above that of his master in the dialectics of world history. This comes as the result of the

realisation that the highroad of human development, the humanisation of man, and the socialisation of the natural condition can only be traversed through work, through that attitude to things, in which their autonomy and regulation by laws of their own become manifest by virtue of which things force man, under the threat of perdition, to cognize them, i.e. to cultivate his organs of cognition; only through work does man become human (YH, 327).[36]

Two moments are of particular importance here. The first one is Lukács's substitution of a 'dialectics of work' for Hegel's dialectics of consciousness. Admittedly, the dialectics of work is a significant moment of the dialectics of consciousness, yet hardly more than a moment. At bottom, Hegel's argument is not about labour as such; it is about the destiny of consciousness to progress through an unavoidable stage of objectification in labour, from which it has eventually to free itself in the utopian process of incorporation of the substance in the subject. Secondly, we can see Lukács adding a new dimension to Hegel's interpretation of the master-servant relation. While Hegel confines himself to underscoring the general (and abstract) condition of the servant's 'having and being a "mind of his own"' (PhM, 239), Lukács goes a long way further, and reads into this emerging independence a desired (and imagined) growth of the human faculty for acquiring knowledge of the world through labour.

HEGEL'S *PHENOMENOLOGY* AS AN OPTIMISTIC *BILDUNGSROMAN*

We can thus see how, in Lukács's interpretation, the episode of the master-slave relations is cleansed of Hegel's suppressed bitterness, which Dilthey and Wahl captured so perceptively. Hegel's explicit insistence that, along with 'formative activity', 'fear' is the other essential presupposition for the growing freedom of human consciousness (PhM, 239–240) is totally excised from Lukács's argument. What we get instead is a version of the *Phenomenology* that reads like an optimistic and dignified *Bildungsroman* of the human race. In an unceremonious footnote in the chapter on the structure of the *Phenomenology*, Lukács recommends that *Geist* be read by the modern readership everywhere as 'species', pure and simple (YH, 470, n. 5). Further in the same chapter, he calls upon the modern reader to think of Hegel's work as concerned with 'the acquisition by the individual of the experience of the species' (YH, 470). One cannot help the feeling that Lukács engrafts onto the texture of *Phenomenology* visions that originate in and attend his own coterminous interpretations of Goethe's *Wilhelm Meister* and *Faust*. This impression is confirmed by Lukács in his numerous parallels between the three works throughout the book.

There is no denial of the fact that the reading of the *Phenomenology* as a *Bildungsroman* and the comparison with *Faust* are invited by Hegel's text itself. To start with, in the preparatory notes toward *Phenomenology* Hegel pays due attention to Goethe's life work, a fact Lukács willingly points to (YH, 566). In the *Phenomenology* itself (1807), Hegel quotes a few lines from the 'Schülerszene' of *Faust, ein Fragment* (1790). To signal the main parameters of his idea of *Bildung*, in the Preface to the *Phenomenology* Hegel sets up a parallel between the development of the individual consciousness and that of Spirit: 'The particular individual, so far as content is concerned, has also to go through the formative stages of the general Spirit, but as shapes once assumed by Spirit and now laid aside, as stages of a road which has been worked over and levelled out' (PhM, 89).[37] Regarded from the side of the individual, Hegel goes on,

Bildung . . . consists in his acquiring what lies at his hand ready for him, in assimilating its inorganic nature in himself, and taking possession of it for himself. Looked at, however, from the side of universal Spirit as substance, *Bildung* means nothing else than that this substance gives itself its own self-consciousness, brings about its own inherent process and its own reflection into itself (PhM, 90).[38]

As one could infer from this passage, there is indeed a solid ground for discussing the *Phenomenology* as an extended scheme of *Bildung*. On closer inspection, however, we can see that Lukács reconfigures Hegel's design. In Hegel, the sole true subject of *Bildung* is Spirit. *Bildung* can be meaningful only as a particular stage on the road to the coming-of-age of Spirit. This is made abundantly clear in section VI B. a. of the *Phenomenology*, whose title ('Der sich entfremdete Geist, die Bildung') already suggests the interchangeability between *Bildung* and the estrangement (*Entäusserung*) of Spirit from the natural state. The product of this process is culture, broadly understood in its intellectual, political and economic aspects. Culture is the outcome of *Bildung*, as much as the latter is the result of the estrangement of the immediate self. Historically, the period of culture (*Bildung*) can be located between the Middle Ages and the French Revolution, with the subsequent domination of Napoleon seeing the complete conversion of the substance into a subject in the absolute self-awareness of Spirit.[39] Thought of in this way, the idea of *Bildung* is indeed amenable to the 'secular' reading Lukács imposes on it, but even so one could hardly tolerate his equation of *Bildung* with the unceasing growth and unfolding of human faculties in labour across history. The insurmountable contradiction in Lukács's argument is that he seems to be usurping Hegel's original meaning of *Bildung* as a limited stage in the history of Spirit to make it stand for a constant process of perfection of man in labour. On the other hand, if we think of *Bildung* as a process involving the consciousness of *the individual*, we will soon be met with Hegel's questioning of the originality of this process. Applied to the individual, *Bildung* has to rely on the mechanisms of repetition; it unfolds in the form of a compulsory following of beaten paths and an assimilation of already available experience. What is more, as far as individual development is concerned, *Bildung* is a rather ambiguous process, for it lets the *Ansichsein* of the individual shine forth only then to cancel it and transform it into universality: 'the pretence of individuality . . . is precisely the mere presumptive existence which has no permanent place in this world where only renunciation of self and, therefore, only universality get actual reality' (PhM, 515–16). For Hegel, *Bildung*, far from being a heroic and uncontested manifestation of individual power, reveals the painful transition from particularity to universality. What in this process might appear to be the talents and force of the individual is indeed a disguised recognition of the supra-individual substance of self-consciousness:

> This world [of universal objective being], although it has come into being by means of individuality, is in the eyes of self-consciousness something directly and primarily estranged, and, for self-consciousness, takes on the form of a fixed, undisturbed reality. But at the same time self-consciousness is sure this is its own substance, and proceeds to take it under control. This power over its substance it acquires by culture (*Bildung*), which, looked at from this aspect, appears as self-consciousness making itself conform to reality. . . What seems here to be the individual's power and force, bringing the substance under it, and thereby doing away with that substance is the same as the actualisation of the substance (PhM, 516–17).

It is this bitter duality of *Bildung* that Lukács is so reluctant to admit in his own analysis of the process. By concentrating on the positive aspects of work as the field in which humans cultivate their faculties and appropriate the outer world, he gives Hegel's idea of *Bildung* a vehement Marxist twist. He refuses to see that in work consciousness undertakes a necessary but by no means final step towards its liberation: it creates for itself its own supporting objectivity from which it has to deliver itself in a next step of emancipation. The *Phenomenology*, then, is a *Bildungsroman* of Spirit not in the sense of a straightforward optimistic blueprint for its progress, but rather in the sense of a narrative about the inescapable yet instructive intermediate phase of unhappy separation of consciousness from both the initial immediacy of certainty and from a final state of absolute self-awareness. Implicitly evoking the tradition

of Dilthey and Wahl, and leaning on W. Moog, in his 1946 introduction
to the *Phenomenology* Jean Hyppolite stresses the difference of Hegel's
pedagogy from that of the Enlightenment: to cultivate oneself is not to
develop along a continuous line of progress, be it even by spontaneous
outbursts of growth, but to 'oppose oneself and rediscover oneself through
a rending and a separation'.[40] Lukács chooses to spare his readers this
drama of development through laceration. For him, Hegel, like Goethe,
remains loyal to the behests of Enlightenment. The *Phenomenology* serves
Lukács as the paramount embodiment of rationalist humanism, in which
work is the centre of the generic powers of humanity and a guarantee for
mankind's never-ending progress.

One has to concede that Lukács occasionally realises the radical
divergence of his own interpretation of the master-slave relation and of
Bildung from Hegel's. In an earlier section, he discusses the concept of
Bildung in Hegel, Goethe and Schiller, and concludes that Hegel, more
than Goethe, accentuates the 'disharmonies and contradictions which
make such a dramatic appearance at this stage of human history' (YH,
263). Like Hegel, here Lukács speaks of *Bildung* as a definite period in
the history of humanity marked by 'dismemberment and bifurcation' that
precede the 'final harmony of Hegel's absolute Spirit' (YH, 263). This,
however, remains an isolated case in *The Young Hegel*. As if frightened by
the direction his analysis might take, in the subsequent paragraphs Lukács
hastens to impress on the reader the safer reading of Hegel as close, despite
all dissimilarity, to Goethe and the project of Enlightenment (YH, 263;
266).[41]

KOJÈVE'S 'THEATRICAL' INTERPRETATION OF THE MASTER-SLAVE RELATIONSHIP

As we have already pointed out in the preceding sections, in the 1930s,
Lukács was not alone in his Marxist interpretation of Hegel. The master-
slave relation and the role of work in the *Phenomenology* are particularly
prominent in Kojève's *Introduction to the Reading of Hegel*. In Lukács's
book the problem of the master-slave relation takes up only a few pages; in
Kojève's, it is the indisputable pinnacle of the entire analysis.[42] When we
define Kojève's interpretation as Marxist, we should not overlook the fact
that it is richly amalgamated with existentialist ideas.[43] The very birth of
the master-slave couple is portrayed as the result of free choice, and, in
this sense, as an existential act. Although Kojève postulates that both the
future master and the future slave are granted equal freedom to create

themselves as such,[44] this seems to be true only for the future slave: he prefers subjugation to demise. The master to be, on the other hand, has to make an altogether different decision. He must decide whether to kill his rival or to let him live. Since each of the two opponents seeks recognition by the other in the fight (PhM, 232–33), the stronger one, if he kills the weaker, will survive the struggle alone, with no one left to recognise him as victor. Therefore, he must spare the life of his adversary and overcome him, in Kojève's account, 'dialectically', that is 'he must leave him life and consciousness, and destroy only his autonomy' (15). If we opt for a post-structuralist reading of Kojève's proposition, we might say that his imagination finds at the start of human history the theatrical scene of a 'struggle to the death' with no bodies left behind.[45] In order for history to go on, the same scene must be repeated over and over again, each time to the same effect. At its origin, Kojève insists, man is always either Master or Slave.[46] History stops at the moment 'when the difference, the opposition, between Master and Slave disappears' (43). This opposition needs be kept in check at all times while History lasts: it should not be given completely free rein, or else the relation between the two will dissolve as the upshot of actual death.

Since, however, Hegel's understanding of History envisages a point where it comes to an end and gives way to a self-sufficient Spirit withdrawn in itself, Kojève has every right to predict that the interaction of Master and Slave 'must finally end in the "dialectical overcoming" of both of them' (9). Where Kojève does injustice to Hegel's project is in the claim that this state will be reached solely through the activities of the slave. In maintaining, moreover, that human history as a whole is 'the history of the working Slave' (20), Kojève comes very close to Lukács's veneration of labour and the oppressed. Yet Kojève's exposition bespeaks a larger conceptual scale and freedom of argument: he starts not from the supposedly inherent advantage of work in the formation of man, but from what he perceives to be the 'existential impasse' of mastery (19; 46). After the master has enslaved his adversary, he realises that 'he has fought and risked his life for a recognition without value for him' (19). He wants to be recognised as master, but he can be recognised as such only by the slave who, for him, is no more than an animal or a thing. Therefore, the master can never be satisfied. Mastery, however, remains a supreme value for him, and he remains fixed in it. There is nothing more he can achieve: 'He cannot go beyond himself, change, progress ... He can be killed; he cannot be transformed, educated' (22). Unlike him, the slave did not desire so strongly to be master (otherwise he would have struggled for this to the death); but he did not want to be slave either: he acquiesced in order to preserve his life. Consequently, neither of these two conditions is binding for him. 'He is ready for change; in his very being, he is change, transcendence, transformation, "education"' (22). The future and History hence belong not to the warlike Master, who either dies or preserves himself indefinitely in identity to himself, but to the working Slave (23; 225).

Like Lukács, Kojève thinks of work as *Bildung* but he accords the latter a double meaning. For one thing, *Bildung* involves work, which, as with Lukács, is a transformation of the world by making it more adapted to the needs of humans. Unlike Lukács, however, the second meaning Kojève ascribes to *Bildung* is not that of growth and development of the generic powers of man in work; rather it is an existentially coloured meaning of bringing man 'into greater conformity with the *idea* that he has of himself, an idea that – in the beginning – is only an *abstract* idea, an *ideal*' (52). This is why, unlike Lukács, Kojève is not afraid of paying due attention to Hegel's claim that the condition of slavery becomes significant not merely through the work accomplished, but rather owing to the fact that this work is carried out in the service and from fear of another (48). Kojève retains the tragic notes of the *Bildungsroman* Hegel's *Phenomenology* enacts. For him, much like for Lukács, the slave is the only true subject of *Bildung*, yet Kojève is not frightened to admit that the noble transformation of the slave entails a long passage through humiliation and undignified submission that reach the core of human existence. Lukács's serene alchemy of ennoblement and cultivation in work is abandoned here for a realistic project of improvement through observance of the basic instincts of anxiety and self-preservation.

For the analysis of what we termed the epistemology of reversal and theatricality, it is of the greatest importance to realise that Kojève's picture of history singles out bourgeois society as a space constituted by the exchange between slaves who do not have masters and masters who do not possess slaves. In bourgeois society, extended in Hegel/Kojève's notion back to the time of nascent Christianity, 'the opposition of Mastery and Slavery is "overcome". Not, however, because the Slaves have become true Masters. The unification is effected in *pseudo* -Mastery, which is – in fact – a pseudo-*Slavery*, a Slavery without Masters' (63). Thus, we can see that the bourgeois world is built upon a principle of pseudo-change that leaves just enough room for the status quo to thrive. Bourgeois society is the ultimate confirmation and example of reversals without upheaval; it is a continuation of the same 'struggle to the death' that leaves no bodies on the stage; it is a theatrical alteration of identities where the master sinks to the position of a slave of his own property, but the slave, while liberated from his slavery, does not rise to mastery.

JEAN HYPPOLITE: THE FOLLY OF LANGUAGE

These almost carnivalesque relations can also be traced in language. The stage in which Spirit alienates itself to create for itself the necessary support of objectivity is marked by dualism and harsh contradictions. Having become alien to itself, Spirit lives a disharmonious life. Even opposites previously thought of as absolute become interchangeable:

> What is found out in this sphere [of objective Spirit] is that neither the concrete realities, state-power and wealth, nor their determinate conceptions, good and bad, nor the consciousness of good and bad ... possess real truth; it is found that all these moments are inverted and transmuted the one into the other, and each is the opposite of itself (PhM, 541).

Both Lukács and Kojève remain, however, largely insensitive to the manifestations of this dialectic in language. It is their contemporary Jean Hyppolite who called attention to this aspect of the *Phenomenology*.[47] For Hyppolite, language remains the only way to go beyond the 'natural alternatives of positing and negating'.[48] In language, Hyppolite writes, we can estrange ourselves without having to die. Language can do the work of sublation by preserving at the same time as it negates. The realm of objective Spirit and culture (*Bildung*) is therefore the realm of language: 'The language expressing the condition of disintegration ... is, however, the perfect language and the true spirit of this entire world of culture' (PhM, 540). Language, being the essence of the self-alienation of Spirit, is not merely the vehicle of the process of 'inversion and perversion of all conceptions and realities' (PhM, 543), but the only way to hold together the products of this process. Hegel quotes a long passage from Goethe's recently published translation of Diderot's *Le Neveu de Rameau* to give a clearer idea of what language ought to be in order to perform this function. A 'fantastic mixture of wisdom and folly', it must resemble

> 'the madness of the musician who piled and mixed up together some thirty airs, Italian, French, tragic, comic, of all sorts and kinds; now, with a deep bass, he descended to the depths of hell, then, contracting his throat to a high, piping falsetto, he rent the vault of the skies, raving and soothed, haughtily imperious and mockingly jeering by turns' (PhM, 543).

It is due to this practice of expressing oppositions and bringing together thoughts which for the innocently subjective consciousness of the 'honest soul' (*Ehrlichkeit*) lie so far apart, that the consciousness of laceration cultivates a language 'full of *esprit* and wit (*geistreich*)' (PhM, 543). The wit of language is testimony to the merciless perversion of 'everything that is monotonous' (PhM, 544), for the self-sameness of the monotonous entity is 'merely an abstraction' which conceals the work of tension and contradiction within it and has, therefore, to be exposed and overcome in the painfully non-identical objectifications of Spirit.

We thus arrive at a picture of the evolution of Spirit largely anticipated by Lukács and Kojève in their analyses of the reversible inequality of Master and Slave, and more distinctly drawn by Hyppolite. The exit of Spirit from the condition of unchallenged yet limited subjectivity, and its setting out on the road of self-education (*Bildung*) is a process, if you will, of in*carn*ation of Spirit in a *carn*ivalesque world which is inarticulable other than through a similarly Protean language capable of expressing at once the entire range of contradictions inherent in this world. The truth about this world can be reached only in the interplay of moments that are as much positive and necessary as negative and transitory. Characteristically, then, this truth is likened by Hegel to a 'bacchanalian revel, where not a member is sober; and because every member no sooner becomes detached than it *eo ipso* collapses straightaway, the revel is just as much a state of transparent unbroken calm' (PhM, 105). We will find similar, and even stronger, imagery in Hegel's analysis of the immediate actuality of self-consciousness as reason. The metaphors of drama and performance are assisted here by a vocabulary that evokes the carnivalesque:

The "depth" which mind brings out from within, but carries no further than to make a presentation (*Vorstellung*), and let it remain at this level – and the "ignorance" on the part of this consciousness as to what it really says, are the same kind of connection of high and low which, in the case of the living being, nature naïvely expresses when it combines the organ of its highest fulfillment, the organ of generation, with the organ of urination (PhM, 372).

CONCLUSION: LUKÁCS'S OPTIONS IN THE 1930S

Let us attempt a brief conclusion after this extensive analysis of Lukács's *Young Hegel* in the context of the 1930s and 1940s left interpretations of Hegel. We have seen behind the relation between master and slave and the objectification of Spirit through alienation in *Bildung* the presence of an epistemology of reversals and turns, but also a theatrical staging of the contradictions governing these relations. Thus we arrive at a notion of – to paraphrase Nietzsche – a 'gay dialectic', which examines the oppositions in their interchangeability and containment. As we have seen, this dialectic is inconceivable without a language of wisdom and folly, of bacchanalian revelry and bodily earthiness. Language is not merely a field for the application of the dialectic; it is the very mode of objectified existence of Spirit, a form of its incarnation, replete with inner contradictions and reproducing them. The being of Spirit in the era of its objectification (culture) is essentially and imperatively linguistic; it is in language that the opposites meet to produce the theatrical blend of sublime and abject, of tragic and comic.[49] The entire history of Spirit, or – speaking in secular terms – the whole history of humankind, proves to be dependent on this necessary stage of self-estrangement, flamboyant and painful at once, and on the provocative inversion of concepts and realities.

Lukács, Kojève and Hyppolite each worked out different aspects of this challenging re-interpretation of Hegel's *Phenomenology*. Against the background of Hyppolite's and especially of Kojève's work, Lukács's revision of Hegel remained more predictable and also more inflexible in its resolute emphasis on the happy end of *Bildung* and the eventual victory of the Slave. Yet Lukács's work, too, can be seen to contain – against his own intention – the germs of a modern approach to philosophy as a narrative structure, not in the sense of Lyotard's later grand narratives, but rather in the sense of organising and strengthening one's philosophical statement through recourse to analogies with literary texts. Lukács's insistent, if, as we have seen, somewhat inflated, parallels between Hegel and Goethe remain strong evidence thereof.

However, Lukács's place in this comparison, as well as the scope and limitations of his position, have to be seen not in abstract academic terms but rather as conditioned by a network of historical and biographical contexts. Lukács's appropriation of Hegel ought to be evaluated against the background of his own intellectual evolution and the options available to him on the Moscow political scene in the 1930s. Unlike Kojève and Hyppolite, who were seen as influential in championing a left – in Kojève's case more pronounced than in Hyppolite's – interpretation of Hegel that mediated between Marxism and Existentialism without originating in or serving any narrow political allegiances, Lukács's own engagement with Hegel was shaped in no small measure by the relentless pressures of the Party orthodoxy in the 1930s and the 1940s, to which he chose to subscribe after penning his 'Bloom Theses' in 1928. After a spell of resilient struggle to defend his freedom as philosopher by reasserting the main theses of his 1923 book *History and Class Consciousness* (even though this reassertion amounted in some cases to strong modification), Lukács eventually succumbed to Stalinism.[50] It is this subscription to Stalinism, however refined and subtle, that eventually compromised Lukács's chance to exercise an (even) wider influence through his interpretation of Hegel. Kojève and Hyppolite, as is well known from existing research on the history of French philosophy after World War Two, proved much more successful in this respect.

In defining Lukács's position, we also have to bear in mind the different course of his intellectual formation and his embrace of a specific elitist Central-European culture dominated by German-language philosophy.[51] In a recent book-length study, Károly Kókai has made a strong case for Lukács as essentially a Central-European intellectual, who – as a *Mitteleuropäer* – turned for solution in succession towards the West and the East, failing in both directions.[52] He did not make it into German academia; his habilitation plans at Heidelberg were frustrated because of what Max Weber's colleagues judged to be an over-essayistic, often unruly writing style and an insufficiently systematic approach. Nor did he make it in Moscow, where he was constantly dogged by a lingering suspicion of elitism and foreignness, which barred his access to the positions of real political and ideological power and culminated in his arrest in 1941.[53] Even in the late 1940s, in Budapest, he would feel a stranger, for whom Budapest was only a stop on the way to Vienna, where he had intended to settle (but did not in the end).[54] Too Eastern for the West and to Western for the East, Lukács looked too cosmopolitan to inspire confidence among the Soviet party officials: a Hungarian by nationality, a Soviet citizen, and – for eight out of his twelve years in the Soviet Union – a member of the German Communist Party.[55]

All this added to Lukács's predicament in the 1930s and severely limited the choices available to him. After accepting the Comintern criticism of *History and Classs Consciousness* and volunteering self-criticism, his intellectual autonomy was substantially eroded. Settling in Moscow only aggravated this process; he was no longer in a position to overthrow the dogma of Stalinized Marxism. He did endeavour to lend this dogma some sophistication and flexibility, but his work, including his book on the young Hegel, bore all the signs of a political and ideological compromise. While remaining as original as possible in his writing on literary history and theory, Lukács's contributions to the history of philosophy were shaped by the prevalent climate of conformity with Stalin. In *The Young Hegel*, this mixture of originality and dogma is particularly indicative: on the one hand, Lukács defies the established Soviet interpretation of Hegel by attempting to demonstrate that not just the mature and the late but also the young Hegel could be grasped as a forbearer of Marxism;[56] on the other hand, his turn to Hegel bears – ironically – the imprint of a reconciliation with Soviet reality and a benevolent attention to the role of the great personality in history. Hegel had glorified Napoleon and the terror of the French revolution as necessary instruments of world history; he was the philosopher summoned by history to reveal the God-like nature of the politician.[57] In the 1930s, Lukács's approval of Hegel's glorification of Napoleon amounted in turn to a silent approval and justification of terror, Stalin, and the Communist Party as 'incarnations of the reason of world history'.[58] Paradoxically, one could perhaps see behind this reconciliation with Stalin, modelled as it was on Hegel's veneration of Napoleon, a more complex motivation: not just a prudent tactical acceptance of the political status quo, but also a loyalty to bourgeois individualism, to its trust in the uniqueness of great personalities – all of which is so close to Lukács's understanding of culture as based on the canon of exclusive individual accomplishments.

Thus Lukács's reading of Hegel was ridden with contradictions reflecting his own unstable position in the 1930s and his rich but controversial political and intellectual baggage. He was enmeshed in – making use of it and being himself used – a carefully orchestrated Soviet Hegel boom in the 1930s that was designed and controlled to endow the ruling Marxist-Leninist ideology with the grandeur of a long-reaching intellectual tradition.[59] This scenario was to change dramatically only a few years later, when in 1944 the Party – no longer requiring Hegel's added clout of intellectual legitimacy for its doctrine, or for its Leader's standing, and certainly concerned amidst the War with populist propaganda more than with serious philosophy – declared an end to the 'idealisation' of the German thinker.[60]

NOTES

1 G. Lukács, *The Young Hegel*, trans. R. Livingstone (London, 1975), xi. Further in the text all references will be to this edition, abbreviated as 'YH', with page numbers given in brackets in the main text. In the Introduction and the first two subsections of the present article, I take up, revise and up-date arguments and information contained in the first half of Chapter 9 of my book *The Master and the Slave: Lukács, Bakhtin, and the Ideas of Their Time* (Oxford, 2000).

2 G. Lukács, *Record of a Life. An Autobiographical Sketch*, ed. I. Eörsi, trans. R. Livingstone (London, 1983), 101.

3   In his short sketch of Lukács's life, Aleksandr Stykalin gives 1938 as the year in which
    Lukács completed his doctoral thesis; whether this should suggest that the text of the
    thesis and that of the book were identical (given their completion at the same time)
    remains unclear (cf. A. Stykalin, 'Derd' Lukach (1885-1971). Biograficheskii ocherk',
    in V. Sereda and A. Stykalin (eds.), *Besedy na Lubianke*, 2nd corrected and enlarged
    edn. (Moscow, 2001), 198). Elsewhere, however, Stykalin gives the completion date of
    the thesis as 1937 (A. Stykalin, *D'erd' Lukach – myslitel' i politik* (Moscow, 2001), 99).
    This earlier dating parallels the inconsistency to be found in the different versions
    of Lukács's autobiographical and autobibliographical submissions in the late 1930s
    (cf. esp. G. Lukács, 'Autobibliographie', *Internationale Literatur*, 1938, no. 6, 155,
    according to which the book was completed in the autumn of 1937).
4   L. Sziklai, *Georg Lukács und seine Zeit, 1930-1945* (Budapest, 1986), 99; the decision of
    the dissertation committee and the text of the certificate have recently been published
    (cf. *Besedy na Lubianke* (Moscow 2001), 124–5). In her introduction to the Russian
    edition (Moscow, 1987), the Hungarian scholar M. Hévesi asserts (incorrectly) that
    Lukács's defence took place only in 1944 and (correctly) that the first edition of the
    book (Zurich and Vienna, 1948) followed further work on the text (cf. M. Hévesi,
    'D'erd' Lukach i ego issledovanie filosofii Gegelia kak teoreticheskogo istochnika
    marksizma', in D. Lukach, *Molodoi Gegel' i problemy kapitalisticheskogo obshchestva*
    (Moscow, 1987), 3; in the preface to the (East) Berlin edition, dated January 1954,
    Lukács himself testifies to having substantially reworked his dissertation in 1947-
    48, in the process of preparing the first book edition.) The first edition of 1948
    (*Der junge Hegel: über die Beziehungen von Dialektik und Ökonomie*) did not, however,
    carry the title of Lukács's choice (*Der junge Hegel und die Probleme der kapitalistischen
    Gesellschaft*); it was restored in the (East) Berlin edition on Lukács's explicit insistence
    (see Lukács's letter to Harich of 4 May 1953 in 'Wolfgang Harich – Georg Lukács.
    Briefwechsel', ed. R. Pitsch, *Deutsche Zeitschrift für Philosophie*, 1997, no. 2, 281–304
    (296).
5   Cf. Lukács's c.v. of 23 January 1945 (*Besedy na Lubianke*, 128).
6   The best account of the early pre-history of Lukács's book can be found in L. Sziklai,
    op. cit., 91–3 and 100–102.
7   For more on Lukács's transition from neo-Kantianism to Hegelianism, see
    G. Tihanov, 'Culture, Form, Life: The Early Lukács and the Early Bakhtin', in
    C. Brandist and G. Tihanov (eds.), *Materializing Bakhtin: The Bakhtin Circle and
    Social Theory* (Basingstoke and New York, 2000), 43–69 (50–52).
8   The list of Lukács's most important writings on Hegel, most of them completely
    neglected by Lukács scholarship, comprises the following published texts: 1. 'Die
    Jugendgeschichte Hegels', *Die Rote Fahne*, 203 (Berlin, 3 May 1922) [A review of
    Dilthey's book of the same title republished as Vol. 4 of Dilthey's collected writings
    (1921)]; 2. 'Der deutsche Faschismus und Hegel', *Internationale Literatur*, 1943,
    no. 8, 60–68; 3. *Der junge Hegel. Über die Beziehungen von Dialektik und Ökonomie*
    (Zurich and Vienna, 1948); 4. 'Les nouveaux problèmes de la recherche hégélienne',
    Bulletin de la Société Française de Philosophie, XLIII, 1949, no. 2, 54–80; 5. 'Hegels
    Ästhetik', *Sinn und Form*, 1953, no. 6, 17–58 (first published in Hungarian in 1952);
    6. *The Ontology of Social Being. Hegel's False and His Genuine Ontology*, trans. D.
    Fernbach (London, 1978) (a chapter from Lukács's *Ontologie*). This list does not take
    into account the numerous reprints of these texts in German and other languages, nor

does it account for the many slight variations resulting therefrom. A good example of this practice is Lukács's article 'Die Nazis und Hegel', *Aufbau*, 1946, no. 2, 278–289, which is largely identical in terms of content and phrasing with the 1943 text from *Internationale Literatur* (indeed, the only changes in the 1946 version, along with the altered title, is the use of the past simple tense instead of the present and the omission of a small number of quotations).

9 The joint discussion and defence of Goethe and Hegel is characteristic of all of Lukács's texts on Goethe in 1932, the year marking the hundredth anniversaries of his and Hegel's death: 'Der faschisierte Goethe', *Die Linkskurve*, Goethe-Sonderheft (June 1932), 32–40; 'Goethe und die Dialektik', *Der Marxist. Blätter der marxistischen Arbeiterschule*, 1932, no. 5, 13–24; 'Goethes Weltanschauung', *Illustrierte Neue Welt*, 2 (1932); 'Was ist uns heute Goethe?', *Linksfront*, 1932, nos. 5–6 (this text was also published in Russian as 'Chem iavliaetsia dlia nas Goethe?', *Oktiabr'*, 1932, no. 4, 130–37). The single exception, for the obvious reason of extreme brevity, is 'Goethe und die Gegenwart', *Arbeiter-Sender*, 1932, no. 2, where the parallel Goethe-Hegel is absent. More on Lukács's interpretation of Goethe and the idea of *Bildung*, see in G. Tihanov, *The Master and the Slave*, 216–27.

10 On this, see Vesa Oittinen's brilliant article 'Die "ontologische Wende" von Lukács und seine *Faust*-Interpretation', in F. Benseler and W. Jung (eds.), *Lukács 2001. Jahrbuch der Internationalen Georg-Lukács-Gesellschaft*, Vol. 5 (Bielefeld, 2001), 67–99.

11 Interestingly, in 1932 Carl Schmitt, at the time one of Germany's most prominent political philosophers and very soon afterwards a proponent of Nazi ideology, wrote with sympathy about Lukács as a thinker, in whose work (the reference is to *History and Class Consciousness*) Hegel's actuality was very much alive (C. Schmitt, *The Concept of the Political*, trans. G. Schwab, Chicago and London, 1996, p. 63). Only a year later, in 1933, Schmitt published a new edition of his book, in which Lukács's name was dropped. This fact was first established by K. Löwith, in H. Fiala (pseud.), 'Politischer Dezisionismus', *Revue Internationale de la Théorie du Droit*, 1935, Vol. 9, No. 2, 119; Schmitt thought that the author of the article was Lukács (cf. K. Löwith, *My Life in Germany Before and After 1933*, trans. E. King (London, 1994), 91).

12 G. Lukács, 'Der deutsche Faschismus und Hegel', *Internationale Literatur*, 8 (1943), 62.

13 K. Rosenkranz, *Georg Wilhelm Friedrich Hegels Leben* [1844] (Darmstadt, 1988), 340.

14 As late as 1970, frail and ill, and with just a bit more than a year left before his death, Lukács was prepared to give a talk for Radio Salzburg on Hegel's significance for Marxism; he stressed to Leo Kofler, who was commissioning the talk, that it was only the importance of the topic that made him consider the invitation so seriously (cf. Lukács's letter to Kofler of 3 February 1970, in D. Redlich (ed.), 'Briefwechsel zwischen Leo Kofler und Georg Lukács, 1962-1970', in F. Benseler and W. Jung (eds.), *Lukács 2001. Jahrbuch der Internationalen Georg-Lukács-Gesellschaft*, Vol. 5 (Bielefeld, 2001), 9–23 (21–2).

15 G. Lukács, 'The History of Hegel's Youth', in G. Lukács, *Reviews and Articles from 'Die Rote Fahne'*, trans. P. Palmer (London, 1983), 55.

16 Even the most extensive account of Lukács's debt to and polemics with Dilthey does not mention Lukács's book *The Young Hegel* (cf. W. Jung, 'Georg Lukács als Schüler Wilhelm Diltheys', *Dilthey-Jahrbuch*, 5 (1988), 240–257; now reprinted in

W. Jung, *Von der Utopie zur Ontologie. Zehn Studien zu Georg Lukács* (Bielefeld, 2001), 58–78).

17 Jean Wahl, on the other hand, knew parts of *The Young Hegel* thanks to Lukács's permission to familiarise himself with the manuscript of the book before its publication (cf. the discussion in G. Lukács, 'Les nouveaux problèmes de la recherche hégélienne', *Bulletin de la Société Francaise de Philosophie*, XLIII, 2 (1949), 77). In this discussion Wahl spoke unequivocally in defence of Dilthey (77–78).

18 Cf. J. Wahl, *Le malheur de la conscience dans la philosophie de Hegel* (Paris, 1929), 158–193. Further quotations are incorporated in the main body of the text, with page references given in brackets.

19 W. Dilthey, 'Die Jugendgeschichte Hegels', *Gesammelte Schriften*, Vol. 4 (Leipzig and Berlin, 1921), 187.

20 *Ibid.*, 40 ff.

21 Kojève stated in a letter to Professor George L. Kline, dated March 30, 1967, that he did not read Wahl's *Le Malheur de la conscience dans la philosophie de Hegel*, but that he did have frequent conversations with Wahl; see 'Preface to the Paperback Edition', in N. Lee and M. Mandelbaum (eds.), *Phenomenology and Marxism* (Baltimore, 1969), vii.

22 For a broad panorama of French interpretations of Hegel in the 20th century, see Roberto Salvadori, *Hegel in Francia: Filosofia e Politica nella Cultura francese del Novecento* (Bari, 1974); Barry Cooper, *The End of History: An Essay on Modern Hegelianism* (Toronto, 1984), esp. chapter 2; Michael S. Roth, *Knowing and History. Appropriations of Hegel in Twentieth-Century France* (Ithaca and London, 1988); M. Kelly, *Hegel in France* (Birmingham, 1992), esp. 31–53; Bruce Baugh, *French Hegel: From Surrealism to Postmodernism* (New York and London, 2003).

23 For a conscise overview of Hegel's rediscovery in Paris in the 1930s and 1940s, see, among others, George L. Kline, 'The Existentialist Rediscovery of Hegel and Marx', in N. Lee and M. Mandelbaum (eds.), *Phenomenology and Marxism* (Baltimore, 1967), 113–38, esp. 114–21.

24 G. W. F. Hegel, *Science of Logic*, trans. A. V. Miller (London, 1969), 747. Lukács quotes this passage as an excerpt from Lenin's *Philosophical Notebooks* (YH, 348–9).

25 On the history of the idea of the 'cunning of reason', see H. Kittsteiner, *Listen der Vernunft. Motive geschichtsphilosophischen Denkens* (Frankfurt am Main, 1998).

26 Cf. Herbert Marcuse, *Hegel's Ontology and the Theory of Historicity*, trans. S. Benhabib (Cambridge, Mass. and London, 1987), 263. Lukács never mentions Marcuse's book. One of the reasons for this is Marcuse's benevolent attitude and obvious debt to Dilthey's philosophy-of-life interpretation of Hegel: 'The ontological concept of Life is the central one around which the problem of historicity unfolds in Hegel's work' (H. Marcuse, *op. cit.*, 319). Lukács's silence is less explicable in the late 1960s when he undertakes his own project of Marxist ontology, a chapter of which deals with Hegel's ontology; see G. Lukács, *The Ontology of Social Being. Hegel's False and His Genuine Ontology*, trans. D. Fernbach (London, 1978).

27 An indication elsewhere in Lukács's book (YH, 417) fosters the conclusion that the idea of a possible connection between Hobbes's *bellum omnium contra omnes* and Hegel's dialectic of master and slave was first revealed to him in a letter by Marx to Engels, in which the former suggests that Hobbes's principle reminds one of

Hegel's 'animal kingdom of the spirit' in the *Phenomenology*. Although the name of Leo Strauss does not appear in Lukács's book, it is very likely that the inspiration to trace the origins of Hegel's dialectics to Hobbes also comes from Strauss's book *The Political Philosophy of Hobbes* (1936) where Strauss announces his and Kojève's plans 'to undertake a detailed investigation of the connection between Hegel and Hobbes' (Leo Strauss, *The Political Philosophy of Hobbes* (London, 1936), 58 n.). On young Hegel's debt to and transformation of Hobbes, see, above all, L. Siep, 'Der Kampf um Anerkennung. Zu Hegels Auseinandersetzung mit Hobbes in den Jenaer Schriften', *Hegel-Studien* 9 (1974), 155–207 (Siep also provides a strong criticism of Staruss's interpretation of the link between Hegel and Hobbes); and A. Honneth, *The Struggle for Recognition. The Moral Grammar of Social Conflicts*, trans. J. Anderson (Cambridge, 1995), 17–18 and 43–5.

28 T. Hobbes, *Leviathan*, London, 1973, 105.

29 T. Hobbes, *op. cit.*, 106.

30 B. Mandeville, *The Fable of the Bees or Private Vices, Public Benefits* (London, 1934), 230.

31 B. Mandeville, *op. cit.*, 85.

32 Cf. B. Mandeville, *op. cit.*, 32 and remark E, 72–74.

33 Cf. Leibniz, 'On Natural Law', *Political Writings*, trans. and ed. P. Riley (Cambridge, 1988), 78; on a parallel between Leibniz and Hegel, see H. Holz, *Herr und Knecht bei Leibniz und Hegel* (Neuwied and Berlin, 1968), 83 ff.

34 On Aristotle, Rousseau, and the dialectics of lordship and bondage, see J. Shklar, *Freedom and Independence: A Study of the Political Ideas of Hegel's* Phenomenology of Mind (Cambridge, 1976), 59–70.

35 G. W. F. Hegel, *Phenomenology of Mind*, tr. J. B. Baillie (London, 1961), 235. While I think that Miller's more recent translation of the *Phenomenology* is more adequate as the result of his decision to render *Geist* as 'Spirit', I consider Baillie's translation on the whole to be stylistically better than Miller's. For this reason references will be made to the former rather than to the latter (with some infrequent modifications); Baillie's translation will be abbreviated as 'PhM', with page numbers given in brackets.

36 Here I modify the existing English translation of Lukács's German text. The German original reads: '[zu der Erkenntnis], daß der große Weg der Menschheitsentwicklung, das Menschwerden des Menschen, das Gesellschaftlich-werden des Naturzustandes nur über die Arbeit geht, nur über jene Beziehung zu den Dingen, in der deren Selbständigkeit und Eigengesetzlichkeit zum Ausdruck kommt, durch die die Dinge den Menschen bei Strafe seines Untergangs zwingen, sie zu erkennen, d. h. die Organe seiner Erkenntnis auszubilden; nur durch die Arbeit wird der Mensch zum Menschen' (G. Lukács, *Werke*, Vol. 8 (Neuwied and Berlin, 1967), 408). The English translation renders this as follows: 'realisation that the high-road of human development, the humanisation of man, the socialisation of nature can only be traversed through work. Man becomes human only through work, only through the activity in which the independent laws governing objects become manifest, forcing men to acknowledge them, i.e. to extend the organs of their own knowledge, if they would ward off destruction'.

37 I have slightly modified Baillie's translation here: I everywhere replace 'mind' by 'Spirit', and I also simplify his 'has also to go through the stages through which

the general mind has passed', with which he renders the German 'muß... die Bildungsstufen des allgemeinen Geistes durchlaufen'.

38 With 'assimilating its inorganic nature in himself' I translate the German 'seine unorganische Natur in sich zehre', which Baillie renders as 'making its inorganic nature organic to himself'. I have also modified Baillie 's 'from the side of universal mind *qua* general spiritual substance', with which he renders the German 'von der Seite des allgemeinen Geistes als der Substanz', into 'from the side of universal Spirit as substance'. Whereas I invariably use *Bildung* (as in the German text), on the first of these two occasions Baillie prefers 'culture or development of mind'; on the second one, he uses simply 'culture'.

39 Cf. J. Hyppolite, *Genesis and Structure of Hegel's* Phenomenology of Spirit, trans. S. Cherniak and J. Heckman (Evanston, 1974), 377.

40 *Ibid.*, 385.

41 More on the problematic nature of the Hegel-Goethe parallel in Lukács, see in V. Oittinen, *op. cit.*, 74–9; In the late 1940s, the time of the first publication of Lukács's *The Young Hegel* (1948), the *Faust-Phänomenologie* parallel also occupied Ernst Bloch (cf. his 'Das Faustmotiv in der *Phänomenologie des Geistes*', *Neue Welt* 1949, no. 4, 71–86); Oittinen considers Bloch's essay but suggests that it was published only in 1961 (cf. Oittinen, *op. cit.*, p. 77 n. 24).

42 For a brief orientation in the current debates on the master-slave relation and Kojève's place in them, see L. O'Neill, 'Introduction: A Dialectical Genealogy of Self, Society, and Culture in and after Hegel', *Hegel's Dialectic of Desire and Recognition. Texts and Commentary*, ed. J. O'Neill (Albany, NY, 1996), 1–25.

43 For a critique of Kojève's (and Lévinas's) existentialist reading of Hegel from the agenda of intersubjectivist moral philosophy see, above all, A. Honneth, *op. cit.*, pp. 48–49. Interestingly, just two years before the start of Kojève's lectures on the *Phenomenology* at the Sorbonne, Heidegger gave a lecture course (1930-31) on the *Phenomenology* in Freiburg, without, however, focusing on the master-slave relation (cf. M. Heidegger, *Hegel's "Phenomenology of Spirit,"* trans. P. Emad and K. Maly (Bloomington and Indianapolis, 1988)). Kojève himself never concurred with those seeing his interpretation of Hegel as existentialist; cf. Kojève's letter to Carl Schmitt of 16 May 1955, in P. Tommissen, 'Zeimal Kojève', *Schmittiana. Beiträge zu Leben und Werk Carl Schmitts*, ed. P. Tommissen, Vol. 6 (Berlin, 1998), 103. (On the contacts and the intellectual intersections between Kojève and Schmitt, see G. Tihanov, 'Regimes of Modernity at the Dawn of Globalisation: Carl Schmitt and Alexandre Kojève,' in D. Kadir and D. Löbbermann, *Other Modernisms in an Age of Globalisation* (Heidelberg, 2002), 75–93.)

44 Cf. A. Kojève, *Introduction to the Reading of Hegel*, ed. A. Bloom, trans. James H. Nichols, Jr. (New York and London, 1969), 43. Further page references to Kojève follow this edition and are given in brackets in the main body of the text.

45 A post-structuralist reading of Kojève would not be ungrounded. Kojève radicalises Hegel's motif of desire for recognition as a desire that desires not an object but the desire of another up to a point where human history becomes 'history of desired Desires' (A. Kojève, *op. cit.*, 6). Elsewhere, this statement is expanded in the following way: 'To be anthropogenetic, then, Desire must be directed toward a nonbeing – that is, toward another *Desire*, another greedy emptiness, another *I*. For Desire is absence of *Being* ...' (A. Kojève, *op. cit.*, 40). It is not difficult to recognise in this

thought a proto-image of Lacan's later interpretation of desire: 'man's desire finds its meaning in the desire of the other, not so much because the other holds the key to the object desired, as because the first object of desire is to be recognised by the other' (J. Lacan, *Ecrits: A Selection*, trans. A. Sheridan (London and New York), 1977, 58); Lacan, among others, attended Kojève's lectures on Hegel at the Sorbonne (cf. J. Heckman's Introduction to J. Hyppolite, *Genesis and Structure*, xxiii). Apparently, in 1936 Kojève and Lacan decided to write together a study on Hegel and Freud ('Hegel et Freud. Essai d'une confrontation interpretative'), of which only about 15 pages were written, all by Kojève (cf. D. Auffret, *Alexandre Kojève. La philosophie, l'Etat, la fin de l'Histoire* (Paris, 1990), 447). Lacan's debt to Kojève is brought into relief by Macherey in his article 'The Hegelian Lure: Lacan as Reader of Hegel' (P. Macherey, *In a Materialist Way. Selected Essays*, ed. W. Montag, trans. T. Stolze (London and New York, 1998), 59–60)). For a disagreement with Kojève's exegesis of *desire*, see H. G. Gadamer, *Hegel's Dialectic. Five Hermeneutical Studies*, trans. P. Christopher Smith (New Haven and London, 1976), 62, n. 7.

46 At this point one can clearly see how Kojève's existentialist premises transfigure the classical Marxist philosophy of history. The Marxist scheme presupposes a proto-stage of indiscernibility between master and slave, exploiter and exploited, followed by a protracted era of class struggles making up the 'pre-history' of humanity; finally, a short hour of eruptive break heralds the advent of an eternal realm of justice and dignity for everyone. In Kojève, however, the long spell of history dominated by master-slave relations and filled up with the theatrical dramatism of compromise and negotiation is not preceded by an initial phase of solidarity. The entire history of the human race seems to fall apart into an era of evolutionary transformations (*Bildung*) within the prevailing pattern of inequality and a radical moment at which the 'struggle to the death' finally claims a real victim in the person of the (former) master. There is no stage of primordial equality in Kojève's scenario, for his existentialist perspective precludes any point of aboriginal purity: even 'in his nascent state, man is never simply man. He is always, necessarily, and essentially, either Master or Slave' (A. Kojève, *op. cit.*, 8).

47 Here I concentrate exclusively on Hyppolite's *Genesis and Structure*, leaving aside his later work on Hegel's *Logic*. Curiously, and somewhat contrary to expectations, Kojève stated in the letter to Professor George L. Kline quoted above (n. 21) that Hyppolite (and Sartre) did not attend any of his lectures on the *Phenomenology* (but that Merleau-Ponty did, and regularly so); see 'Preface to the Paperback Edition', in N. Lee and M. Mandelbaum (eds.), *Phenomenology and Marxism* (Baltimore, 1969), vii.

48 J. Hyppolite, *Genesis and Structure*, 402. In stressing the importance of language, Hyppolite seems to be following Alexandre Koyré's identification of language and Spirit: 'The history of language and the life of language is at the same time the history of the Spirit'; see A. Koyré, 'Hegel à Iéna', *Revue philosophique de la France et de l'étranger* 118 (1934), 274–83 (282).

49 For a suggestion that Hegel's *verkehrte Welt* in the *Phenomenology*, interpreted as both 'inverted and perverted world', could be closely linked with the genre of satire as a potential manifestation of the comic, see H. G. Gadamer, *Hegel's Dialectic. Five Hermeneutical Studies*, trans. P. Christopher Smith (New Haven and London, 1976), 48.

50 For Lukács's reassertion of *History and Class Consciousness* in the mid-1920s, see his *A Defence of 'History and Class Consciousness'. Tailism and the Dialectic*, trans. E. Leslie (London and New York, 2000), most likely written in 1925 or 1926. For a cogent attempt to explain Lukács's turn to Stalinism, see J. Rees, 'Introduction', *ibid.*, 1–38 (34–8). See also Fr. Jameson's review in *Lukács-Jahrbuch*, Vol. 6 (Bielefeld, 2002), 129–36.

51 Lukács's closest friend and collaborator from his Moscow period, Mikhail Lifshits, reminisced decades later with a certain suspicion: 'And Lukács attached himself to us ('primknul k nam') as a representative of Western thought and the crisis-riddden German culture'; see M. Lifshits, 'Lukács', ed. V. Arslanov, *Voprosy filosofii*, 2002, no. 12, 105–40 (138). Lifshits even questioned Lukács's transition from Kantianism to Marxism ('Lukács, Bloch and many others – a whole generation of half-Marxists'), submitting that this was actually a transition from Kant to the historicism of the Hegel-influenced Baden School of neo-Kantianism (*ibid.*, 125–6).

52 K. Kókai, *Im Nebel. Der junge Georg Lukács und Wien* (Vienna, 2002), 235–6.

53 Lukács was arrested on 29 June 1941 and spent the time until 26 August 1941 at Lubianka, in the institutional prison of the NKVD.

54 See Z. Tarr, 'Georg Lukács zur Judenfrage', in F. Benseler and W. Jung (eds.), *Lukács 2000. Jahrbuch der Internationalen Georg-Lukács-Gesellschaft*, Vol. 4 (Bielefeld, 2000), 207–24 (220).

55 Lukács became a member of the German Communist Party on 1 July 1931; in April 1941 he was registered in the Hungarian Communist Party (cf. L. Sziklai, ' "41 bin ich doch aufgeflogen". Das Verhör Georg Lukács's in der Lubjanka', in F. Benseler and W. Jung (eds.), *Lukács 2001. Jahrbuch der Internationalen Georg-Lukács-Gesellschaft*, Vol. 5 (Bielefeld, 2001), 215–42 (229–30).

56 This is why the publication in 1956 by Il'enkov (himself one of the most distinguished Soviet philosophers of the 20th century) of a portion of *The Young Hegel* (cf. D. Lukach, 'Ekonomicheskie vzgliady Gegelia v ienskii period', *Voprosy filosofii*, 1956, no. 5) became such an important event in Soviet academic philosophy, perceived by the orthodoxy as an act of revisionism. In the GDR, Lukács's book appeared only after the death of Stalin, in 1954. The editor, Wolfgang Harich, had initially thought of publishing Lukács's book together with Hegel's *Jugendwerke*, but Lukács opposed this suggestion; cf. Lukács's letter to Harich of 16 September 1952 in 'Wolfgang Harich – Georg Lukács. Briefwechsel', 285.

57 'If Napoleon is God revealed ('der erscheinende Gott'), Hegel is the one who reveals him' ('Hegelian Concepts. Alexandre Kojève. Saturday, December 4, 1937', in *The College of Sociology (1937-39)*, ed. D. Hollier, trans. B. Wing (Minneapolis, 1988), 88).

58 Cf. U. Tietz, 'Lukács und der Stalinismus', *Deutsche Zeitschrift für Philosophie*, 1990, no. 10, 960.

59 A Party resolution of 1930 envisaged the speedy publication of a fifteen-volume edition of Hegel's works by 1932; although the edition was completed only well after World War II, by 1940 the Russian readership had at its disposal an imposing body of Hegel's texts comprising thirteen volumes.

60 The official Party line was stated in 'O nedostatkakh i oshibkakh v osveshchenii nemetskoi filosofii kontsa XVIII i nachala XIX v.', *Bol'shevik*, 1944, nos. 7–8. Concerning the Central Committee meeting that propmpted the adoption of this

policy, see M. Voslensky, *Sterbliche Götter* (Frankfurt am Main, 1991), 195. By 1947 Zhdanov considered 'the Hegel issue long settled'. He made the announcement at a formal meeting of Soviet philosophers; see C. Warnke, 'Ich lasse auf Hegel nicht scheißen!' Wolfgang Harichs Vorlesungen zur Geschichte der Philosophie 1951-1954', in S. Dornuf and R. Pitsch (eds.), *Wolfgang Harich zum Gedächtnis. Eine Gedenkschrift in zwei Bänden*, Vol. 2 (Munich, 2000), 507–47 (524). All this also meant that the chance of Lukács publishing *The Young Hegel* in the Soviet Union before the end of World War Two swiftly disappeared, even though his trusted collaborator Igor Satz had been engaged in the preparation of a Russian translation as early as 1942, in the atmosphere of the 'War thaw' (cf. L. Sziklai, *Georg Lukács und seine Zeit*, 99).

Comparative Criticism **XXV**, pp. 97–122. © 2004 Edinburgh University Press
Printed in the United Kingdom

Proust and Italian painting

MALCOLM BOWIE

On a first reading of Proust's *A la recherche du temps perdu*, one may have the impression that knowledge of Italian painting suffuses the whole texture of the novel, and that any reader who is himself or herself in possession of such knowledge will have a privileged path to the inner recesses of the work's meaning. Proust's characters, including notably his narrator, certainly name specific painters and paintings often, and in so doing display an enlarged curiosity about the major traditions of Italian art: Luini is here as well as Leonardo, Gozzoli as well as Fra Angelico, and Gentile Bellini as well as his more celebrated younger brother Giovanni. Yet it would be unwise to let oneself be carried away by the animation and copiousness of Proustian art-talk. A subsequent reading of the novel, or even a brief perusal of the monumental index to its new Pléiade edition, is likely to bring its eclipses and exclusions into view. Much more attention is paid to Venice, Padua and Florence than to Siena, Rome or Naples, and the Italian masters who figure prominently in the novel are often inspected through a docilely admired Ruskinian optic. Simplifying matters somewhat, we could say that, for Proust, Italian painting springs fully formed into life as Giotto paints the Scrovegni Chapel in the early fourteenth century and expires some two hundred and fifty years later during the old age of Titian. Baroque and eighteenth-century painting exist only fitfully in his compendious novel, and later Italian painting not at all.

Moreover, visual sensation-seekers are likely to be disappointed by many of Proust's descriptions. Works of art often enter the narrator's consciousness by way of conversation and reading, and even when they are not obviously mediated by other people's verbal performances, their presence in the book is as easily triggered by reproductions in gallery guides and artist's monographs as by first-hand experience. Proust's narrator pays generous tribute to the modern technologies involved in this widening of access to the masterpieces of the past, in sharp contrast

97

to Mme de Villeparisis, say, who seems capable of being moved only by paintings that have come into her possession by family inheritance:

On aurait dit qu'il n'y avait pas pour elle d'autres tableaux que ceux dont on a hérité. Elle fut contente que ma grand-mère aimât un collier qu'elle portait et qui dépassait de sa robe. Il était dans le portrait d'une bisaïeule à elle, par Titien, et qui n'était jamais sorti de la famille. Comme cela on était sûr que c'était un vrai. Elle ne voulait pas entendre parler des tableaux achetés on ne sait comment par un Crésus, elle était d'avance persuadée qu'ils étaient faux et n'avait aucun désir de les voir. (II, 68; II, 332)[1]

Overall, the novel is minutely attentive to the commodification of works of art, and to the manifold lives that paintings lead outside the visual field of spectators. In a work where imaginary paintings are described with fierce particularising intensity, real paintings are often seen to disappear. They become tokens of social standing, objects of ostentatious learned discussion, or compliant pictorial surfaces overprinted with the memories, motives and intentions of desire-driven individuals. Titian is swallowed into the inscrutable darkness of the Villeparisis family history; Veronese is transformed into the stage-designer for the Verdurins' seaside house-parties at La Raspelière (III, 330, IV, 391), and Carpaccio into the dramatic portraitist of the adult narrator's troubled devotion to his mother (IV, 225; V, 742). More often than not, Proust's Italian painters enter the force-field of his fiction at the point where their works have ceased to be visually arresting or exigent. They are the custodians of artistic meaning that has been lost, diluted or trivialised, and their works are plundered by an all-consuming literary imagination in search of re-usable, re-workable building materials for its own grand project.

In the remainder of this discussion I shall concentrate on the minority of cases in which the sensuous bite of visual experience is in part at least preserved by Proust's text, and artists allowed a brief period of absorption in the pleasures of paint and associated media before being recruited into the service of an emerging literary work. These examples will be arranged, as far as possible, in an ascending order of complexity, beginning with a group of artists who each appear once only, and are confined to single sentences. In his reverie on place names at the end of *Du côté de chez Swann*, the narrator switches suddenly from dreams of storm and seascape to a contrary dream of inland spring:

non pas le printemps de Combray qui piquait encore aigrement avec toutes les aiguilles du givre, mais celui qui couvrait déjà de lys et d'anémones les champs de Fiesole et éblouissait Florence de fonds d'or pareils à ceux de l'Angelico. (I, 379; I, 465)

The golden backgrounds used by Fra Angelico in his Bosco ai Frati altarpiece and elsewhere are here wittily remotivated, and repositioned in the history of art. The artist's use of gold leaf is determined not by the continuing force of a widespread medieval workshop practice but by the quality of Tuscan sunlight. Fra Angelico is resanctified as one of the supreme Florentine painters not simply because he lived in Fiesole and worked there and in Florence itself but because he distilled into certain of his paintings the local springtime weather.

The second extract is taken from *La Prisonnière*, from the episode of the first performance of Vinteuil's posthumous septet. The recital has been arranged by the Verdurins, but the role of chief adviser on the guest-list has been assigned to Charlus, who is eager to further the career of the violinist Morel. Charlus is speaking with pride rather than with distaste or jealousy of Morel's success with women:

Je ne peux pas aller avec lui au restaurant sans que le garçon lui apporte les billets doux d'au moins trois femmes. Et toujours des jolies encore. Du reste, ça n'est pas extraordinaire. Je le regardais hier, je les comprend, il est devenu d'une beauté, il a l'air d'une espèce de Bronzino, il est vraiment admirable. (III, 723; V, 241)

We could say that Bronzino appears here simply as shorthand for sexual ambiguity in males, and that the languid elongations of the Mannerist style are being summoned up by Charlus for his familiar purpose of erotic provocation. He seems to know exactly what Bronzino was at when he painted those beautiful feminised youths whose displaced virility is returned to them by a sword, an armoured codpiece, or a nearby marble figurine.[2] If we wished to associate this passage with a single Bronzino painting – one that, as it were, fitted the facts of Morel's bisexuality – we should need to look no further than the Louvre's *Portrait of a Sculptor*, in which a beautiful youth clasps a female statuette by the buttocks while casting a drooping gaze outwards towards the spectator. (Plate I) Like Morel, the youth is a lover of women whose eyes go elsewhere too. Like Charlus, but with a greater show of ironic reservation, the narrator teases the sexual appetites of his addressee.

A final example takes us forwards to eighteenth-century Italian art, and back to the earliest extended description of Combray in *Du côté de chez Swann*. The narrator reports on his fascination with architectural features that seem to have been detached from one building in the townscape and imposed upon another – with church towers, for example, that seem to grow from domestic rooftops. From Combray his associations take him to Normandy, and thence to Paris:

Plate I. Bronzino, Agnolo (1503-72): *Portrait of a Sculptor, possibly Baccio Bandinelli* (1493-1560) (oil on panel).

Même à Paris, dans un des quartiers les plus laids de la ville, je sais une fenêtre où on voit après un premier, un second et même un troisième plan fait des toits amoncelés de plusieurs rues, une cloche violette, parfois rougeâtre, parfois aussi, dans les plus nobles 'épreuves' qu'en tire l'atmosphère, d'un noir décanté de cendres, laquelle n'est autre que le dôme de Saint-Augustin et qui donne à cette vue de Paris le caractère de certaines vues de Rome par Piranesi (I, 65; I, 71).

As in both earlier cases, the naming of an Italian artist is given a complex closural force. The artist's name, placed in the final or almost final position in the sentence, on the one hand enlarges its scope, releases us from parochial concerns and the territory of France, but on the other hand recapitulates the burden of the sentence and sharpens it into a memorable propositional point. The radiance of an imagined spring, the allure of a sexual partner and the interleaved planes of the Parisian skyline are all encapsulated in the same way. Piranesi closes his sentence with particular summative force. What better way could there be of marking the passage from *colore* to *disegno* in the changing urban scene than by naming a great etcher? Proust's latecoming Piranesi learns his lessons from the darkening air, which applies itself to the dome of Saint-Augustin with consummate craftsmanship and moves patiently through successive proof stages towards the definitive print. A gentle art-historical comedy is again present here: the play of light and shadow upon Haussmann's city-plan and Victor Baltard's unlovely Italianate edifice is so powerful that this corner of the new Paris is for a moment transformed into the domed Baroque city celebrated by Piranesi in his *vedute*. (Plates II and III) By an opposite current of suggestion Piranesi has been turned into the *parisien* that his name harbours anagrammatically.

References of this kind, while adding piquancy to the transient textures of the novel, have no weight-bearing role in its overall narrative structure. These Italian artists help to create zones of semantic intensity, but do not reach out into the temporal dimension by marking significant staging-posts in the narrator's personal history. At the next level of complexity, however, exactly this begins to happen. Painters start to operate, in quiet ways, as devices of plot. Pisanello, for example, appears on three occasions and can be thought of as creating a micro-circuit of association inside the larger movement of the narration from youthful exuberance to death-haunted middle age. In *A l'ombre des jeunes filles en fleurs*, the narrator, already fascinated by the 'little band' of girls but as yet scarcely able to tell them apart, reports on the changing spectacle of the sea as seen from the window of his hotel room:

la mer, sertie entre les montants de fer de ma croisée comme dans les plombs d'un vitrail, effilochait sur toute la profonde bordure rocheuse de la baie des triangles empennés d'une immobile écume linéamentée avec la délicatesse d'une plume ou d'un duvet dessinés par Pisanello [. . .] (II, 160; II, 442).

This is one of countless passages in this volume of the novel where the narrator's erotic absorption in the girls themselves spills out on to the

Plate II. Baltard, Victor (1805–74): Eglise Saint–Augustin: photograph by Carole Rodier

Plate III. Piranesi, Giovanni Batista (1720-78): *Vedute di Roma: Piazza Navona* (detail)

natural scene, imparting a new charge to what would otherwise be its unremarkable geographical details. Feathers and down are exquisitely depicted in the Pisanello ink-drawings of birds to be found in the Louvre, but Proust's reference here is likely to include also a memory of the artist's most famous panel painting, which is owned by the same museum. For Pisanello, in his *Portrait of Ginevra d'Este*, effects his own bold displacement of attention from the human subject to nature. (Plate IV) In the essay 'Un professeur de beauté' Proust drew particular attention to this portrait, with its background of blossoms, butterflies and juniper leaves.[3] Robert de Montesquiou, the subject of the essay, possessed the art of seeing distinctly what others saw indistinctly, and in this respect had a special affinity with Pisanello. The analogy between Albertine and Pisanello's princess in their respective natural settings is a powerful one. From the undifferentiated surfaces of Ginevra's neck, temple and brow, the spectator's gaze moves into a profuse and particularised world: pistils, stamens, insect antennae and the serrated fringes of petals speak of desires and sensations that maidenly modesty cannot be supposed to know. Before Albertine has acquired character and sentience of her own the sea, distinctly seen, has already spoken of the turbulent desire-world that she is to inhabit in due course, and into which she is to usher the narrator.[4]

In *Le Côté de Guermantes*, Pisanello's differentiating eye and brush are rediscovered in a scene of broad salon comedy. 'Ah! Vous laissez bien loin derrière vous Pisanello' (II, 511; III, 242), says Legrandin, congratulating Mme de Villeparisis on her powers as a flower-painter and unctuously dismissing the minute detail and alleged deadness of her distinguished predecessor's draughtsmanship. But it is in *Le Temps retrouvé* that Pisanello's precision is to make its final appearance, in one of the episodes of much darker comedy devoted to the first World War. Mme Verdurin and her fellow society hostesses have found ingenious ways of contributing to the war effort. Under their benign supervision, younger women are now public-spiritedly wearing outfits that pick up the military theme, and jewellery that may have originated at the front. Bracelets can be made from fragments of shell-casing, and cigarette-lighters from 'deux sous anglais auxquels un militaire était arrivé à donner, dans sa cagna, une patine si belle que le profil de la reine Victoria y avait l'air tracé par Pisanello' (IV, 302; VI, 40). Proust's reference here is not to the profile of Ginevra d'Este but to those found on Pisanello's portrait medals, which were his other great contribution to late Gothic art. (Plate V) The delicacy and precision of Pisanello's line are again the main features of his artistry, and again they have been caught into a grotesque social comedy having precision of its own. The text is alive with cruel comparisons. The fortunes of soldiers at the front are set against those of Parisian salon-keepers; copper coinage against precious metals; works of art against gewgaws;

Plate IV. Pisanello, Antonio (1395-1455): *Portrait of Ginevra d'Este* (c. 1436-38; panel).
Louvre

and real queens – whether Victoria herself or Pisanello's original sitters –
against Mme Verdurin '[qui] était avec Mme Bontemps, une des reines
de ce Paris de la guerre' (IV, 301; VI, 40). Yet, Pisanello, remembered

Plate V. Pisanello, Antonio (1395-1455): *Portrait medallion of Cecilia Gonzaga*

in the patient exercise of his art, also helps to recreate here the sense of pathos that so often permeates the Proustian comic vision: the soldier, shining his halfpennies under the threat of violent death, is a close kinsman of Proust's narrator who, in *Le Temps retrouvé* as a whole, surrounds himself with living *vanitas* emblems as he polishes his own artistic project.

A further long-range refrain of this kind is, on the face of it at least, the most parsimonious of them all, for the artist concerned, the elder Tiepolo, is admitted to the novel on the strength of his name, and one only of his characteristic colours. Throughout, Tiepolo is associated with fashion, with elaborate feminine clothing in particular, and he helps to merge the novel's three most alluring female characters into a composite figuration of the 'eternal feminine'. At the start of *A l'ombre des jeunes filles en fleurs* the narrator, having only recently been admitted to the circle of the Swanns, already feels himself entitled to have views on Odette's attire:

Elle allait s'habiller elle aussi, bien que j'eusse protesté qu'aucune robe 'de ville' ne vaudrait à beaucoup près la merveilleuse robe de chambre de crêpe de Chine ou de soie, vieux rose, cerise, rose Tiepolo, blanche, mauve, verte, rouge, jaune, unie ou à dessins, dans laquelle Mme Swann avait déjeuné et qu'elle allait ôter. (I, 531; II, 131)

Very much later in the novel, at the start of *Sodome et Gomorrhe*, the duchesse de Guermantes arrives at an evening reception wearing a cloak 'd'un magnifique rouge Tiepolo' (III, 61; IV, 71) and, before leaving, fifty pages later, poses in the same garment before her admiring fellow guests: 'Droite, isolée, ayant à ses côtés son mari et moi, la duchesse se tenait à gauche de l'escalier, déjà enveloppée dans un manteau à la Tiepolo' (III, 117; IV, 137-8). But it is only at the end of *La Prisonnière* that this slightly uncertain shade of pink or red acquires a definition and full cadential force. At a time when Venice is still an impossible destination for the narrator, Albertine is wearing a tantalising Fortuny dress that breathes Venice from its very fabric and from its every decorative device:

Si je n'avais jamais vu Venise, j'en rêvais sans cesse depuis ces vacances de Pâques, qu'encore enfant, j'avais dû y passer, et plus anciennement encore par les gravures du Titien et les photographies de Giotto que Swann m'avait jadis données à Combray. La robe de Fortuny que portait ce soir-là Albertine me semblait comme l'ombre tentatrice de cette invisible Venise. Elle était envahie d'ornementation arabe comme Venise, comme les palais de Venise dissimulés à la façon de sultanes derrière un voile ajouré de pierre, comme les reliures de la bibliothèque Ambrosienne, comme les colonnes desquelles les oiseaux orientaux qui signifient alternativement la mort et la vie, se répétaient dans le miroitement de l'étoffe, d'un bleu profond qui au fur et à mesure que mon regard s'y avançait se changeait en or malléable, par ces mêmes transmutations qui, devant la gondole qui s'avance, changent en métal flamboyant l'azur du Grand Canal. Et les manches étaient doublées d'un rose cerise qui est si particulièrement vénitien qu'on l'appelle rose Tiepolo (III, 895-6; V, 450).

Thus Proust's paragraph ends: upon the artist's name and upon a colour singled out for emphasis from the shimmering Venetian palette. Two currents of sensuous suggestion reach their point of convergence here. On the one hand pink is the colour of Odette's clothing during her career as a courtesan, and the colour of Albertine's arousal, noted during all the main scenes of love-making between her and the narrator. On the other hand, Venice is the most desirable of cities and the richest in erotic provocation, and Tiepolo the last of its great narrative painters. There is an omen in the naming at this point of the presiding artistic genius of the Republic in its declining years, for the narrator's journey to Venice, as recounted in *Albertine disparue*, contains its own story of irreversible decline and unassuageable loss. The Venice he finally discovers is beautiful still, but fatefully trapped in nostalgia for its own past glories. The city is a versatile mnemonic instrument and a fitting stage-set for the narrator's own exercises in the remembering of lost love. What Proust is doing, therefore, in this overdetermined Tiepolo cadence is putting colour to dramaturgical use in a manner that is altogether worthy of Tiepolo himself. Proust sends his flamboyant pink on an echoing journey across the vast internal spaces of his fiction, rather as Tiepolo projected his blues, golds and indeed, occasionally, his pinks across the huge vault of his ceilings in the Residenz at Würzburg or the church of Santa Maria dei Gesuati in Venice.

At first sight the next level of complexity hardly seems complex at all, for it involves a simplistic reduction of artistic meaning and a wilful refusal to attribute depth, subtlety and guile to the art of depiction. For Proust's fictional commentators on art, people in paintings often resemble people in real life. Painted figures seem to release themselves from the captivity of their frames and to wander free in salon society; and, by an opposite but equally unsubtle movement, friends, neighbours and acquaintances from the everyday world retreat into the artificially stabilised world of paint upon canvas. The search for such equivalences spreads by contagion among the characters of the novel. For Swann, Bloch resembles Mahomet II as painted by Gentile Bellini (I, 96 and 349; I, 115 and I, 427), and Mme Blatin Fra Bartolommeo's portrait of Savanarola (I, 525; II, 125). For Saint-Loup, the chambermaid of Mme Putbus is 'Follement Giorgione!' (III, 94; IV, 111). For the narrator, Albertine in profile suddenly resembles a Leonardo grotesque (III, 587; V, 83), while at the final 'matinée de Guermantes' one of the sclerotic guests seems to belong in a study by Mantegna or Michelangelo (IV, 518; VI, 310) rather than in a modern drawing-room.

Reading paintings in this simplifying way does not, however, necessarily produce simple effects within the narrative texture. The narrator, criticising Swann in *A l'ombre des jeunes filles en fleurs* for his excessive devotion to resemblances of this kind, already suggests one of the main ways in which they can be rescued and redeemed:

Si on avait écouté Swann, les cortèges des rois mages [in the Palazzo Medici-Riccardi], déjà si anachroniques quand Benozzo Gozzoli y introduisit les Médicis, l'eussent été davantage encore puisqu'ils eussent contenu les portraits d'une foule d'hommes, contemporains non de Gozzoli, mais de Swann, c'est-à-dire postérieurs non plus seulement de quinze siècles à la Nativité, mais de quatre au peintre lui-même. Il n'y avait pas selon Swann, dans ces cortèges, un seul Parisien de marque qui manquât. (I, 525-6; II, 125)

As Swann repeats the artist's gesture by projecting his contemporaries back into the past, and is taken to task by the narrator for doing so, the troubled temporal medium in which the narrator himself dwells comes clearly into view, and in its two contrary dispensations. On the one hand, that medium contains improbable survivals, invariant structures of society or of individual minds that seem to migrate across the centuries: the magi, the Medici and the moderns can be expected to resemble each other in their passions if not in their facial features. On the other hand, time-bound meanings have an alarming propensity to wane and decay, or to be ousted by the changing individual's latest emotional demands: the Medici have to disappear in order to allow the moderns to become visible.

The survival and decay of prototypes give Proust one of his essential themes and a reliable organising device in his recklessly distended narrative. His army of Italian painters has all the flexibility of response needed for the execution of this split-level project: they supply continuity and change, repetition and innovation, symmetry and surprise.[5] Even the simplest equivalences between characters in the novel and painted images external to it can prove rich in ambiguity, and produce strange syncopations within the onward flow of narrative time. The case of Giovanni Bellini is particularly instructive from this point of view. In *A l'ombre des jeunes filles en fleurs*, describing the fluting tones to be found in the voices of young girls, the narrator speaks of them playing upon their vocal instrument 'avec cette application, cette ardeur des petits anges musiciens de Bellini' (II, 262; II, 564). It seems likely that Proust's reference here is to the two tiny figures who appear at the feet of the enthroned madonna in Bellini's Frari triptych—one playing the lute and the other a pipe. (Plate VI) In *La Prisonnière*, on the other hand, the narrator speaks of 'un ange doux et grave de Bellini, jouant du théorbe' (III, 765; V, 294) and seems to have in mind the older and more serene lutenist who stands beside the virgin in Bellini's votive picture for Doge Agostino Barbarigo, in the church of San Pietro Martire on Murano.[6] (Plate VII) There is no need to consult either image, however, in order to register the contrast between childish and youthful musicianship, and between the early and late epochs of the narrator's infatuation with Albertine. In a sense, Bellini merely provides optional external scaffolding for the narrator's self-analysis. But when, at the end of *La Prisonnière*, these musical angels return they can easily produce in the reader a complex spasm of remembrance. Albertine is not a work of art, the narrator reminds himself, and he must not fall into the trap of imagining things otherwise, as Swann before him so often had. Even when he began to think of her as 'un ange musicien merveilleusement patiné' (III, 885; V, 438), he was on the verge of being bored by her. This is one of countless moments in the novel where the narrator's precepts are borne out in the act of narration. For this musical angel belongs not to one earlier moment in

Plate VI. Bellini, Giovanni (c. 1430-1516): *Madonna and Child and Saints* (triptych altarpiece). Santa Maria Gloriosa dei Frari, Venice

the text but to several; it is not a simple equivalence between person and painted image, but an amalgam of earlier artistic references, a compromise formation, as psychoanalysis might say, between the Frari and San Pietro Martire panels, an apparently static motif that yet has a temporal pulse

Plate VI. Bellini, Giovanni (c. 1430-1516): *Madonna and Child and Saints* (triptych altarpiece). Santa Maria Gloriosa dei Frari, Venice

Plate VII. Bellini, Giovanni (c. 1430-1516): *Madonna and Child* (Barbarigo Altarpiece). San Pietro Martire, Murano

Plate VIII. Botticelli, Sandro (1444/5-1510): *The Youth of Moses*, Sistine Chapel
(1481; fresco) (detail)

running inside it. Bellini and his angels have re-entered the composite, heterogeneous, open-ended flux of human time.

This use of art-works as aids to self-analysis, and the relentless secularising of Judaeo-Christian iconography that such a process entails, are vigorously sketched in the first volume of the novel, and the sprung temporal rhythms resulting from remembered paintings are articulated from a very early stage. Swann's emotional history, like the narrator's in due course, is one of demented connoisseurship, of 'reported sightings', as John Ashbery delightfully calls them, that are shot through with impending calamity.[7] Swann's passion for Odette is confirmed and stabilised when he first identifies her with Jethro's daughter Zipporah as painted by Botticelli in his Sistine *Life of Moses*, and Swann embarks soon after on a shocking reinterpretation of the characteristic Botticelli female face as it migrates from work to work. (Plate VIII) All such figures have a 'visage abattu et navré qui semble succomber sous le poids d'une douleur trop lourde pour elles' (I, 276; I, 337) and this, Swann suddenly realises, is the expression that Odette assumes when she is lying about her own wishes and intentions: she internalises the pain that her lie will cause her partner and then re-expresses it facially in feigned solidarity with him.

Botticelli is being reinterpreted from within the jealous lover's delusional system. Just as the *Life of Moses* self-consciously parallels the *Life of Christ* on the opposite wall of the Sistine Chapel, all the works enlisted by Swann, including the Uffizi *Madonna of the Pomegranate*, parallel the demeaning history of his love affair with a courtesan. (Plate IX) Christianity prefigures the martyrdoms brought on by modern romance. Botticelli is the proleptic portraitist of a self-dramatising amatory style much favoured by the fin-de-siècle bourgeoisie.

The violence that Swann, and the narrator in his turn, do to works of art, their greedy appropriation of other people's masterpieces to their own emotional ends, and the entire play of anticipation and retrospection that these aberrant interpretations introduce into Proust's narrative, while being pathological symptoms when looked at in one perspective, are signs of a newly emerging aesthetic integrity when looked at in another. The narrator's own artistic project, when he begins to sketch it in detail in the later volumes of the novel, will involve the deployment of prophetic and historical devices on a colossal scale. By the time we reach *La Prisonnière*, the narrator is already speaking with great warmth of the retroactive unity imposed upon their works by Hugo in *La Légende des siècles*, Balzac in the *Comédie humaine* and Wagner in the *The Ring* (III, 666; V, 176), and sketching for himself a method of composition that will be freely inventive yet strict, forward-flung yet backward-looking, wayward yet purposeful. The narrator's commentaries on Bellini and on Swann's version of Botticelli, are an experimental workshop in which this prospective and retrospective method is sketched in miniature. From the wilful misreading and misappropriation of other people's art-works the narrator begins to formulate the animating principle that will underlie his own.

To illustrate my final level of complexity, I have chosen two artists who appear in all four volumes of the new Pléiade edition, and whose works are implicated more intimately in the plotting of the novel than those of any other painter, Italian or not, real or imaginary. I am referring to Giotto and Carpaccio. In both cases the narrator eventually emancipates himself from reproductions and verbal reports: after long periods of anticipation, he actually travels to see the Scrovegni Chapel in Padua, and the Accademia in Venice. Remembering André Breton's definition of the imaginary as 'that which tends to become real', we could say that Giotto's frescoes and Carpaccio's panels tend more determinedly to become real as the book proceeds than any other Italian painting.[8]

In the early stages of the novel, the narrator knows only the monochrome wall-paintings depicting the Virtues and Vices that appear

Plate IX. Botticelli, Sandro (1444/5-1510): *Madonna of the Pomegranate*, Galleria degli Uffizi, Florence

along the lower portion of the side walls of the Scrovegni Chapel, and he knows these only from photographs. Giotto's Charity, Envy, Injustice and Idolatry become, even so, active generators of textual meaning and an

Plate X. Giotto di Bondone (c. 1266-1337): *Angels*, from *The Lamentation* (c. 1305 fresco) (detail). Scrovegni (Arena) Chapel, Padua

important element in the novel's elaborate pattern of internal echoes and cross-references. The adolescent Albertine, for example, playing diabolo at Balbec reminds the narrator of the Idolatry or *Infidelitas* panel, which also contains a strange gadget on a string. Menacing pre-echoes of her later diabolic behaviour and her suspected infidelities are already beginning to sound in this seaside idyll (II, 241; II, 539). When the narrator finally enters the polychrome world of the chapel itself in *Albertine disparue*, he finds not only that the characteristic energy of these allegorical emblems is present at the upper levels too, but that the distinction between art-objects and the everyday world of sense experience is beginning to dissolve:

après avoir traversé en plein soleil le jardin de l'Arena, j'entrai dans la chapelle des Giotto où la voûte entière et le fond des fresques sont si bleus qu'il semble que la radieuse journée ait passé le seuil elle aussi avec le visiteur et soit venue un instant mettre à l'ombre et au frais son ciel pur; son ciel pur à peine un peu plus foncé d'être débarrassé des dorures de la lumière, comme en ces courts répits dont s'interrompent les plus beaux jours, quand, sans qu'on ait vu aucun nuage, le soleil ayant tourné ailleurs son regard, pour un moment, l'azur, plus doux encore, s'assombrit. (IV, 226-7; V, 743)

Just as the blue of Giotto's walls and ceiling seem to have been imported into the chapel from the sunny day outside, so his flying angels seem to be the kinsmen of modern aviators learning how to loop the loop. (Plate X) This double reminder of what lies outside the art-work is entirely characteristic of Proust's novel and of the authority it bears: it is exactly at the moment when the Scrovegni Chapel is finally revealed in its aesthetic

Plate XI. Carpaccio, Vittore (c. 1460/5-1523/6): *The Healing of the Madman* (oil on canvas). Galleria dell'Accademia, Venice

splendour that it rejoins the real world, becomes a habitable space, and speaks to the spectator of his passions, their uncertain future and the course they have already run.

A reminder of the same kind had already been present in the *tableau vivant* that Proust builds upon Carpaccio's Ursula cycle and *The Healing of the Madman*. (Plate XI) This last-named panel offers a Venice seen in the multitude of its perspectives, colours, trades and human types, a theatre of ethnic diversity and of intricate social performance and display:

Je regardais le barbier essuyer son rasoir, le nègre portant son tonneau, les conversations des musulmans, des nobles seigneurs vénitiens en larges brocarts, en damas, en toque de velours cerise. (IV, 226; V, 743)

However, even as the narrator feasts upon the Venetian manifold held motionless by a festive painting, another order of sensation suddenly intrudes:

[. . .] je sentis au cœur comme une légère morsure. Sur le dos d'un des compagnons de la Calza, reconnaissable aux broderies d'or et de perles qui s'inscrivent sur leur manche ou leur collet l'emblème de la joyeuse confrérie à laquelle ils étaient affiliés, je venais de reconnaître le manteau qu'Albertine avait porté pour venir avec moi en voiture découverte à Versailles, le soir où j'étais loin de me douter qu'une quinzaine d'heures me séparaient à peine du moment où elle partirait de chez moi (IV, 226; V, 743)

The narrator's long description of Carpaccio's paintings had until this point teemed with other works, artists and media. Ruskin, Whistler, Richard Strauss and José-Maria Sert had joined forces with the nameless architects, bridge-builders, mosaic-makers and leatherworkers upon whom the fame of Venice in large part rests. The whole throng of these artists and artisans had been gathered into a *summa* on the aesthetic imperative, and on Venice as its living monument. Yet now, in the middle of this ecstatic catalogue, jealousy, pain, panic, loss and mourning have been reborn. *The Healing of the Madman* lapses from its moment of aesthetic integrity, finds its healing work undone, and for a moment draws the narrator back towards the jealous madness of which he had imagined himself purged, but there is promise as well as pain in this sudden revaluation of the Carpaccio panel. Perhaps the best thing about great works of art, Proust's narrator suggests, is that they can in the end afford us an exit from art. Perhaps the sense of necessity and inevitability with which they address us as readers, hearers or spectators comes from their insistence on returning us to the real world, even if this means making us mad again. What can be said with greater confidence, however, is that Proust is fascinated by the afterlife of aesthetic experience, and that his grand set-piece descriptions of real and imaginary art-works contain not just intimations but dramatic pre-enactments of art brought face to face with its own extinction.

Proust's Italian artists, even those who are particularly prized by the narrator and intricately woven into the novel's plot, find themselves subjected, therefore, to a law of intermittence, and have about them an air of strangely combined fullness and vacancy. They inhabit an oscillatory intermediate world in which painters acquire authority and then promptly lose it, offer a secure source of value and then retract it. As is so often the case in Proust's novel, the narrator himself provides a perfect expression in which to encapsulate this tantalising quality of in-betweenness. Characterising the procession of Albertines extended back in time, scanning them, seeking to make sense of their multiplicity, the narrator speaks in *La Prisonnière* of a stratified mental space:

Je la voyais [Albertine] aux différentes années de ma vie occupant par rapport à moi des positions différentes qui me faisaient sentir la beauté des espaces interférés, ce long temps révolu, où j'étais resté sans la voir, et sur la diaphane profondeur desquels la rose personne que j'avais devant moi se modelait avec de mystérieuses ombres et un puissant relief. Il était dû, d'ailleurs, à la superposition non seulement des images successives qu'Albertine avait été pour moi, mais encore des grandes qualités d'intelligence et de cœur, des défauts de caractère, les uns et les autres insoupçonnés de moi, qu'Albertine, en une germination, une multiplication d'elle-même, une efflorescence charnue aux sombres couleurs, avait ajoutés à une nature jadis à peu près nulle, maintenant difficile à approfondir. (III, 577; V, 70-1)

Memories of Albertine at different ages occupy an 'espace interféré', or an 'interference zone', as we might nowadays say;[9] the narrator's sexual partner has become a palimpsest of superimposed planes and troubled meanings, an incitement to knowledge but one who herself can be known only in transit and on the wing.

Even here, on the threshold of the novel's most extended and most ingenious erotic tableau, and even as the narrator's eye becomes an instrument of specifically sexual arousal, Italian art and the pleasures of connoisseurship steal upon the scene. As the passage continues, an artist first mentioned in 'Combray' reappears in a new guise:

Car les êtres, même ceux auxquels nous avons tant rêvé qu'ils ne nous semblaient qu'une image, une figure de Benozzo Gozzoli se détachant sur un fond verdâtre, et dont nous étions disposés à croire que les seules variations tenaient au point où nous étions placés pour les regarder, à la distance qui nous en éloignait, à l'éclairage, ces êtres-là, tandis qu'ils changent par rapport à nous, changent aussi en eux-mêmes. (III, 577; V, 71)

Early in the novel, Gozzoli had made a brief appearance during the episode of the withheld goodnight kiss. The narrator's father, giving permission – with a show of patriarchal solemnity – for his wife to spend the night in their child's room, reproduces a gesture from one of Gozzoli's murals for the Campo Santo at Pisa.[10] In *A l'ombre des jeunes filles en fleurs*, as we have already seen, the narrator's attention had turned to the chapel of the Palazzo Medici-Riccardi and to the *Journey of the Magi* with which Gozzoli adorned its interior.[11] It is to this work that he now returns, or so it would seem: nowhere else in the artist's surviving output are human figures so consistently arrayed upon backgrounds of green. (Plate XII)

Yet the text here undermines one of its own claims at the very moment of making it. Gozzoli's figure is present to exemplify flatness. One celebrated lower portion of his mural is a mere frieze of full faces and profiles, a refusal of depth and mobility. Yet the name of the artist, like that of Albertine herself, triggers associations between a scene of sequestered

Plate XII. Gozzoli, Benozzo di Lese di Sandro (1420-97): *Portraits of Piero de' Medici*
(on a mule), *Cosimo de' Medici* (centre) *and the Duke Salviati*. Palazzo Medici-Riccardi,
Florence

love-making and those earlier scenes of domestic drama and sharp-edged
salon conversation in which his name had also appeared. Gozzoli occupies
an 'espace interféré' of his own. Even as he emblematises a weak, two-
dimensional, insufficiently complex mode of artistic representation, he is

being reabsorbed into the textual manifold and revealing new dimensions of himself. He is present in three guises at once: as a painter of flat processionals, as an epic dramatist of family life, and as a market-driven artist eager to please his patrons by painting them into the Christian story. Gozzoli's career echoes Albertine's as an 'être de fuite' (III, 599; V, 98). He too has become a stratigraphic map, a spatial device for measuring, and re-experiencing, the passage of time. Again like Albertine, however, he is even in this respect an ambiguous textual construction: his different personalities are laid out as a chronological series, each of them corresponding to a phase in the narrator's own life-story, but he is also a timeless cluster of potentialities all gathered about a vacant core and all surveyable at once, in a moment of rapturously inclusive perception. At one moment Gozzoli summons the narrator back to a pitiless time-bound world, in which all creatures age and die, and at the next releases him from the limitations of that world into a new sense of fecundity and well-being. Memories of him 'germinate and multiply'.

Proust's account of Italian painting in *A la recherche du temps perdu* is governed by a more general ambiguity of the same kind. On the one hand the works of Giotto, Botticelli and the Venetian masters are relentlessly returned to the dimension of human time, and made porous to the desires and fears of individuals. Proust's characters use paintings for their own worldly ends, handle them with carefree impropriety, and have only a fleeting sense of their independent aesthetic dignity. Proust's novel is a disorderly imaginary museum in which no exhibit has a fixed position or a stable value. The Italian galleries of this museum have their own fluttering population of ghostly grandees, whether artists or sitters. Those who paint and those who are painted are alike seen *en fuite* and *en profil perdu*. On the other hand, Italian painting as glancingly figured in this elaborate fiction still has a monumental quality that sets it apart from the other national traditions to which Proust refers. Chardin, Delacroix, Manet and Monet have important roles in the work, as do Turner and Rembrandt. A single detail from Vermeer's *View of Delft* becomes a magical Proustian palimpsest and leitmotif.[12] But it is only in Italy, and only in the period between Giotto and Titian, that Proust discovers a whole compacted archive of painterly preoccupations and achievements. When it comes to the art of painting, Italy is Europe's treasury and its bulwark against frivolity and transience. Even when selected Italian masterpieces have been textualised by Proust and placed under the sign of ambiguity, the corpus of late Medieval and Renaissance painting in Italy retains its copiousness, complexity of vision and power of endurance. Sooner or later all art-works perish, Proust's narrator announces (IV, 620-21; VI, 445), and even now a chill wind of mortality is blowing through the workshops, palaces and academies in which pictures are produced and preserved. Yet Proust's Venice is not 'merely born to bloom and drop', and neither does it merely blaze out in a last moment of Tiepolesque splendour, for in this novel Proust has invented a new form of custodianship for the characteristic artistic productions of the city.[13] He has placed them inside an ever-mutating fictional texture in which their own mutability is given a new poignancy, and their own improbable tendency to 'become real' echoed and reinforced.

NOTES

1 My Proust quotations are taken from the new Pléiade edition of *A la recherche du temps perdu* (4 volumes under the general editorship of Jean-Yves Tadié, Paris, 1987-9), and accompanied in my text and notes by volume number and page. In each case, the second reference given is to the six-volume Scott Moncrieff/Kilmartin/Enright translation (London, 1992).

2 Works by Bronzino conforming to this pattern include his portrait of Ludovico Capponi in the Frick Collection, New York and the portrait of Gianrettino Doria in the Galleria Doria-Pamphilj in Rome.

3 See the editorial note to be found on II, 1422 of the new Pléiade edition of Proust's novel, and, for Proust's account of Montesquiou on Pisanello, *Contre Sainte-Beuve précédé de Pastiches et mélanges et suivi de Essais et articles*, ed. Pierre Clarac (Paris, Bibliothèque de la Pléiade, 1971), 515.

4 In *La Prisonnière* the particularising vocabulary here devoted to the natural world is reapplied to the person of Albertine herself. The 'triangles empennés' of foam upon the sea are at that later stage to be rediscovered in the large locks of Albertine's hair: 'les cheveux, noirs et crespelés, montrant d'autres ensembles selon qu'elle se tournait vers moi pour me demander ce qu'elle devait jouer, tantôt une aile magnifique, aiguë à sa pointe, large à sa base, noire, empennée et triangulaire, tantôt massant le relief de leurs boucles en une chaîne puissante et variée, pleine de crêtes, de lignes de partage, de précipices, avec leur fouetté si riche et si multiple semblant dépasser la variété que réalise habituellement la nature, et répondre plutôt au désir d'un sculpteur qui accumule les difficultés pour faire valoir la souplesse, la fougue, le fondu, la vie de son exécution, faisaient ressortir davantage, en l'interrompant pour la recouvrir, la courbe animée et comme la rotation du visage lisse et rose, du mat verni d'un bois peint.' (III, 885).

5 Speaking of Leconte de Lisle's rhyming, Baudelaire wrote: 'Ses rimes, exactes sans trop de coquetterie, remplissent la condition de beauté voulue et répondent régulièrement à cet amour contradictoire et mystérieux de l'esprit humain pour la surprise et la symétrie' (*Œuvres complètes*, Vol. II, ed. Claude Pichois (Paris, Bibliothèque de la Pléiade, 1976), 179.

6 A similar adolescent musician appears in the San Giobbe altarpiece, now in the Accademia in Venice.

7 *Reported Sightings* is the title Ashbery gave to his collected art chronicles (1957-1987) (Manchester, 1989).

8 'L'imaginaire est ce qui tend à devenir réel' ('Il y aura une fois', in *Le Revolver à cheveux blancs*, Paris, 1932), 11.

9 *Interférer* is an anglicism, the first use of which in this transitive form is ascribed in Robert's dictionary to Proust.

10 See I, 36. The scene mentioned by the narrator appears neither in the book of Genesis nor in the (now destroyed) Gozzoli frescoes at Pisa. For a full account of the possible sources, and of Proust's ambiguous phrasing at this point, see Jo Yoshida's masterly footnote (I, 1114).

11 See above, pp. 108–9

12 A penetrating survey of Proust's treatment of painters from Italy and elsewhere is to be found in John Cocking's essay 'Proust and Painting', in *Proust. Collected Essays on the Writer and his Art* (Cambridge, 1982), 130-63.

13 The phrase quoted is used of Venice in Browning's 'A Toccata of Galuppi's'. For a comprehensive account of Proust's Venetian source-materials, and of his intricate reprocessing of these, see Peter Collier's admirable *Proust and Venice* (Cambridge, 1989).

Comparative Criticism **XXV**, pp. 123–159. © 2004 Edinburgh University Press
Printed in the United Kingdom

Visual musical poetry: the feeling of Pallaksch in Bacon, Clean, and Kurtág

BEATE PERREY

I

PREMISSES

Imagine György Kurtág's hysterical singer: terrified and terrifying, visibly horrified by something we cannot see, afflicted by his own *Sprechgesang*, stuttering, choking, and expelling 'in utmost rage and desperation'[1] something that is beyond words.[2] Within this aesthetic of emotional excess, there are a number of songs by Kurtág of which both tone and structure create an atmosphere that transforms the traditionally intimate sound space of the German art song into an extravagant operatic scene and the solitary singer into an extrovert theatrical character. Sheer exaltation of an intensely declamatory style turns stage into sanctuary and singer into 'deranged priest'.[3] When these songs are performed alongside works by J. S. Bach, as Kurtág suggests, the concert hall becomes a bizarre place of worship. But who is worshipped here? For in Kurtág's music God is nowhere. Nevertheless, his singer seems to have a message that has been treated by the composer as if it were sacred. It is in the absolute intent to transmit this message, and in the sharp urgency behind its voice, that Kurtág's singer recalls for us the figure of Bach's Evangelist. Yet, struck blind at the vision of a disappearing God, Kurtág's singer is trembling to the tip of his tongue: he stutters and stumbles, he disperses sense in a paroxysm of words, or loses it in delirious ululations, or is unable to make any sound at all. Left with nothing and unable to name the void, Kurtág's singer, like Francis Bacon's famous screaming pope, stands there, eyes and mouth wide open, in the midst of a seizure that is apocalyptic.

In this study I shall compare the work of three artists, the poet Celan, the composer Kurtág and the painter Bacon, in their respective searches to capture invisible forces when they seize the body until it generates a violent scream. I shall begin with a close reading of Celan's famous poem

Figure 1: *Study after Velasquez's Portrait of Pope Innocent* X, Francis Bacon, 1953. Oil on canvas, 153 × 118,1 cm. © DACS London 2003

Tübingen, Jänner from the poem collection *Niemandsrose* written in 1961, to compare it with one of Kurtág's most astonishing vocal compositions, the as yet unpublished song of 1997 for baritone solo based on Celan's poem,[4] making us hear speechlessness, noise and non-sense as part of the modalities of the scream.[5] If the *song* can be said to be exceptionally challenging in its treatment of the human voice in twentieth-century song, the poetic voice of the *poem* is, as we shall see, no less so. In exploring both works, my focus will be on how each – the one musico–poetic, the other poetic – achieves its end, the culminating moment in both poem and song. I want to reflect on two issues: on the one hand, the human *figure* as the work's agent vis-à-vis the *figuration* of that persona's sensations through words and sound. This includes *dis-figuration* triggered by the intensity of a sensation coming over at the most acute point, the end in both poem and song; on the other hand, I want to focus on the scream and how it stands for the de-formations of the body. Here Bacon's famous shrieking mouth is the catalyst. The speechlessness that lies behind the 'very special violence'[6] we can perceive in poem, song and painting, whether linguistic, acoustic or visual, is all the more fascinating as it bespeaks the invisibility of the cause of the horror in the blinded poet, singer and priest. Neither reader, listener or viewer, nor indeed these works' agents, exasperated poet, shouting priest, or shrieking painterly pope, are able to see their predicament.[7] In these works, no reason for the horror is given. It is this lack of reason which attracts us to this space and within which we may explore the shapes and meanings of the Unknown.

Reading Celan's poem alongside three chosen images by Francis Bacon, Kurtág's vocal setting as well as a number of literary, philosophical and psychoanalytic sources, I hope to enrich this enterprise with an explanatory, and especially visual dimension that lends to all of the works and passages discussed more depth, more subtlety, and more critical relevance. The examples are all to do with the complexities of vision, whether it concerns the vision of internal images or, more to the point, the difficulty or even impossibility of visualizing either an extreme emotional experience, or images triggered by a visual literary description or, again, images in the general sense of the word. Setting these different types of images side by side, I want to explore the hermeneutic value in the interfaces of visualizing words as well as sound, and reading images. The three paintings by Francis Bacon are not mere illustrations; rather they focus our attention and bring to the surface an extreme affective side in Celan's poem, a very special kind of violence, through a *visual poetics*.[8]

Celan's poetry is notorious for its semantic difficulty. Mainly due to its rarefied symbolism and the use of partly invented vocabulary, it has the reputation, hardly ever openly declared except by a few, of a 'hermetic' poetry. However, as Adorno pointed out with reference to Peter Szondi's important work on Celan's poetry, 'its hermeticism is not synonymous with incomprehensibility'.[9] While engaged in a poetic project that seems at first sight to fit the cliché of post-war art, namely to express the inexpressible ('Celan's poems want to speak the utmost horror by remaining silent'[10]), Celan nevertheless asserted the strength of poetry when commenting on the condition of contemporary poetry in his seminal text *Der Meridian*: 'The poem shows a strong tendency towards silence. [. . .] The poem holds its own on the edge of its own margins.'[11]

My interest is to follow up this relatively recent, highly self-conscious as well as risk-conscious flirtation with what Celan called 'a strong tendency towards silence' in order to explore the formal achievements of this struggle; that is, to see if and where and in what form and material this 'tendency towards silence' has been represented. My emphasis is thus on material presence, on the figuration of a 'tendency towards silence'; on how silenced content breaks through, how it forges itself a path and turns, if not into words, then into sound or thing or noise, however inarticulate or de-formed. The form this creative dynamic takes in the imagination of the three artists I have chosen to consider here – Kurtág, Celan, Bacon – leads away from the human figure. Although still in the service of the humanistic ideal of figurative art, the figurations we encounter in Kurtág, Bacon and Celan are not anthropomorphic. As will be seen from the works which I shall discuss – Kurtág's singing priest, Bacon's pope, and Celan's patriarchic poet – each artist uses the human figure in order to work out its disfigurement, its dehumanization, to turn it into something eminently able to catalyze the extra-human experience. In this comparative study, my interest is both to measure in Kurtág's song the formal and expressive possibilities of poetry and music under the pressures of extremism; and also to see whether the 'vocal' setting adds a significant dimension to an experience that has already been powerfully captured by words alone. To explore notions of identity as we encounter them in Celan and Kurtág – across their explorations of memory, the un-nameable, the unthinkable, the Unknown, the realms of the inhuman and the animalistic – I shall refer to a number of texts by Nietzsche, Benjamin, Kafka, Ortega y Gasset, Freud and Bion, among others.

My narrative features three paintings by Francis Bacon: first his *Study after Velasquez's Portrait of Pope Innocent X* , 1953; second the right-hand panel of *Three Studies for Figures at the Base of the Crucifixion* of 1944; and third, *Head II* of 1949. These paintings are powerful elaborations of one of Bacon's favourite and most haunting themes: the mouth, wide open in a shriek. As will be obvious, my use of Bacon's images on this theme is neither accidental, nor simply in the name of synchronicity. Within this study on forms of decay – poetic as well as sonic – generated by the artistic aim and imagination to represent what cannot be represented, Bacon's images add a crucial level of tactile visuality.[12] His work shows radical forms of disfigurement, of mutilation as well as uneasy animalistic ebullience similar to those we experience in the fierce elaborations of the same theme by Celan and Kurtág. Trying to trap what is beyond words, beyond metaphor or symbolism, we are confronted with 'visual thoughts', Benjamin's thought-images (*Gedankenbilder*) re erring to an unnamable reality. These images, whether poetic, sonic or visual, are charged with that voracious energy that Christopher Bollas's notion of 'the unthought known'[13] captures so well on a conceptual level. Bacon's paintings can thus be seen to be part of a modernist project of image-making shared by both Celan and Kurtág. They enter our frame of reference in order to render vivid, through their immediacy, my central concern: the perception, conceptually and sensually, of that tremendous sense and impressive material reality of the dynamics of regression that characterize both Celan's poem and Kurtág's song. Such regression is visible in Bacon's images, leading from the famous priest depicted as recognizably human, if hysterical figure (*Study after Velasquez's Portrait of Pope Innocent X* of 1953) to a diminished, mutated human remnant that is nothing more than a neck, a throat and a roaring mouth (*Three Studies for Figures at the Base of the Crucifixion* of 1944, detail of right-hand panel) to, finally, the fully decomposed, less than human and much more animalistic remains of a mouth barely to be made out by the small row of glaring teeth inhabiting Bacon's *Head II* of 1949. This tri-partite visual tableau is based not on chronology, but on the idea of intensification in a fierce struggle for articulacy.

Here the human figure no longer takes on the representational or narrative thrust of song, poem or painting, but shrinks away from a horrifying sight, to disappear into an increasingly afflicted voice. This voice, symbolized by the shrieking mouth, functions as a synecdoche to efficiently dispense with the human figure. It captures the figure's descent into an animalistic realm. In developing my comparative tableau, I shall begin with a close reading of Celan's poem, its imagery and language. Here I shall be particularly concerned with possible readings of the last line's multiple resonances. In this context, I shall also refer to a number of unpublished manuscript sources that suggest reviewing or complementing existing readings.

II

CELAN'S POEM

In 1962 Celan comments on Paul Klee's painting *Der Schöpfer* (The Creator): 'Above all I looked at. . . and admired, from the depths of my discouragement, this immense courage: "The Creator". . . against a violet background, labyrinths of lines trying to carry on inside an extra-human, infra-human, animal-like framework'.[14]

Remarkable in its linguistic artifice, Celan's comment carries strong resonances for those familiar with his poetry. Celan's own ways with words resemble Klee's labyrinthine lines in this painting. Like these, Celan's poetic lines try to carry on, against the background of the Holocaust, inside the monstrous linguistic framework that the German language was destined to become for him. And as if etched into the surface of this language, it is with his lines of poetry that Celan, certainly aesthetically,

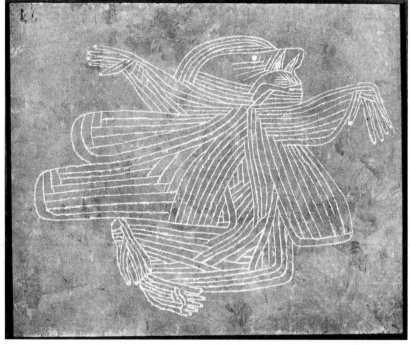

Figure 2: *Der Schöpfer (The Creator)*, Paul Klee, 1934 , 213 (U 13), oil with lines stamped on canvas; original 42 × 53,5 cm, Paul-Klee-Stiftung Kunstmuseum Basel
©DACS London 2003

finally breaks free: he cleaves through a given linguistic space – the German language – as he invents or re-invents words and images, and by so doing, he emerges into space and finally takes possession of it. But how could this be done? And what were the risks? These are the kind of questions this study attempts to address. What might seem at a first glance like a 'poetics of exile' eventually reveals itself to be triumphant over the loss of a native place, home of a mother tongue; yet a rather peculiar kind of blindness is needed that allows this new land and language, Celan's 'Celania'[15], to come into full view. The search for such a place the poet himself, fleetingly and hesitatingly, once described in his notes to the Meridian as 'sprachblind'.[16]

Language on the Edge

Celan's vision of the self and the world are confrontations with the fugitive line separating the two: the self from the world, the inside from the outside, the I and the you. This also implies a test of limits, the attempt at fusion, or its failure. The boundary between the self and the world being nothing other, of course, than language, the language chosen by Celan delineates a kind of wasteland where traditional means of lyrical expression have been pushed to extremes.

   Lyric expression can turn extreme when confronted with an image/word-dichotomy,[17] when seeing extreme internal or external images exceeds the word, that is, when in the attempt to capture this experience, words are either not enough, or there are not enough of them: words are overwhelmed and turn into non-sense, noise or silence. While one may think that, strictly considered, the maximal aesthetic effect of such versions of non-symbolism would amount to zero, this may on reflection turn out to be an overestimate. For after Romantic poetry had aimed at the profound while already verging on the rhapsodically obscure, and before poetry might hypothetically reach for total linguistic dissolution, lyric language may nevertheless pass through a non-verbal sound-language first of all, that is a language located somewhere in between poetry on the one hand and hardly articulate sonics on the other, *prior to* turning into total nonsense, noise, or silence. This is when lyric language may show 'a strong tendency towards silence'.

Hölderlin's Heir

In German lyrical poetry, two major poets, Friedrich Hölderlin and Paul Celan, have explored this 'tendency towards silence'[18]. As if seeking to fill this tendency towards silence with sound, Kurtág's *Hölderlin-Gesänge* must be considered one of the most intense and intriguing compositional responses to such poetry. However, *Tübingen, Jänner,* although clearly experimenting with a 'tendency towards silence', takes on yet another kind of significance and offers wide-ranging interpretative possibilities if read as a 'sonic setting', in the musical sense of the term whereby Celan offer us a highly individualized reading of a pivotal phrase quoted from Hölderlin's poetic œuvre as well as one highly eccentric verbal expression reported by Hölderlin's contemporaries from his years of madness. The *Tübingen, Jänner* poem is therefore a sonorous reflection upon the formidable transformation the lyric faced in the hands of Hölderlin, whose poetic experiments on the edge of lyric language have haunted the condition of German poetry ever since. So, two threads of major lyrical thought – Hölderlin's and Celan's – come together in *Tübingen, Jänner,* where they tightly intertwine to lock verbal sense into a semantically intricate poetic knot. What is more, if we think of Celan's literal quotation from Hölderlin's hymn *Der Rhein* in *Tübingen, Jänner,* Celan's poem explicitly stands under the sign of song, the lyricist's age-old preoccupation, sacred for Hölderlin, nearly impossible for Celan, uncertain for Kurtág. Kurtág's song *Tübingen Jänner* in its predominantly melismatic idiom thus becomes a space in which the whole idea of song, this strange textual amalgam interlacing sense and sound, and the whole idea of voice, prime means to speak, reverberate in the deformed and anguished sonorities that the memory of a forgotten hymnic past imposes upon some artists of a twentieth-century that itself was experienced as extravagantly trying, in both senses of the word.

Few poets hold the attention of today's artists and intellectuals as Hölderlin does. One of the last writers to have had the Orphic ambition to write a hymnic poetry that would also succeed as a philosophical proposition, as another way of thought, Hölderlin's biographical 'tendency towards silence' through madness for the last 37 years of his life has been interpreted as a kind of sincerity that sees real value in what lies beyond poetry, namely the act of renunciation.[19] As George Steiner wrote: 'Silence here stands for the word surpassing itself, it stands for the realization not in another medium, but in that which is its echoing antithesis and defining negation, silence.'[20]

If Hölderlin's poetic collapse came from within as he had pushed linguistic and syntactic possibilities of the early nineteenth-century German language to their absolute breaking point,[21] the twentieth-century was to provide the kind of phenomena capable of pushing language to breaking point from without. Overwhelmed by a hitherto unknown degree of brutality, amazed and dazzled by the passion for death characterizing the Holocaust, language found itself *wanting*: wanting words to speak, and yet lacking them altogether. However, when Maurice Blanchot, citing Nietzsche, reminds us that 'we have no words for the extreme; dazzling joy and great pain burn up every term and render them all mute',[22] he may well be speaking of a crisis of communication that had already preoccupied the early Romantics and others, including Hölderlin, as they tried to widen their linguistic horizons to capture a sensibility that would take account of the irrational aspects of both lived experience and language itself. By loosening the causal chain between word and image, all that which keeps a language together, and by exalting language to mere 'acoustic configurations of thoughts' (Novalis) instead, or by transforming it into 'pure movement, freed of the object', language was invited to let go of referentiality and aspire to the condition of music.

The events of the twentieth century put this enterprise to the test when the Romantic fascination with a language modeled on the presumed abstract nature of music 'freed of the object' was shocked into a less voluntary awareness of the limits of a language originally committed to a figurative rendering of the world and now confronted with one that seemed to have lost its face. The issue for some twentieth-century artists, among them Paul Celan, Francis Bacon and György Kurtág, was thus to find a language strong enough to carry the experience of a world they felt to be itself undone.

Like the Inferno: 'si che dal fatto dir non sia diverso'[23]

Paul Celan's lyrical poetry is at times said to exhibit a language that has surrendered to what it describes, and it is this perception of potential linguistic dissolution that has become a shared concern among Celan scholars throughout the critical literature. This is understandable: the curiosity over what seems like a near-defeat of language in response to the real defeat of humanity corresponds perhaps to the spectacular nature and singular vehemence of the encounter in question, namely when language finally catches up with life, or rather with what is left of it. It is in this sense, I think, that Celan makes note of Dante's proposition that 'thing and word shall not be divided.'[24] The persistent issue that his poetry raises is that of an apparently unprecedented proximity of life and art. For such poetry to succeed requires an extreme degree of stylistic as well as semantic abstraction, similar to the concerns of non-figurative art. Such rarefaction of both figure and concrete image can indeed, when it does succeed, have a special poignancy, due perhaps to the high degree of stylistic risk involved. As can be seen in *Tübingen Jänner*, Paul Celan's poetry is, I shall suggest, an attempt to rarefy the German language.[25]

TÜBINGEN, JÄNNER	TÜBINGEN, JANUARY

1	*Zur Blindheit über-*	Eyes talked in-
2	*redete Augen.*	to blindness.
3	*Ihre – 'ein*	Their – 'a
4	*Rätsel ist Rein-*	riddle is pure-
5	*entsprungenes' – ihre*	ly arisen' –, their
6	*Erinnerung an*	memory of
7	*schwimmende Hölderlintürme, Möven-*	floating Hölderlintowers, gull-
8	*umschwirrt.*	enswirled.
9	*Besuche ertrunkener Schreiner bei*	Visits of drowned carpenters to
10	*diesen*	these
11	*tauchenden Worten:*	plunging words:
12	*Käme,*	Came, if there
13	*käme ein Mensch,*	came a man,
14	*käme ein Mensch zur Welt, heute, mit*	came a man to the world, today, with
15	*dem Lichtbart der*	the light-beard of the
16	*Patriarchen: er dürfte,*	patriarchs: he could,
17	*spräch er von dieser*	if he spoke of this
18	*Zeit, er*	time, he
19	*dürfte*	could
20	*nur lallen und lallen,*	only babble and babble,
21	*immer-, immer-*	ever-, ever-
22	*zuzu.*	moremore.
23	*('Pallaksch. Pallaksch.')*	('Pallaksch. Pallaksch.')

In the opening 'Zur Blindheit über-/redete Augen' ('Eyes talked in-to Blindness'), the hyphenated 'über-redete' ('talked in-to') separating 'Blindheit' and 'Augen' is the dividing line separating the linguistic from the visual realm. On the one hand the phrase suggests that an excess of the word defeats the visual sense; on the other it presumes the perception of blinding images, impossible to name. Lines 3–5 contain the quotation from Hölderlin's famous poetic hymn *Der Rhein*. In the original, 'ein Rätsel ist Reinentsprungenes' ('a riddle is purely arisen') is followed by 'Auch/Der Gesang kaum darf es enthüllen' ('Also/ Gesang may hardly reveal it'),[26] a covert generic reference of considerable significance for Celan. From 'ein Rätsel ist Reinentsprungenes' onwards the poem recedes into the past, with the keyword 'Erinnerung' ('memory') in line 6 introducing a floating of sense and blurring of sight that the 'schwimmende Hölderlintürme, Möwen-/umschwirrt' ('floating Hölderlintowers, gull-/enswirled'), as well as the obvious homophony of Rein with the river 'Rhein' confirm. 'Tauchende Worte' ('plunging words') in line 11 announces the poem's crux, leading into the last stanza (lines 12–22), made up of various forms of repetition and rhythmic hesitation, of pauses and syllabic clusters. This final stanza vibrates in discord with the whole idea of lyrical poetry. And it is this discord that finds its strongest expression in the poem's closing, enigmatic '("Pallaksch. Pallaksch.")', a bizarre line ending, parenthetically kept apart from the main body of the poem, yet dominating it.

Words Written into Water

Let us first, before turning to 'Pallaksch', consider more closely the image of 'plunging words'. Placed at the symmetrical divide between the poem's first and second part, juxtaposing eleven lines against eleven (if we consider the colon as closing the poem's first part),[27] this image already figuratively contains those tentative, afflicted utterances which are about to become audible in the poem's last stanza. The image of 'Tauchende Worte' ('Plunging words') forms a pivot, in the mechanical sense of poetic rhetoric, upon whose annunciatory colon everything turns: the 'Hölderlin-towers' mirrored onto the water's surface, gull-enswirled by memory. In this same way Celan's 'plunging words' will step into their own image on the water's surface, but inverted and unfamilar. Yet when stepping into their own image, these words no longer contain metaphorical meaning or even semantic potential, for this is what they are precisely lacking: images. Hollowed out in this way, Celan's 'plunging words' are nothing more than scattered reflections of themselves. They are de-figured, dys-figured shapes, transformed into scattered letters flickering on the glittering, passing surface movement. Similar to the voices in Celan's line 'Stimmen, ins Grün/der Wasseroberfläche geritzt' (of which a literal translation might be 'voices, etched into the green of the water's surface') on which Werner Hamacher offered such artful commentary,[28] it is words themselves in *Tübingen, Jänner* that memory transforms into a 'Wasserspiegelschrift' (mirror writing on water), and which are literally defaced and emptied out through an essential void of images held within. These are disembodied words. But the sense of loss evoked at this pivotal point in the poem is in fact explicit from the beginning, if we consider that words written into water are much like words written into the sand; and the notion of transience is even more acute with the movement of Celan's river adding to the idea of the loss of sense that of the loss of time. The riddle of Hölderlin's words is in the river's flowing.

In the last analysis, Celan's 'plunging words' are a powerful metaphor for the moment of de-metaphorisation, undoing the idea of an interlocking between word and world. The possibility of naming a world is lost, except for the naming of loss itself – through the very image of the loss of image. Thus with utmost linguistic precision Celan succeeds in naming the nameless. But the image of 'plunging words' for Celan also speaks of an entranced gaze *at* words. For these are not words that will ever speak the truth, but whose hidden truth – de-creation – is the same truth that was revealed to Narcissus: gazing at his own image reflected in the water, he steps into this, his own image, to pull him into death.

Words Undone

'Erinnerung' (memory) is for Celan no neutral word. It seems to be the experience of memory as well as its projective inversion, hypothesis or speculation (note 'käme', 'dürfte', and 'spräch'), which provokes throughout the poem's last stanza a radical expression of faltering speech and fractured signification. If the 'lallen und lallen' ('babble and babble') in line 20 as a form of inarticulate speech is decidedly onomatopoetic, the triple repetition of 'käme' in lines 12, 13 and 14 is acoustically the first sign of a stutter that lines 21 and 22 impressively evoke ('immer-, immer/ zuzu').

The temporalities within this poem are equally indicative. While the poem's first part (lines 1-8) is clearly directed towards the past, with 'Erinnerung' at its centre, the second part (lines 12–22) swings to the future, with the opening 'käme' denoting grammatically a wished-for reality as much as it accommodates actual visions of future and possibility.[29] The use of the subjunctive in 'käme', 'dürfte' and 'spräch' has the function and effect of transcending the present to invest in a future. As part of a distinct mode similar to litany (see the triple repetition of 'käme') the radiant image of 'Lichtbart der Patriarchen', representing a divine authority, reminds us of a prayer addressed to a messianic listener.[30] Certainly, in view of the darkness evoked by the poem's opening line followed by the increasingly fragmented speech of the poem's second part, such nocturnal imagery and stuttered verse recall with remarkable negativity the best known of all biblical messages: 'Let there be light: and there was light' as well as 'In the beginning was the Word'.[31] Celan's babbling and stuttering denies the word the power to build a future, or to construct at all. Instead it is locked within a short-circuit of senselessness ('immer–immer'), forced to semantic standstill by 'zuzu' indicating closure and futile circularity at once.[32] If there is a mounting sense of contradiction between the forward-looking 'käme' and the end-stopping 'zuzu' enclosing the poem's second part, the consistency with which all words indicating loss of speech – from 'lallen' onwards – have been doubled marks Celan's intent to symbolize infinite multiplicity and, as to 'immer-, immer-/zuzu', everlasting timelessness.

A Grayer Language

The final 'Pallaksch. Pallaksch' is a linguistic fabrication – Hölderlin's, as we shall see. It is an intensification as well as an abstraction of the earlier, already highly strenuous forms of communication, the babbling and the stuttering. Nonetheless, just as slurred speech can mean both the sound of yet unformed speech as well as the utterance of delirious decline, the stutter carries a similar semantic ambiguity of becoming and unbecoming within itself, situated at the equipoise of the 'was' and the 'will be'. Onomatopoeia, on the other hand, as we might hear it in 'Pallaksch', clearly catches the human language in *statu nascendi*, not in a state of decline. It is sound yet to become word, itself a force field of potentiality. In this sense 'Pallaksch' is a password of hope. As a sonorous entity within the context of lyricism, however, it may strike one as an aesthetic failure. Thus, in the light of Celan's citation of Hölderlin's hymn tacitly alluding to *Gesang* (song) as the central characteristic of Hölderlin's poetry, consider the following statement by Celan made in 1958 about the condition of contemporary poetry:

German lyric poetry, [...] while still remembering darkest matters [...] can no longer, despite its awareness of the tradition to which it belongs, speak the language which many a sympathetic ear still seems to expect from it. Its language has become more sober, more factual; it is suspicious of the 'Beautiful'; it attempts to be true. To look for a word in the visual realm, while keeping an eye on the polychrome of what seems to be in fashion today, it is so to speak a 'grayer' language. It is a language which – among other things – wishes to place its 'musicality' where it will no longer share that 'melodiousness' which still resounds more or less unconcernedly in accordance as well as side by side with the greatest horrors.[33]

Working from within the German language after it had been steeped so deeply in the rhetoric of the inhuman, from within a language paralysed as it were by all it remembered, Celan's attempt was to unlock somewhere within it a linguistic potential that could open it up once again and speak the 'truth' of the world as he saw it. In this attempt, memory and the idea of forgetting – as thematized in the poem *Tübingen, Jänner* – played an essential role.

'Forgetting grants you Memory'[34]

More than a decade before Freud's first publications on the subject, Friedrich Nietzsche, in his late psycho-philosophical text *Zur Genealogie der Moral*, spoke about the functions and, more importantly, the burden of memory and the uses of forgetting:

Forgetfulness is no mere *vis inertiae* as is assumed by the superficially-minded; it is much rather an active, in the strictest sense a positive capacity of inhibition. . . [Let us] occasionally close the doors and windows of [our] consciousness. . . [let us have] a little silence, a bit of *tabula rasa* of consciousness so that there will be space again for something new. . . – this is the use of active forgetfulness.[35]

The conditions of Celan's poetry may appropriately be viewed in terms of the Nietzschean sense of a *tabula rasa*, that is in Celan's own phrasing, a language that is 'aware of', that 'consciously remembers' 'the tradition to which it belongs' – and that therefore must be re-invented. Celan's notebooks and papers of the 1950s – as yet unpublished and housed in the Deutsches Literatur Archiv in Marbach – contain hundreds of alphabetically organised lists of verbal inventions, derived from words that he severely deformed.[36] He created a new vocabulary, as unknown as words of a foreign language. With this, Celan created his own linguistic territory, his 'Celania'.[37] Here, only tone and resonance remain resolutely German. His screening of specialized dictionaries and his consistent preoccupation with etymology, taking words back into an unknown past, as well as his restless concern for verbal invention reaching into a wholly new linguistic future, all this informs Celan's language with a real sense of uncanny strangeness: it sounds familiar; yet it is incomprehensible.

In this way Celan's poetry, perhaps more than any since Hölderlin, recalls to the German ear the sounding magnificence of its legacy. And in the effort to escape the shadow which Celan felt recent history cast over it, the German language is revivified – or so one might think. For such radical manipulation of language also contains risks: as Celan presses to disfigure words polluted by a recent past in order to either create new words or discover words so old and distant as to seem new again, brand-new, as if no human touch had yet tarnished their shine, or no human voice had yet distorted their resonance, so the poet risks aiming for a *pure* language, a language cleansed of its past, purified at last. As Celan calls back to life words long lost and forgotten or conjures up words as yet unheard, the attempt is to make them confess a truth which coincides no less however with a corresponding degree of mystery. And it is in this restless movement into a distant past or forwards into a far-off future that Celan's 'Celania' obtains its full sense: as an act of linguistic estrangement in a constant attempt to take root in lost origin or absolute utopia, to live a time before all time. Such striving locks the mind in an absolute past or an absolute future, both sites of a kind of irreality whose powerful attraction, however, is to keep the present in eternal abeyance.

A Non-Word

It is the *resonance* of 'Pallaksch' combined with its complete absence of sense that gives this word its enigmatic fabric and makes for its uncanny sonorous strangeness. Not lexicalised in any language, 'Pallaksch' seems a lingo-creature without semantic identity, a wraith of a word, a linguistic cripple.

Kafka, whom Celan much admired, describes in one of his short stories, 'Die Sorge des Hausvaters', the shape and action of a similarly unknown word or 'entity'. It is Kafka's subtle shift of tone, gliding from harmlessness into morbidity, that eventually captures the eeriness of its intrinsic indeterminacy: 'Odradek', a 'strange' word at first, a 'thing' next, then something like an 'animal' and yet like a child, before it suddenly disappears, evaporating as quickly as it descended from a meta-world of sub-humanity:

There are some who say the word Odradek is of Slavonic origin, and they try to account for its formation on that basis. Others again believe that it derives from the German and is merely influenced by Slavonic. The uncertainty of both interpretations, however, probably justifies the conclusion that neither is correct, especially since neither permits one to attach a meaning to it.

No one, of course, would occupy himself with such studies if a creature called Odradek did not in fact exist. [. . .] the whole thing certainly appears senseless, and yet in its own way complete. It is not possible to state anything more definite on the matter since Odradek is exceptionally mobile and refuses to be caught.

He resides by turns in the attic, on the stairs, in the corridors, in the entrance hall. Sometimes he is not to be seen for months; [. . .] Sometimes when one comes out of one's room and he happens to be propping himself up against the banister down below, one feels inclined to speak to him. Naturally one doesn't ask him any difficult questions, one treats him – his diminutive size is itself sufficient encouragement to do so – like a child. 'What's your name?' one asks him. 'Odradek,' he says. 'And where do you live?' 'No fixed abode,' he says, and laughs; but it is only the sort of laughter that can be produced without lungs. [. . .][38]

Walter Benjamin has called Kafka's Odradek 'eine Figur des Vergessens', a 'figure of what has been forgotten', in other words a form which contains, in its very formlessness or strangeness, the forgotten past.[39] The past is remembered as a malformation, like some of Kafka's other great figures of forgetting, Gregor Samsa for example, turned infra-human in *Die Verwandlung* (Metamorphosis), the crossbred cat and lamb in *Die Kreuzung* (The Crossbreed), or indeed Benjamin's own extra-human figure of forgetting *Das bucklicht' Männlein* (The little Hunchback) developed from a German children's song of the same name.[40] Within this scenario, and as if emerging out of Celan's linguistic *tabula rasa*, 'Pallaksch' appears in a somewhat sharper light as something like a Benjaminian 'Figur des Vergessens'. Speaking about memory and forgetting, in the *Meridian*, Celan stated: 'Perhaps – I am only asking –, perhaps poetry turns, with a self-forgotten 'I', towards [. . .] this uncanny strangeness and foreignness, and [thereby] sets itself [. . .] again free?'[41]

If a figure such as Kafka's Odradek seems like an incarnation of the *Unheimliche*, of uncanny strangeness, Celan's 'Pallaksch', presented with such singular formal concern at the poem's end marks the decisive moment when poetry turns strange or foreign. Throughout the poem's second part, Celan has been announcing this moment of change, with 'babbling' and stuttering signifying a gradual linguistic erosion even before the eventual and conclusive relinquishing – through 'Pallaksch' – of the poet's articulate enactment of identity. This is what is at issue here. And the question to be asked is, could the non-identity thus achieved then be considered an effective means in the search for poetic freedom?

Hölderin's *'Tendency towards Silence'*

If Hölderlin is occasionally held to have achieved 'poetic freedom', arguably in its most absolute form, by surpassing the poetic word through silence,[42] it should not be overlooked, however, that Hölderlin's partial silence *also* coincided with his years of madness. Let us note, too, that the defining absence of meaning confers on the word 'Pallaksch' not only the status of a *non-sense* -word, but also the status of a *non*-word – a word that isn't a word because it is not part of any language. This brings 'Pallaksch' close to the Hölderlinian 'tendency towards silence' sometimes equated with 'poetic freedom'. Notions of mad non-sense and notions of a 'tendency towards silence' begin to blur, however, once we think of Celan's remark 'Verstummen: vieles ist in Klammern gesetzt' ('Falling Silent: much is put within brackets'),[43] and 'The poem shows a strong tendency towards silence. [. . .] The poem holds its own on the edge of its own margins' as quoted earlier. Where, then, can we still make out here a distinction between 'a strong tendency towards silence' and non-sense? And between art and life? 'Pallaksch' provides an opportunity to explore the question on a strictly linguistic level, since in fact it is borrowed literally from Hölderlin's years of madness, of which it is emblematic. And within this specific historical context, Celan's poem comes to be seen as the artistic framework for an imaginary world into which the reality of madness has made its *entrée*: for, as can be seen from the typed manuscript of Celan's poem *Tübingen, Jänner*, Celan added in handwriting 'Waiblinger, der kranke Hölderlin' ('Waiblinger, the sick Hölderlin') in the upper right hand corner.[44]

Celan's note refers to *Der kranke Hölderlin*, a volume of documents describing 'the sick Hölderlin' after his retreat into the so-called 'Hölderlinturm' ('Hölderlin tower') in Tübingen from 1806 until his death in 1843. These documents were assembled by Erich Trummler and published in 1921.[45] As has been pointed out many times, Celan came across the word 'Pallaksch' in an article contained in this book, 'Aus dem Bericht von Christoph Theodor Schwab (1846)' ('From the report of Christoph Theodor Schwab (1846)'), in which the author Schwab states that 'one of [Hölderlin's] favourite expressions was the word pallaksch'.[46] While there has indeed never been any doubt, among scholars at least, about the textual source for Celan's 'Pallaksch' – conveniently traceable given Celan's almost ostentatious indication that it came from *without* his own poetic discourse – this particular piece of hard evidence has nevertheless remained curiously unhelpful in the effort to understand

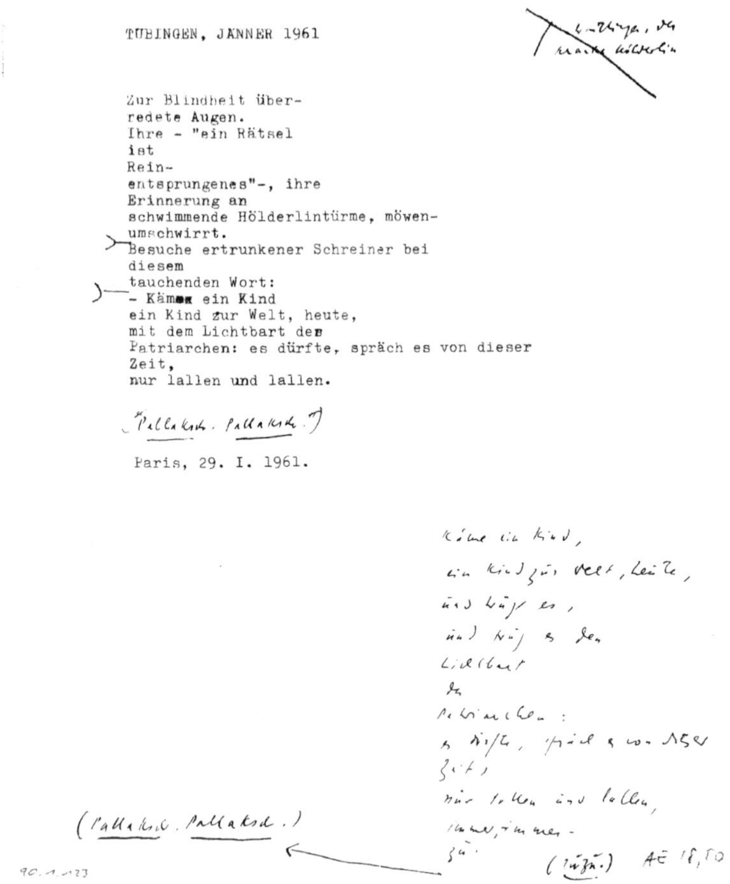

TÜBINGEN, JÄNNER 1961

Zur Blindheit über-
redete Augen.
Ihre - "ein Rätsel
ist
Rein-
entsprungenes"-, ihre
Erinnerung an
schwimmende Hölderlintürme, möwen-
umschwirrt.
Besuche ertrunkener Schreiner bei
diesem
tauchenden Wort:
- Käm[illegible] ein Kind
ein Kind zur Welt, heute,
mit dem Lichtbart des
Patriarchen: es dürfte, spräch es von dieser
Zeit,
nur lallen und lallen.

Paris, 29. I. 1961.

Figure 3: Celan's typed manuscript of *Tübingen, Jänner* with additions in his own hand, Literaturarchiv Marbach

better the meaning of 'Pallaksch'. This surely has to do with the intrinsically enigmatic nature of 'Pallaksch' itself first of all; secondly, however, this interpretative helplessness also lies in the fact that it is in this case particularly ineffective to simply state the origin of 'Pallaksch' since, by doing so, nothing has been said at all – be it about a possible meaning for 'Pallaksch', or its use by Hölderlin, or its sense in the poem – precisely because no such critical questioning has been undertaken. Yet, already Schwab's report provides us with a number of informative remarks about 'Pallaksch' of which Celan, reader of the report, was most probably aware when he singled out 'Pallaksch' to become the most distinctive feature in his poem. We must also assume that Schwab's comments about

'Pallaksch' played a crucial role in Celan's motivation to use it in the first place, apart from the inherently intriguing shape and sound that characterizes 'Pallaksch'. Schwab's comments are noteworthy not least for their patent interpretative insecurity:

'If [Hölderlin] used in his answers incomprehensible, senseless words, then he did so partly capriciously, but partly also, and more frequently so in order to take a rest from strenuous, sensible thinking.'

'His favourite word was pallaksch!'

'One time one could take it to mean 'yes', another time 'no', but usually he wasn't thinking of anything at all, but used it rather when his patience or the remains of his rational capacities were exhausted and when he didn't want to take the pains of reflecting whether it were 'yes' or 'no' that were to be said.'[47]

This makes for interesting reading. While the word's sense remains unclear – determined by its very indeterminacy, sitting hyperflexibly between an arbitrary yes and no – the *gesture* for which it stands is not. Indeed, the only feature described by Schwab with consistency is that of exhaustion and the lack of Hölderlin's desire to hold on to 'sensible thinking'. This, he asserts, is what lay behind Hölderlin's use of 'Pallaksch'. In wondering how Schwab might have reached this conclusion with such confidence, given that the word on its own discloses few clues, it becomes clear that it must have been Hölderlin's physical and psychic state, as witnessed by Schwab, that determined Schwab's interpretation. In this sense, 'Pallaksch' grows out of the loss of intellectual interest and energy, to become the gesture of loss itself.

'Pallaksch' thereby appears to be Celan's word of verbal defeat. The emotionally charged state of apparent exhaustion, or so-called madness, has poetically found an appropriate linguistic equivalent in the onomatopoetic 'lallen' within which it is still just about contained. Linguistically already less contained, however, are 'immer-, immer' as well as 'zuzu', bits of a language consumed by the emotional drain of which they still attempt to speak. Finally, 'Pallaksch' is fragmented by the extreme emotional force to which this word still tries to give verbal expression. In the end, 'Pallaksch' cannot contain this violent force; emotion breaks through and disperses it.[48] By inserting Hölderlin's 'Pallaksch' Celan clearly chose to reflect Hölderlin's depleted world, a world subsumed under the sound of 'Pallaksch'. Yet by reflecting it, Celan did not attempt to adopt it. On the contrary. 'Pallaksch' has been left entirely unchanged. For assimilation would go beyond literal quotation, would organically incorporate as well as transform, and thus change the original shape of what had been taken in. As such, then, 'Pallaksch' remains outside the poem, and indeed Celan has indicated as much by adding parentheses to the quotation marks, a means of self-imposed restraint and distance – a distance that is rather put on display. It is this that makes for a paradoxical dynamic between the relatively loose attachment of this last line to the rest of the poem, and it being by the same token its eye-catcher and structural base. The semantic intricacies involved in Celan's reference to Hölderlin are reflected in the word's relative notational complications which can be followed up in the poet's manuscript (see reproduction above), that revealed the amount of deliberation which went into Celan's typographical handling of Hölderlin's 'Pallaksch'.

Yes/No = No

Let us consider for a moment Schwab's impression that 'Pallaksch' was to mean at one time 'yes' and at another time 'no'. Within a context of speech and voluntary action, such serene equivalence of 'yes' and 'no' must be recognized as probably the most radical form of negation, as the sign of an extreme and deliberate negativism, thereby joining the reality of loss (and loss of reality). In a poetic context, however, its function is different, if not opposite. For Celan's desire to remain equivocal in *Tübingen, Jänner* through the use of 'Pallaksch' can seem an 'act of freedom in which the poetic 'I' denies its subordination, or at least its awe of the ontological solemnity of language', as John Jackson remarks. The invention and celebration of such meta-language is like 'a mockery of the verbal fixity of being, it is a gesture through which the decision of non-sense prevails [. . .] over the permanence of the principle of identity'.[49] It is perhaps in this regard that Celan spoke of an 'anonymous, nameless poetry' and of 'poetry's innate tendency to remain nameless'.[50] Nevertheless, the poetic anonymity Celan achieved by creating with 'Pallaksch' a semantic gap could also be seen to have been 'repaired', so to speak, by an explicit naming of the author's identity in *Tübingen Jänner* precisely through the very omission of naming, be it a poetic 'I' or any other kind of substitute.

The Mirror-Invertedness of the You

Celan's famously frequent use of the pronoun 'you' and its self-referential implications in terms of pronominal reversal – saying 'you' when meaning

'I' – is, as one of his most characteristic poetological procedures, strikingly absent in *Tübingen, Jänner*. Indeed, there is no address of any kind: the first part (lines 1–11) consists of two plain statements, enclosing within the related second one the Hölderlin quotation; the second part (lines 12–22) is a statement in the subjunctive but set in direct speech, which, nonetheless, still addresses no-one; and '("Pallaksch. Pallaksch")' is itself, as a quotation, withheld by parenthetical reservations, and as I suggested earlier, a sign saturated with referential equivocation. So, no 'you', no 'I', no direct appeal. Yet, this absence of *pro*-nouns in *Tübingen, Jänner* seems to expose that Celan avoids them most when they concern him most. For to use pronominal reversal and to speak of oneself as 'you' clearly dissolves the distinction between 'me' and 'not-me'. Celan himself spoke of a 'mirror-invertedness of the you'.[51] And it is a constant revocation of fixity for the sake of flux or fusion, a determined evasion of self, that is at the heart of *Tübingen, Jänner*. The internal movement of such identificatory instability corresponds to an 'immer noch da – schon nicht mehr' ('still there – already no longer'), and to a 'Selbstaufhebung des Subjekts = möglich in der Dichtung???' ('Self-neutralization of the subject = possible only in poetry???'), two formulations for the same concern that, as we know from his Notes to the *Meridian*,[52] preoccupied Celan for many years. By carving out a seemingly impersonal space in *Tübingen, Jänner*, Celan may be addressing himself more directly than ever, and well beyond mere poetological significance.

III

KURTÁG'S SONG

Kurtág stands out in his persistent preference for literary and poetic texts whose nerve-structure is organized around as well as empowered by a forward drive and intent to tackle silence and the more noisy articulations this silence provokes.[53] What happens to such radical denial of lyricism and logic as expressed by 'Pallaksch' when confronted with musical sound or thought? If Celan's language were at this very moment of the poem well and truly wrecked, with sense suspended in the absence of both image and verbal meaning, would '*Gesang*' still be possible for Kurtág? And, if so, what would become of the non-symbolic of 'Pallaksch'?

Figure 4: Manuscript of Kurtág's *Tübingen, Jänner*, part of the *Hölderlingesänge* op. 35 composed 1997, Paul Sacher Foundation Basel

Figure 4: (Continued)

Lyricising Slackening Speech

The 'Pallaksch' in Kurtág's *Tübingen, Jänner* follows one of the more lyrical passages in his vocal œuvre. Set off from the song's second *Arioso* part, Kurtág's 'Pallaksch' cuts five times through the smooth and expansive vocal stream that reached its greatest lyrical intensity with 'lallen und lallen'. Based on the step-wise, falling motion of minor seconds (A natural-G sharp, then B natural-A sharp), the tenor voice celebrates each 'lallen' with a few grace notes, adding to the indicated *dolce* a somewhat more dolorous shade.[54] A sense of nostalgia enrobes the second 'lallen', set a step higher as a sequence of the first, rhyming musically. What makes Kurtág's 'lallen und lallen' a poignant moment is its stylistic singularity as the only place in the song to sound conventionally lyrical. It comes about rather unexpectedly in the midst of a seemingly erratic environment, itself much more extensive in time so that the lyricism of 'lallen und lallen' stands in contrast with everything before or after, and with 'Pallaksch' in particular.

Kurtág exploits this lyrical effect and the tension it generates by setting 'immer-, immer-/zuzu' also to a falling minor second (E flat-D natural; C sharp-C natural; F flat-E flat), but in an increasingly agitated mode, with the voice gradually rising in both volume and register (*allmählich erregter werden; sempre cresc.*). His repeat of 'zuzu' represents a significant textual change of the original poem which, poetically speaking, undermines Celan's carefully-constructed symbolization of infinite multiplicity and timelessness as discussed earlier.[55] The reason must be aesthetic: only by repeating 'zuzu' is Kurtág able to maintain the sequential rhyming pattern, since Celan's clustered 'zuzu' is based on the monosyllabic 'zu', unlike 'lallen', 'immer' or 'Pallaksch'. In order to lyricize it like 'lallen und lallen' and 'immer-, immer', Kurtág chose to double Celan's single 'zuzu'. Thus, Kurtág is very deliberately drawing out Celan's words of verbal defeat with a *cantabile* voice. The gain is on the side of expression: if words originate in sensation, then states of exhaustion or madness have poetically found an appropriate linguistic equivalent in the onomatopoetic 'lallen' within which such states are still containable. Linguistically already less contained, however, are 'immer-, immer' as well as 'zuzu', bits of a language consumed by the emotional strain of which they still attempt to speak. Then 'Pallaksch' is scattered compositionally by sounding the first of its two syllables at the extreme upper end of the vocal register, and the second at its extreme lower end. 'Pallaksch' is thus not only split, but also dragged in opposite directions.

And it is also hollowed out by a temporal space, a split second's gap, since Kurtág, for the first time in this song, no longer links the syllables by *legato* slurs: on the contrary, as can be seen in the score, Kurtág uses reversed accent signs to ensure the markedly dissociated pronunciation of 'Pallaksch'.

In Celan, the capacity of words to contain extreme emotion has been tested and shown to fail. In Kurtág, a similar experiment is taking place, not only as to the projection of emotion beyond ordinary language, such as is signaled by the non-sensical 'Pallaksch', but as to the idea of a singing voice as a whole: the stylized voice of the German Lied, to which Kurtág refers when setting the 'lallen' in a lyrical mode, fails at the moment of greatest emotional disarray, that is with 'Pallaksch'. A number of compositional procedures used for 'Pallaksch' generate a gradual vocal regression and contribute to a highly dramatized disappearance not only of the lyrical voice, but the voice altogether, especially in its human quality: at first, the singing voice ceases to be lyrical and melismatic. Eventually it tips over into what seems like a primitive mode marking the imminent risk of a turnabout towards bestialization. The end of Kurtág's song is a whisper. With hardly any voice left to utter the last 'Pallaksch', these desperate final noises manage to efface any trace of a human presence.

In the song's manuscript, significantly, the fourth and last of Kurtág's arrowed *crescendo* signs, further heightened by a *molto* indication as well as a *fermata*, intensifies what couldn't be further from 'Gesang', or even from merely lyrical fragments. Here Kurtág highlights noise, produced by what is not yet or is no longer a voice: 'geräuschvoll, gleichsam erstickend einatmen' ('noisily, breathing as if to suffocate'), the performer is to accelerate into and magnify the intermediary zone of sonic debris produced by the mere attempt to breathe. By throwing into relief the distressing noises of suffocation, Kurtág dramatizes what is in truth a pleading for respiration – the prime condition of speech. At the same time there is a lessening of distance until the listener seems within the singer's proximity, and even closer still, inside the stutterer's throat in order better to seize the peculiar clucking sound of 'Pallaksch'. With Kurtág's 'Pallaksch', as I hear it, we find ourselves within the greatest proximity to the stuttering singer, and even closer still: *inside* his throat so as to touch and taste and feel the peculiar clucking sound of this strange word. Kurtág's 'Pallaksch' seems to suggest a close-up into the physicalities of the *making* of noise – *any* noise – in order to be heard at all, to ensure the

very basics of life, without any metaphysics. Ortega y Gasset described
the sense behind this kind of artistic procedure:

> To satisfy the desire for dehumanization one need not alter the inherent nature of things. It
> is enough to upset the value pattern and to produce an art in which the small events in life
> appear in the foreground with monumental dimensions. Here we have the connecting link
> between two seemingly very different manners of modern art, *the surrealism of metaphors
> and what may be called infrarealism*. Both satisfy the urge to escape and elude reality.
> Instead of soaring to poetical heights, art may dive beneath the level marked by the
> natural perspective. How it is possible to overcome realism by merely putting too fine
> a point on it and discovering, lens in hand, *the micro-structure of life* can be observed
> in Proust, Gomez de la Serna, Joyce [. . .] The procedure simply consists in letting the
> outskirts of attention, *that which ordinarily escapes notice, perform the main part in life's
> drama* .[56]

Compositionally, Kurtág magnifies 'Pallaksch' and thereby transposes
it into a sound world that, linguistically and poetically, seemed already
strongly implied by Celan: if the uncanniness of the Germanic 'Pallaksch'
is the shape that takes on the past, remembered as well as de-formed
by the unconscious (Benjamin), it also signifies the total devaluation of a
sign as a carrier of sense. No longer functioning as a symbol, but working
in the name of de-symbolization as the poem's driving force, it instead
'takes over the full function and significance of the thing it symbolizes'.[57]
'Pallaksch' thus becomes an entity. Isolated in this way it is no longer
arbitrary at all: it now represents something that is fully and wholly
imaginary, without any reference to the reality to which it might, as a
sign, be attached. 'Pallaksch' then corresponds to what Freud described
as 'the over-accentuation of psychical reality in comparison with material
reality'.[58] To be sure, 'Pallaksch' is a much more severe version of Kafka's
almost still sympathetic mental creature Odradek, that abject little figure
of memory. With Celan's 'Pallaksch' the loss of words is total. Coming full
cycle by naming what cannot be named, it expresses a degree of anxiety
that Bion admirably explored in the psychotic personality as 'nameless
dread': a primitive, infantile kind of anxiety, prior to the acquisition of
language, and close to mental death.[59] Both *sprachblind* as well as,[60] then,
as it reaches beyond words once the thinking process has been reversed,
yet knowingly resonant, Kurtág's 'Pallaksch' becomes all but evacuatory
speech as it is expelled *fortissimo* and with maximum emotional intensity
'in utmost rage and desperation'.[61]

In Bacon's image, anxiety takes hold of the human body and renders it
sprachblind, until this force transforms the human into the animal: the body

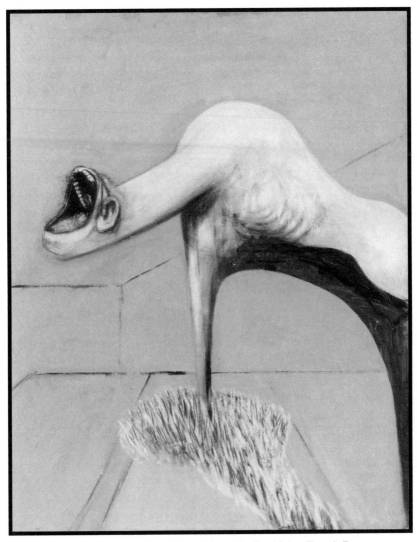

Figure 5: *Three Studies for Figures at the Base of a Crucifixion*, Francis Bacon, 1944 (detail of right-hand panel). Oil and pastel on hardboard, 94 × 74 cm, part of a triptych, each panel 94 × 74. ©Tate Gallery, London 2003

turns into a tumoresque thorax, tumescent neck and a Chapmanesque eared mouth standing in for a head or a face. 'Music', Deleuze writes

is faced with the same task [as painting], which is certainly not to render the scream harmonious, but to establish a relationship between the sound of the scream and forces that sustain it. In the same manner, painting will establish a relationship between these forces and the visible scream (the mouth that screams). But the forces that produce the scream, that convulse the body until they emerge at the mouth as a scrubbed zone, must not be confused with the visible spectacle before which one screams, nor even with the perceptible and sensible objects whose action decomposes and recomposes our pain. If we scream, it is always as victims of invisible and insensible forces that scramble every spectacle, and that even lie beyond pain and feeling. [. . .] Alban Berg knew how to make music of a scream in the scream of Marie, and then in the very different scream of Lulu. But in both cases he establishes a relationship between the sound of the scream and inaudible forces. [. . .] Bacon creates the painting of the scream because he establishes a relationship between the visibility of the scream (the open mouth as a shadowy abyss) and invisible forces, which are nothing other than the forces of the future.[62]

The Mouth of Hell

At this level of raw vocal energy leading up to the song's end, perhaps Kurtág's *Gesang* is just this, the noisy drama of a naked desire to speak. But it is about the heightened desire of someone condemned to stutter, whose every word is traded at a high price, spitting out syllables one by one, brutally voiced under the pressure of an agonizing, strangely syncopated respiration, between moments of suffocating silence. And it is in these moments of silence, forced upon a voice hell-bent to speak that Kurtág's music obtains its tremendous tension and greatest poignancy. It is this utter *desire* to speak, stripped to its physical core, which may indeed be more important, more significant, than the *knowledge* of what might be said.

Kurtág's advantage in leaving the 'Pallaksch' undefined may well be to allow it to work more directly on the nervous system. On the printed page, the violence explicit or implicit in 'Pallaksch' is highlighted by the quotation marks. As if to cancel such expressive as well as graphic flashing-up, it is also, as mentioned earlier, framed and contained on either side, almost stylishly so, by the sobriety of parentheses. Such detailed formal rigour, setting 'Pallaksch' apart from the rest of the poem, indeed enhances the word's inherent energy. Once set free in Kurtág's song, however, 'Pallaksch' is explosive. The way Kurtág exceeds what is generally considered a vocal rendering of words, let alone song, releases the violence inherent in 'Pallaksch' and introduces into this art the moment of human degradation, when sense gives over to pure sensation, when the voice is stripped and performs obscene sounds expelled by a shrieking and roaring mouth, much like those painted by Francis Bacon whose interest was, like Kurtág's I suggest, 'to make the animal thing come through the human'.[63] But 'it is more than that: it has a cosmic dimension, as if it were

Figure 6: *Head I*, Francis Bacon, 1948. Oil and tempera on hardboard, 103 × 75 cm
Richard S. Zeisler Collection, New York. © DACS London 2003

a Mouth of Hell. It seems to suck in and expel every particle of energy in the air'.[64]

Like Bacon's move from the human–become–animal in the *Three Studies for Figures at the Base of a Crucifixion* (Figure 5 above) where our gaze is directed from thorax to neck to screaming mouth with its striking row of teeth, to *Head I*, a severely deformed lump of flesh where little more is discernable than two rows of irregular, sharp (dog-like) teeth like gates to an internal hell, the perspective that Kurtág offers here is one of telescoping us acoustically into a deeply guttural and violently uttered 'Pallaksch', is one where the human voice, like in Bacon, has been pushed to the edge ('äußerster'), and where it breaks more fundamentally than is already the result with those extreme intervals the voice is asked to manage. The 'animal' finally comes through in the very last 'Pallaksch' which is put to us[65] in a most peculiar voice: the indications read *pianissimo* and 'plötzlich, flüchtig' ('suddenly, fleetingly'), the interval separating the syllables could hardly be greater, the separation itself between the two syllables hardly be neater (note the caesura signs before each syllable). And so, suddenly, there appears this little voice, almost toneless in its attempt to reach the extreme high and low pitch which it has been assigned. But in contrast to all we heard up to this point, this little voice sounds surprisingly content with what it has to say: a last 'Pallaksch', drained of all emotion, blank, depleted, before fading away into nothingness 'plötzlich, flüchtig'. Is this perhaps the voice of Kafka's last heroine 'Josefine', the dying songstress of her fellow mouse people? Only at the moment of her death – just like at the vocal turning point in this Kurtág song – can we finally hear her piping voice aloud. As the sign of a thoroughly negative poetology, Kurtág thus entrusted, like Kafka in his final novel,[66] the human voice to the animal.

NOTES

1 Kurtág's performance indications for the singer ['in äußerster Wut und Verzweiflung'] in the manuscript of his song 'Tübingen, Jänner', part of the *Hölderlin-Gesänge* op. 35, reproduced p. 144–45. Unless indicated otherwise, all translations are my own.

2 Ideas for this essay have been developing over a period of two years; I owe thanks to those who encouraged my work, and who, in giving me the benefit of their insight in many conversations or written exchanges, have immensely enriched the experience of writing this piece. The first to thank for their support of this essay since its inception are the members of the research seminar on Paul Celan at the École Normale Supérieure in Paris during 2000–2001 whose weekly meetings were an invaluable source of illumination, and especially to its inspired leader Jean-Pierre Lefebvre. I am equally grateful to Bertrand Badiou, editor, together with Eric Celan, of the *Correspondence*, and director of the Centre de Recherche Paul Celan at the École Normale Supérieure in Paris for their permission to reproduce the manuscript of Celan's poem *Tübingen, Jänner* as well as refer to material housed

in the Literaturarchiv Marbach. Once begun, my work was further assisted by an invitation to present it conference on Poésie et Musique organized by Michel Delville at the Centre Interdisciplinaire de Poétique Appliquée of the Faculté de Philosophie et Lettres, University of Liège, Belgium; by a second invitation to present this work at a conference celebrating Kurtág's 75th birthday in the summer of 2001 in Balatonföldvar in Hungary organized by Rachel Beckles-Wilson and Peter Halazs. To Peter Halazs special thanks also for inviting me to submit an earlier and shorter version that appeared in *Studia Musicologica Academiae Scientiarum Hungaricae* 43/3–4, 2002, pp. 451–467; and thanks also to a third invitation to the British Bicentennial Conference of Twentieth-Century Music at Goldsmith College London, organized by Keith Potter. I also had the privilege of presenting my work as research papers in the Colloquia series of the Faculty of Music of Cambridge University as well as King's College London. I wish to thank a number of friends and colleagues whose support, conversation and comments have been especially valuable: Malcolm Bowie, Andrew Brown, Esteban Buch, Leonard Olschner, Robert Pascall, Marjorie Perloff, George Steiner, Andrew Webber, and Arnold Whittall.

3 A. Whittall (2001), 100.

4 The song *Tübingen, Jänner* is part of Kurtág's recent 'work in progress', the *Hölderlin-Gesänge* op. 35.

5 See the *Tübinger Ausgabe*, ed. Heino Schmull and Michael Schwarzkopf (Frankfurt 1996), 36–7.

6 Deleuze (2003), x.

7 Ibid. 42.

8 See Mieke Bal 1991, 1997 and 2001.

9 Th. W. Adorno, *Ästhetische Theorie*, GS 7: 475–6. See for further comments G. Steiner.

10 Ibid. 477.

11 P. Celan, *Meridian* (1983), 197 [*Das Gedicht zeigt eine starke Neigung zum Verstummen. Das Gedicht behauptet sich am Rande seiner selbst*].

12 For a particularly insightful discussion of the notion of decay and the forms it took in twentieth-century French art, see Mathews (2000), in particular the chapter 'The offering of decay: Jean Fautrier, *Les Otages*'.

13 Ch. Bollas, (1987).

14 P. Celan, G. Celan-Lestrange (2001) I, 153 [J'ai surtout regardé ... et admiré, du fond de mes découragements, cet immense courage: 'Le Créateur' par example, sur fond violet, labyrinthes de lignes cherchant à se perpétuer à l'intérieur d'un contour extra-humain, infra-humain, animalier].

15 See P. Celan, G. Celan-Lestrange (2001) I, 214 (letter no. 207).

16 *Tübinger Ausgabe*, 'Meridian', Bibliographical notes by Celan, 212.

17 See Kristeva (1989), in particular the first two theoretical chapters (3–68) and the final chapter on the language of Marguerite Duras (219–259).

18 P. Celan, *Meridian* (1983), 197.

19 For instructive commentary about this proposition, see M. Blanchot (1949).

20 G. Steiner (1985), 47.

21 Th. W. Adorno (1974), 447–491.

22 M. Blanchot (1995), 106.

23 Dante, *Inferno*, Canto XXXII, 12, as quoted in Celan's 'Bibliographical Notes to the Meridian', *Tübinger Ausgabe*, 5. See below for translation.

24 Dante, *Inferno*, Canto XXXII, 12, as quoted in Celan's 'Bibliographical Notes to the Meridian', *Tübinger Ausgabe*, 5.

25 One wonders whether Celan wasn't indeed unusually well suited to explore how far one linguistic world might stretch. Let us note in this context his immediate as well as his acquired linguistic universes: born in Czernovitz, Romania in 1920 of Jewish parentage, Celan's mother tongue was German which remained the language he used for his poetic output, this preference lasting beyond his family's disappearance in the Holocaust, and throughout his life in Paris for almost 25 years until his death in 1970. That said, Celan seems to have been driven by a rather exceptional interest in foreign languages, as well as blessed with uncanny linguistic abilities for he translated (mainly poetry) into German from no less than seven languages: French, English, Russian, Italian, Rumanian, Portuguese and Hebrew.

26 Fr. Hölderlin (1992), 329. See Böschenstein (1997), 123.

27 See Böschenstein (1997), 119.

28 W. Hamacher (1998), 342.

29 G. Steiner (2001), 5–6.

30 See Lacoue-Labarthes (1986) as well as J. Felstiner: *Paul Celan: Poet, Survivor, Jew* (1995), 170–173, who suggests, presumably after Lacoue-Labarthes, that 'the patriarch's odd *zuzu*... even has a forebear in the stammering prophet Moses, who told the Lord, 'I am heavy of mouth and heavy of tongue' (Exod. 4:10)'.

31 *Genesis* 1,3 and St John 1,1.

32 The German 'zu' means 'closed' or 'shut' as well as 'further on', especially in combination with 'immer', as is here the case.

33 P. Celan (1983), 167 [Die deutsche Lyrik ... Düsterstes im Gedächtnis ... kann ... bei aller Vergegenwärtigung der Tradition, in der sie steht, nicht mehr die Sprache sprechen, die manches geneigte Ohr immer noch von ihr zu erwarten scheint. Ihre Sprache ist nüchterner, faktischer geworden, sie mißtraut dem 'Schönen', sie versucht, wahr zu sein. Es ist also, wenn ich, das Polychrome des scheinbar Aktuellen im Auge behaltend, im Bereich des Visuellen nach einem Wort suchen darf, eine 'grauere' Sprache, eine Sprache, die unter anderem auch ihre 'Musikalität' an einem Ort angesiedelt wissen will, wo sie nichts mehr mit jenem 'Wohlklang' gemein hat, der noch mit und neben dem Furchtbarsten mehr oder minder unbekümmert einhertönte].

34 Celan (1997), 272 ['Das Vergessen schenkt dir Gedächtnis'].

35 Nietzsche (1967), 291–2 [Vergesslichkeit ist keine blosse vis inertiae, wie die Oberflächlichen glauben, sie ist vielmehr ein aktives, im strengsten Sinne positives Hemmungsvermögen ... Die Thüren und Fenster des Bewusstseins zeitweilig schliessen ... ein wenig Stille, ein wenig tabula rasa des Bewusstseins, damit wieder Platz wird für Neues [...] – das ist der Nutzen der, wie gesagt, aktiven Vergesslichkeit].

36 See one of Celan's notebooks in the Deutsches Literaturarchiv Marbach: D 90.1. 3258 (*Lektürenotizen, Wendungen, Vokabeln*).

37 See P. Celan, G. Celan-Lestrange (2001) I, 214 (letter no. 207). See also the commentary by Bertrand Badiou concerning the word 'Celania', first used by Gisèle Lestrange, in terms of Celan's German as the poet's 'nomadic language',

'Notice éditoriale' in P. Celan, G. Celan-Lestrange (2001), 10–11. For a particularly brilliant exploration of the notion of 'Celania' by way of opposing Heidegger and Celan, affirming that the philosopher chose to 'be at home' in his language while the poet, 'radical foreigner', attempted to 'hold his own' ('tenir') in the sense that poetry is 'a held tension within the fragmentation of all languages, of all beings and of extreme solitude', see an article by Julia Kristeva in a forthcoming multi-authored publication, ed. Bertrand Badiou (Paris: Éditions du Seuil).

38 Kafka (1983), 129–30. For the English translation, see F. Kafka (1992), 176–177 [Die einen sagen, das Wort Odradek stamme aus dem Slawischen und sie suchen auf Grund dessen die Bildung des Wortes nachzuweisen. Andere wieder meinen, es stamme aus dem Deutschen, vom Slawischen sei es nur beeinflußt. Die Unsicherheit beider Deutungen aber läßt wohl mit Recht darauf schließen, daß keine zutrifft, zumal man auch mit keiner von ihnen einen Sinn des Wortes finden kann. / Natürlich würde sich niemand mit solchen Studien beschäftigen, wenn es nicht wirklich ein Wesen gäbe, das Odradek heißt. [. . .] das Ganze erscheint zwar sinnlos, aber in seiner Art abgeschlossen. Näheres läßt sich übrigens nicht darüber sagen, da Odradek außerordentlich beweglich und nicht zu fangen ist. / Er hält sich abwechselnd auf dem Dachboden, im Treppenhaus, auf den Gängen, im Flur auf. Manchmal ist er monatelang nicht zu sehen; [. . .] Manchmal, wenn man aus der Tür tritt und er lehnt gerade unten am Treppengeländer, hat man Lust, ihn anzusprechen. Natürlich stellt man an ihn keine schwierigen Fragen, sondern behandelt ihn – schon seine Winzigkeit verführt dazu – wie ein Kind. 'Wie heißt du denn?' fragt man ihn. 'Odradek', sagt er. 'Und wo wohnst du?' 'Unbestimmter Wohnsitz', sagt er und lacht; es ist aber nur ein Lachen, wie man es ohne Lungen hervorbringen kann. . .].

39 See W. Benjamin, 'Franz Kafka (1934)', *GW II/2*, 430–32, as well as the notes to his Kafka essay in *GW II/3*,1153–1276.

40 See W. Benjamin, 'Das bucklichte Männlein', *Berliner Kindheit*. *GW IV/1*, 303–4, also in comparison with Benjamin's famous text 'Engel der Geschichte' (Angel of history) in connection with Paul Klee's drawing *Angelus Novus*, where Benjamin's characterization is strikingly similar to the 'bucklicht' Männlein', GW I/2, 697. Cf. also Benjamin's notes on Kafka, II/3, 1153–1276. See also P. Szondi (1978), 275–294.

41 P. Celan (1983), 193 [Vielleicht – ich frage nur –, vielleicht geht die Dichtung [. . .] mit einem selbsvergessenen Ich zu jenem Unheimlichen und Fremden, und setzt sich [. . .] wieder frei?].

42 See G. Steiner (1985), 47.

43 P. Celan, *Meridian*, Tübinger Ausgabe, 208.

44 Reproduction of the first known manuscript of *Tübingen, Jänner* (D AE 18, 49) with the kind permission of the Deutsches Literaturarchiv Marbach and Eric Celan.

45 The same text is reprinted under the title 'Friedrich Hölderlins Leben, Dichtung und Wahnsinn', *Hölderlin StA 7/3*, 50–1.

46 See for example Böschenstein (1997), 122.

47 Schwab (1846), 109–110. Another document, Schwab's diary of January 1841, of which Celan was probably unaware, reads: 'I asked [Hölderlin] to read me a passage but he spoke only incomprehensible words; the word *pallaksch* seems to mean yes for him.' See Schwab in *StA 7/3*, 202.

48 See W. R. Bion (1993), 93–95.
49 Cf. J. Jackson (1987), 217 and 219, for an illuminating exploration, although without reference to *Tübingen, Jänner*, of various forms of metathesis in Celan's poetry.
50 See unpublished manuscript D 90.1.230 in Celan's hand from 'Dossiers "-i-"' ['anonyme, namenlose Poesie/Der Dichtg innewohnender Hang zu*m Namenlosen*' ('anonymous, nameless poetry/poetry's intrinsic tendency toward the *nameless*')], Deutsches Literaturarchiv Marbach, an extract from a collection of handwritten notes. Personal communication Bertrand Badiou. Underlining original.
51 P. Celan, 'Notes to Meridian', *Tübinger Ausgabe*, 204 [Spiegelhaftigkeit des Du –].
52 P. Celan, 'Meridian', *Tübinger Ausgabe*, 205.
53 Reproduction of Kurtág's song with kind permission by the Paul Sacher Foundation where the original manuscript is housed. Cf. also another 'nearly vocal' piece, *What is the Word*, based on Samuel Beckett's poem *Comment dire*, which also shows Kurtág's sustained preoccupation with silence. As his most uncompromising attempt to oppose words and silence, *What is the Word* does not hesitate to let the physicalities involved in the business of regaining speech gain ground over the expressive capacities of an artificially re-enacted experience, as the piece's performer coincides with the handicapped person of whom it speaks, and for whom it was written.
54 This feature may remind some readers of 'Der kranke Mond' from Arnold Schoenberg's *Pierrot Lunaire*.
55 See page 135 above.
56 Ortega y Gasset (1948), 35–36. My emphasis.
57 S. Freud (1919), 267 ['Wenn ein Symbol die volle Leistung und Bedeutung des Symbolisierten übernimmt'].
58 ibid. ['Überbetonung der psychischen Realität im Vergleich zur materiellen'].
59 Bion, *Clinical Seminars and Other Works* (London, 1994), 309. Let us note in passing that Bion was the psychoanalyst of Beckett, author of *The Unnameable*.
60 See Celan's comment p. 129 above.
61 See note 1.
62 Deleuze (2003), 60–1.
63 See D. Sylvester (1987), 54 on Francis Bacon.
64 D. Sylvester (2000), 49.
65 Cf. Kurt Widmer's interpretation of this song at the Edinburgh Fesitival 2001, transmitted by BBC4. Widmer is Kurtág's preferred performer and prepares all his works interpretations in close collaboration with the composer.
66 F. Kafka, 'Josefine, die Sängerin oder Das Volk der Mäuse', see F. Kafka (1983), 200–216.

BIBLIOGRAPHY

Th. W. Adorno: 'Parataxis. Zur späten Lyrik Hölderlins', *Noten zur Literatur III*, *GS 11*, ed. R. Tiedemann (Frankfurt a.M. 1974), 447–491.
Th. W. Adorno: passages on Celan in *Ästhetische Theorie*, GS 7, ed. R. Tiedemann (Frankfurt a.M. 1974), 325, 475, and 477.
D. Anzieu, *Beckett* (Paris 1998).
B. Badiou: Notes Éditoriales', in P. Celan and G. Celan-Lestrange, *Correspondence (1951-1970)*, ed B. Badiou, 2 vols (Paris 2001).

M. Bal, *Reading 'Rembrandt': Beyond the Word-Image Opposition* (New York: 1991).

M. Bal, *The Mottled Screen: Reading Proust Visually*, transl. by Anna-Louise Milne (Stanford: 1997).

M. Bal, *Looking In: The Art of Viewing*, with an introduction by Norman Bryson (Amsterdam: 2001).

W. Benjamin: 'Franz Kafka (1934)', *Gesammelte Schriften II/2*, ed. Tiedemann (Frankfurt a.M. 1967), 409–438.

W. Benjamin: 'Notizen zu Kafka', *Gesammelte Schriften II/3*, ed. Tiedemann (Frankfurt a.M. 1967), 1153–1276.

W. Benjamin: 'Das bucklichte Männlein', *Berliner Kindheit. Gesammelte Schriften IV/1* ed. Tiedemann, (Frankfurt a.M. 1978), 303–4.

W. R. Bion: *Attention and Interpretation*, (London 1993).

W. R. Bion: *Clinical Seminars and Other Works* (London 1994).

M. Blanchot: 'La parole "sacrée" de Hölderlin', *La part du feu* (Paris 1949), 115–132.

M. Blanchot: *The Writing of Disaster*, transl. by Ann Smock (London 1995).

Y. Bonnefoy, 'Paul Celan', *La vérité de parole et autres essays* (Paris 1992), 545–553.

B. Böschenstein: commentary of Celan's 'Tübingen, Jänner', *Kommentar zu Paul Celans 'Die Niemandsrose''*, ed. Jürgen Lehmann (Heidelberg 1997), 119–124.

B. Böschenstein: 'Hölderlin und Celan', in W. Hamacher and W. Menninghaus, ed., *Paul Celan* (Frankfurt a.M. 1988), 194–196.

S. Bogumil: 'Celans Hölderlinlektüre im Gegenlicht des schlichten Wortes', *Celan-Jahrbuch* 1 (1987), 81–125.

Ch. Bollas, *The Shadow of the Object: Psychoanalysis and the Unthought Known* (New York 1987).

M. Broda: *L'amour du nom: essai sue le lyrisme et la lyrique amoureuse* (Paris 1997).

M. Broda: *Dans la main de personne: essay sur Paul Celan* (Paris 1986).

P. Celan, G. Celan-Lestrange, *Correspondence (1951–1970)*, 2 vols. ed. Bertrand Badiou, assisted by Eric Celan (Paris 2001).

P. Celan: ' 'Die Niemandsrose'. Vorstufen – Textgenese – Endfassung', prepared by Heino Schmull with the assistance of Michael Schwarzkopf, *Paul Celan Werke. Tübinger Ausgabe*, ed. Jürgen Wertheimer, (Frankfurt a.M. 1996), 36–37.

P. Celan: 'Antwort auf eine Umfrage der Librairie Flinker, Paris (1958)', in *Celan Gesammelte Werke III* (Frankfurt a.M. 1983).

P. Celan: *Meridian*. Rede anläßlich der Verleihung des Georg-Büchner-Preises Darmstadt, am 22. Oktober 1960', in *Celan Gesammelte Werke III* (Frankfurt a.M. 1983).

P. Celan: *Die Gedichte aus dem Nachlass*, ed. B. Badiou, J.-C. Rambach and B. Wiedemann (Frankfurt a.M. 1997).

D. Cooper: *The Language of Madness* (London 1987).

G. Deleuze: *Francis Bacon: Logique de la sensation* (Paris 2002 originally 1981), transl. by Daniel W. Smith as *Francis Bacon: The Logic of Sensation* (The Continuum International Publishing Group Ltd 2003).

J. Felstiner: *Paul Celan: Poet, Survivor, Jew* (Yale 1995).

S. Freud: 'Das Unheimliche' (1919), *Psychologische Schriften*, Studienausgabe IV, ed A. Mitscherlich, A. Richards, J. Strachey, I. Gubrich-Simitis, (Frankfurt a.M. 1996).

Ortega y Gasset, *Dehumanization* (Princeton, 1948).

A. Gellhaus: 'Erinnerung an schwimmende Hölderlintürme. Paul Celan "Tübingen, Jänner", *Spuren 24* (Marbach 1993).

W. Hamacher/W. Menninghaus: ed, *Paul Celan* (Frankfurt a.M. 1988).

B. Hamacher: 'Sekunde', *Entferntes Verstehen. Studien zu Philosophie und Literatur von Kant bis Celan* (Frankfurt 1998).

Fr. Hölderlin: *Sämtliche Werke, Dokumente 1822-1846, vol. 7/3*, 50–88, (Stuttgart 1974).

Fr. Hölderlin: *Sämtliche Werke und Briefe I*, ed. by Jochen Schmidt (Frankfurt a.M. 1992).

J. Jackson: 'Paul Celan's Poetics of Quotation', *Argumentum e Silentio*, ed. Amy D. Colin, (Berlin, New York 1987), 214–222.

J. Jackson: 'Paradoxe et division chez Paul Celan', La poésie et son autre: essai sur la modernité (Paris 1998), 77–97.

F. Kafka: 'Die Sorge des Hausvaters', *Erzählungen. Gesammelte Werke*, ed. Max Brod (Frankfurt a.M. 1983), 128–31. Also available as 'A Problem for the Father of the Family', *Metamorphosis and other Stories*, trans. and ed. by M. Pasley (London 1992), p. 176–177.

F. Kafka: 'Josefine, die Sängerin oder Das Volk der Mäuse', in 'Ein Hungerkünstler', *Franz Kafka Gesammelte Werke*, ed. M. Brod (Frankfurt a. M. 1983), 200–216.

J. Kristeva, *Black Sun: Depression and Melancholia*, transl. by L. Roudiez (New York 1989).

Ph. Lacoue-Labarthe: 'Deux poèmes de Paul Celan', *La poésie comme expérience* (Paris 1986), 11–51.

J.-P. Lefebvre: 'Ich verulme, verulme–. Paul Celan rue d'Ulm (1959-70) (autour d'un cours sur Tübingen, Jänner ', in *L'École normale supérieure et l'Allemagne, Deutsche-Französische Kulturbibliothek*, ed. Michel Espagne (Leipzig 1994), 263–288.

J.-P. Lefebvre: *'Tübingen, Jänner'*, personal manuscript copy.

P. de Man: 'Lyric and Modernity', *Blindness & Insight. Essays in the Rhetoric of Contemporary Criticism* (New York 1971).

T. Mathews, *Literature, Art and the Pursuit of Decay in Twentieth-Century France* (Cambridge 2000).

R. Nägele: 'Paul Celan: Konfigurationen Freuds, *Argumentum e Silentio*, ed. Amy D. Colin, (Berlin, New York 1987), 237–265.

Fr. Nietzsche: 'Zweite Abhandlung: "Schuld", "schlechtes Gewissen" und Verwandtes', *Zur Genealogie der Moral, Sämtliche Werke. Kritische Studienausgabe*, ed. Giorgio Colli and Mazzino Montinari, (Berlin/New York 1967).

Olschner, Leonard: 'Adorno und das totgesagte Gedicht. Nachforschungen zur Genese einer Provokation', *Passagen: Literatur – Theorie – Medien. Feschrift für Peter Uwe Hohendahl* . Ed. manuel Köppen und Rüdiger Steinlein (Berlin 2001), 277–292.

M. Perloff: *The Poetics of Indeterminacy: Rimbaud to Cage* (Princeton 1981).

C. Th. Schwab: 'Aus dem Bericht von Christoph Theodor Schwab (1846)', *Hölderlin Sämtliche Werke, Dokumente 1822–1846 vol 7:3* (Stuttgart 1974), 202–207.

Th. Sparr: 'Celan und Kafka', *Celan-Jahrbuch 2* (1988), 139–154.

G. Steiner: *Language of Silence* (London 1985).

G. Steiner: After babel: Aspects of Language and Translation (Oxford, 1998, 3rd ed.).

G. Steiner: *Grammars of Creation* (London 2001).

P. Szendi: 'Musique et texte dans les œuvres de György Kurtág', in P. Albéra, ed., 'György Kurtág: entretiens, textes, écrits sur son œuvre', *Contrechamps*, nos. 12-13 (1990), 266–284.

P. Szondi: *Der andere Pfeil. Zur Entstehungsgeschichte von Hölderlins Spätstil* (Frankfurt a.m. 1963).

P. Szondi: 'Hoffnung im Vergangenen. Über Walter Benjamin (1961)', *Schriften II*, Frankfurt a. M. 1978), 275–294.

W. Waiblinger: 'Friedrich Hölderlins Leben, Dichtung und Wahnsinn', *Hölderlin Sämtliche Werke, Dokumente 1822–1846, vol 7 / 3* (Stuttgart1974), 50–88.

W. Waiblinger: *Der kranke Hölderlin. Urkunden und Dichtungen aus der Zeit seiner Umnachtung zum Buche vereinigt durch Erich Trummer* (München 1921).

A. Whittall: 'Laments and Consolations: Kurtág', *Musical Composition in the Twentieth Century* (Oxford 1999), 357–359.

A. Whittall: 'Plotting the Path, Prolonging the Moment: Kurtag's Settings of German', *Contemporary Music Review* 2001, vol. 20, 89107.

Comparative Criticism **XXV**, pp. 161–202. © 2004 Edinburgh University Press
Printed in the United Kingdom

'A Relic of an age still capable of a Romantic outlook': Musical biography and The Master Musicians Series, 1899-1906

CHRISTOPHER WILEY
Royal Holloway, University of London

Musical biography proliferated in England in the hagiographical climate of the later nineteenth century. The exemplary nature of mature Victorian biography and the hero-worship it correspondingly promoted found much resonance in the field of music in the emerging aesthetic of the idolised Great Composer: the creative genius who ruled the concert hall and (in exceptional circumstances) the opera house, whose pieces continued to be popularly performed even after their own day, while those of more minor individuals lay essentially forgotten to history.[1] This domination of the field by an elite handful of exalted figures and their works led to the construction, and subsequent perpetuation, of canons of wider historical and ideological (rather than merely practical) significance. Encompassing the broad period from J. S. Bach to Mozart to Beethoven to Brahms, and comprising the masterworks of the eighteenth and nineteenth centuries now familiarly recognised as 'classical', musical canon remained a largely uncontested phenomenon, at least in terms of the academy at large, prior to the recent critical scholarship of Joseph Kerman, William Weber, and others.[2] Its core constituency was, however, by no means established even by the end of the nineteenth century, and the claims of certain composers and their works to the available cultural ground continued to be fervently debated through the time-honoured method of promotion through the written word, in such forms as music criticism and, of course, biography.

Nineteenth-century England also witnessed the elevation of the genre of biography to institutional status, exemplified in the field of music by such publications as, in their initial incarnations, George Grove's edited *Dictionary of Music and Musicians* (1879-90)[3] and the 'Master Musicians' series (1899-1906).[4] As we shall see in the course of this article, the latter project represents an early and significant attempt to establish, through a set of full-length composer monographs, a closed musical canon of lasting historical importance. Proceeding via a case study of the Master Musicians series, I examine the methods through which late Victorian writers of musical biography attempted to canonise their subjects. Comparative analysis of the constituent volumes of this metabiography reveals striking correspondences in terms of the biographical and musical paradigms to which its authors consistently subscribed in order to construct the composers as relevant to the interpretative communities for which the texts were produced. Some of these paradigms were relatively new when the biographies were written, and were quite specific to England in the late nineteenth (and early twentieth) century. Others were longer-standing and Continental in origin – though adapted in the present context to Victorian needs, and therefore reflective of their particular values – for at the time, the musical scene was very much dominated by Germany. As such, this investigation also serves the wider purpose of demonstrating how musical biography (and, in certain respects, biography in general) functions, in terms of the stage that the genre had reached by the late Victorian Period. My exposition of the paradigms at work therein acts as a kind of scholarly forensic examination of the assumptions of its practitioners, since the study of biography can reveal as much about its writers and readers as about the subjects themselves. Such an enquiry necessarily hinges not so much on the factual information offered by the authors as on the precise ways in which those details are expressed. I have therefore endeavoured to provide, through quotation, a representative cross-section of the rich and extensive evidence in support of my reading.[5]

While responding to the general dearth of critical research examining composer biography *per se* and its documentary significance to music historiography, this preliminary article also seeks to situate the form within the wider context of life-writing in theory and practice.[6] To this end, the ensuing analysis places specific emphasis on three interrelated thematic issues of especial importance to musical biography as compared with that of other disciplines (drawing principally on the example of literature, with which field music has a strong tradition of having been associated in terms both of historiography and analysis). Firstly, musical canon essentially excluded women as composers, and biography became complicit in their historical effacement by denying them the possibility of artistic creation, while simultaneously linking them inextricably to such activities undertaken by their associated male 'geniuses'.[7] Secondly, music's great classical canons offered biography no heroes of English origin, owing to the absence of native composers of significance between the late seventeenth-century Baroque school headed by Purcell, and the emergence of the so-called English Musical Renaissance in the later nineteenth century. Finally, the specialist nature of the discipline of music necessarily influenced the scope for discussion within biography of the subjects' works and achievements, particularly in relation to their life, in terms meaningful to the general readers for whom the genre is typically intended.

1. THE MASTER MUSICIANS SERIES: BACKGROUND

The Master Musicians series began as a set of twelve biographies edited by Frederick J. Crowest and published between 1899 and 1906 by J. M. Dent & Co. of London and simultaneously by E. P. Dutton & Co. of New York, the long-standing relationship between the two businesses having been established for the purposes of distributing Dent's volumes in America.[8] The editor, who wrote the first book of the set, *Beethoven* (1899), possessed a background in musical biography evident from such publications as *The Great Tone-Poets* and his monographs on Cherubini and Verdi.[9] Two other contributors also had notable previous experience in the genre: Stephen Stratton, who prior to his volume *Mendelssohn* (1901) had co-authored the celebrated dictionary *British Musical Biography* with James D. Brown;[10] and Cuthbert Hadden, the writer of *Haydn* (1902) and *Chopin* (1903), who had previously published monographs on Handel and Mendelssohn in addition to biographical texts outside the field of music.[11] Many of the Master Musicians authors were music critics for provincial and London papers and contributors to musical journals and dictionaries. Notably, Edwin Evans produced *Tchaikovsky* (1906) towards the start of an influential career as a leading writer of criticism and programme notes; and Eustace Breakspeare, a student of Stratton, wrote many articles for major music periodicals in addition to his volume *Mozart* (1902). Most of the biographers were performers (notably on the organ) and minor composers, in which latter category Edmondstoune Duncan, who contributed *Schubert* (1905), deserves special mention for his activity and output. Charles Lidgey, the pianist and composer, was little known as a writer except for his early offering to the series, *Wagner* (1899); Lawrence Erb, author of *Brahms* (1905), was a music educator of significance in America, and the only Master Musicians biographer not active primarily in the British Isles.

Finally, two of the contributors were noteworthy scholars of music: Abdy Williams, author of *Bach* (1900) and *Handel* (1901), held a musical post at Bradfield College from 1895 and published on subjects including rhythm and ancient Greek music;[12] and Annie Patterson, who wrote *Schumann* (1903), researched and promoted Irish folk music for many years and lectured towards the end of her life at University College, Cork.[13]

The primary publishing house for the Master Musicians series was founded by its eponymous director, Joseph Malaby Dent, in 1888 and was best known at the time for producing popular editions of the classics at affordable prices (notably the 'Everyman's Library' series) as well as biographies.[14] Judging from authorial comments in its volumes and the reviews they received in periodicals, including *Nation*, *Athenaeum* and *The Musical Times*, the original Master Musicians series similarly endeavoured to provide a set of inexpensive, accessible books offering the reader a concise yet comprehensive outline of the life, character and works of their subjects.[15] As such, its significance lay primarily in filling a gap in the English-language literary market and, unlike Grove's *Dictionary*, it did not purport to present substantial original research or hitherto-unknown information. Indeed, its authors relied considerably on secondary literature previously published both in its country of origin and elsewhere – notably, certain monumental German-, French- and English-language biographies now regarded as classics – and they readily acknowledged this indebtedness within their volumes. Moreover, and eminently in keeping with the spirit of other Dent publications, the series was pitched to appeal to a wide, general readership.[16] Crowest set the agenda in writing of his intention to produce a monograph 'which, while it would appeal to the average musician, would provide the large public of ordinary readers with a complete and proper view' of his subject.[17] The frequency of accompanying musical quotations (a relatively expensive venture for publishers at the time) in some of the biographies indicates that a degree of background knowledge in music would have enhanced one's understanding of the texts. But in practice, the series' readership was sufficiently broad to justify the frequent reprints of its volumes in succeeding years, not to mention its revival after nearly three decades, under the editorship of Eric Blom. Nine of the twelve biographies were revised by the editor – or, in the case of Evans's *Tchaikovsky*, by the original author – and republished in 1934-5, together with three (those on Beethoven, Wagner, and Mozart) written anew, the latter by Blom himself.[18]

The original series is especially interesting to the present study for the fact that the subjects featured in its monographs did not simply accord with those repertories then favoured by the public and receiving performances. In this respect, it differed fundamentally from other sets of composer biographies of the time, including its most celebrated English-language precursor, the 'Great Musicians' series (1881-90).[19] While it is impossible definitively to determine the considerations governing the selection of the Master Musicians canon and the development it received in its volumes,[20] the fact that certain authors had previously produced musical biographies of different subjects, whereas others were assigned to texts that did not intersect with their areas of specialism, alone demonstrates that the choice was not influenced by the availability of suitable writers. Yet several composers then the height of fashion in England, notably Rossini and Verdi, are absent from the set. In fact, its authors repeatedly repudiated music such as theirs, preferring the potentially alienating pursuit of the highest artistic ideals to the (more lucrative) mere conformance to the popular taste of the day.[21] Conversely, the inclusion of certain monographs indicates that the series actively sought to present subjects of wider historical significance. Haydn's popularity in England was fading by the 1900s, Tchaikovsky's music was only just beginning to become fashionable,[22] and the works of Brahms remained, as Erb claimed, 'a matter of the chosen few, the inner circle of the musically elect who can comprehend his message'.[23]

The same trend may be discerned in the biographers' critical treatment of their subjects' works, which were discussed primarily in a separate section to that of their life.[24] The massive monuments of art, which were in many cases those most likely to be known to the public through performance, were inevitably explored, for the genre of biography privileges such large-scale forms. But in addition, within the quite limited space allotted to them, the majority of the authors also attempted a comprehensive sweep of their subjects' output. Two key factors affecting this coverage were the availability of more specific literature to which interested parties could instead be referred,[25] and the likelihood of certain very familiar works needing only brief discussion in comparison to more neglected music. The second point is crucial in determining the difference between a set of biographies that attempted to establish a true canon, and one that merely intersected with, and thus reinforced, current repertories (in which case, the fashionable works would be the ones written about at length or exclusively). Internal evidence would suggest that the latter was emphatically not the case for the Master Musicians series. Evans devoted around two-thirds of his book on Tchaikovsky to introducing the composer's works – many of which were still unknown in England at the time of its first publication – and even suggested that, given the dearth of concert performances, his orchestral music could be experienced by interested readers in arrangements for piano solo or duet.[26] And some of the musical quotations were actually removed from the revised version of the Schubert monograph, as these works had become sufficiently familiar to the reading public, in the thirty years since its first appearance, to render the excerpts unnecessary.[27]

2. PARADIGMS OF MUSICAL BIOGRAPHY

The original Master Musicians series is therefore unique for its time in that it represents a homogeneous group of composer biographies, unified under a single general editor and associated collectively for nearly thirty years. Owing to its conception as a cohesive, closed set, it had the potential to make a far greater impact than could a single biography in terms of establishing a musical canon, especially given that its various volumes were both pitched to a broad, general readership and comparatively long-lived.[28] As the proposed canon was one of lasting historical value, above and beyond the fashionable musical repertories of more immediate concern, the appearance of the set just years after the deaths of Tchaikovsky and Brahms is surely no coincidence. And since its various monographs drew considerably on previous biographies and other literature for their material, the series may reasonably be said to exemplify late nineteenth-century musical biography insofar as this genre was significant to canonicity, as my wider research in the field has largely confirmed. We may now proceed to an exploration of the paradigms contained therein, by which such canonisation was attempted.

Genius in Ancestry, Precocity in Childhood

The Master Musicians volumes typically opened with an exploration of composers' ancestry and childhood, incorporating a glimpse of their life to come. This practice served to justify from the outset the subjects' historical importance and their rights to biographical attention, as well as to pique the reader's curiosity and to flesh out a section of the book that may, in comparison with its later content, have been sparse on fact or not of particular interest.[29] Crowest's biographers seemed especially concerned to 'account for the musical genius of the composer', to use the words of one author, demonstrating its traces in their subjects' forebears and thereby implying a rich inherited musical legacy that further legitimised their claims to greatness.[30] No doubt this practice was partly due to the famous example of J. S. Bach, who was popularly constructed as the grandest member of a line of around sixty professional musicians spanning several centuries, and to Mozart's talented father Leopold, the celebrated violinist and composer.[31] Stratton instead pointed to Mendelssohn's inheritance from his grandfather, the philosopher Moses Mendelssohn – not of the musical variety, but nevertheless a genius.[32] Great Composers born of less exceptional families were discussed with some unease. Patterson, for example, suggested that the encouragement and admiration Schumann received from his father represented a form of passive musicality on his part, even though he was not 'musical in the usually accepted meaning of the term'.[33] This view resonates with Stratton's assessment of Mendelssohn's father, who, though situated generationally between two geniuses, was not himself so remarkable: '[f]or a non-musician', wrote the biographer, his 'insight into the art was wonderful.'[34]

That such speculations on the origins of musical genius considered the male line exclusively immediately raises the question of the role accorded to women in the biographies, especially given that Stratton chose to emphasise the tenuous (and non-musical) contributions of Mendelssohn's father and grandfather while marginalising the very side of the family which played the most important part in the composer's childhood years. His mother Lea was responsible for giving him and his exceptionally gifted sister Fanny – who, as we shall presently see, was herself to possess a significant role in her brother's later biography – their earliest musical tuition. Likewise, whereas Williams explored both Bach's male ancestors and his sons in his lengthy exposition of Bach's family, he simply dismissed the composer's daughters as having shown 'a less positive musical talent' in comparison;[35] and Hadden's assessment of Haydn's forebears similarly privileged his exemplary 'male line' of 'hard-working, honest tradesmen'.[36] As far as the biographies were concerned, female lineage was central to the establishment of composers' genius for entirely different reasons. Hadden alluded to 'the popular idea that genius is derived from the mother';[37] Evans pointed towards the 'mother's side' of the family in the absence of any apparent heredity in the case of Tchaikovsky.[38] (Ironically, though, when a mother did play a demonstrably influential role in the formative development of a subject's abilities, as with Mendelssohn, due recognition was not given.) The authors evidently subscribed to the traditional conception of females as capable only of functioning as a vessel for the inspiration of genius in men, rather than of concrete acts of artistic creation. Genius and musicality were viewed as merely latent in female ancestry but manifest, in some form or other, in male lineages, thereby instituting at the outset of many of the biographies a model that proves crucial, as will be apparent from its subsequent development in the texts.

In discussions of their childhood, composers were typically portrayed as precocious both in performance and composition, which tendency surely followed the celebrated example of Mozart, whose musical talents were so great at that stage of his life that he was literally unbelievable.[39] Breakspeare's contention that Mozart had turned to the writing of music owing to his prowess in performance resonates with similar remarks made by other biographers, whose claims that their young subjects were unusually gifted – sometimes, as in the case of Haydn, with direct comparison to the legendary *Wunderkind* – were more tenuous.[40] Other protagonists were instead presented as precocious in terms of general musicality, with especial tension surrounding Beethoven, whose slow start as a composer was renowned, and therefore unavoidable. Crowest described him as 'comparatively slow in unfolding. . . although he was one of the prodigious piano players of the day, the grandeur and sublimity of his poetic mind had yet to break forth'.[41] Stories of the subjects' childhood were thus used to marshal notions of destiny and to demonstrate the inevitability of their pursuit of a career in music (even if not specifically as a composer), thereby indicating that the child is to become the adult. This idea necessitated a certain amount of justification in cases such as Chopin and Schumann, the ultimate direction of whose life was not so immediately apparent.[42]

Industrious Study as the Path to Genius

The Master Musicians biographers considered that talent was latent or nurtured in childhood, and that their subjects' genius was acquired later in life through nothing other than indefatigable hard work and dedication to their cause – a concept eminently consistent with the Protestant work ethic (which, as we shall later see, was fundamental to the volumes). This paradigm may also account for much of the tension discerned above as to the earliest manifestations of subjects' later genius, in ancestry and childhood: the former testified to composers' pedigree and signalled the ultimate origins of their gifts, and the latter demonstrated that these gifts were not wasted even in their formative years, and that their lives were invested with a higher purpose from the outset. In view of certain undeniable examples amongst the Great Composers, it was clearly important to establish these seeds of genius; but it was also problematic in that ideas of genius as merely inherited or inherent run contrary to the work ethic, since no effort is involved in its realisation. The Master Musicians subjects were therefore also constructed as having engaged from their earliest years in relentless efforts to further themselves and to improve their abilities. Indeed, suggestions were made, in two cases, that they were anxious to commence study even before the time had come for them to be educated. Erb observed that Brahms 'played scales long before he knew the notes', and Evans even implied that Tchaikovsky was drawn to music precisely because of his studiousness, writing that 'as the work expected of him consequently did not absorb all the time at his disposal, he soon occupied himself with the piano.'[43]

The sustained, methodical work commenced by Great Composers in their childhood was charted as having continued, unremittingly, throughout their lives, as the only means (in the eyes of the biographers) by which their genius could be developed and brought to fruition. Williams speculated that, given the 'prodigious rapidity' with which Handel wrote music, the composer must have devoted the majority of his time to 'the most strenuous labour'; Crowest wrote of Beethoven that '[a] more industrious, painstaking, earnest student never breathed – one who, instead of hazarding short cuts to perfection... laboured away at his studies as if heaven and earth depended upon his industry.'[44] Such relentless hard work testified to composers' unwavering dedication to their perceived vocation as it necessitated self-discipline and strict daily routines involving many of their waking hours, notably in those cases where time was divided between these studies and other commendable activities, such as instrumental practice. Suggestions that they worked for the majority of the day and, in fact, the night as well are frequent in the Master Musicians volumes, as are indications that they rose early and made specific use of the morning, perhaps to demonstrate the importance of maximising daylight hours. Self-discipline was also significant to the improvement of biographical subjects in terms of the furthering of their musical skills, which involved an enormous amount of work undertaken alone. This point engendered a certain emphasis on self-teaching, particularly as composers were portrayed as having remained students unceasingly throughout their lives. The associated implication was that autodidactic approaches should be regarded above formal instruction, especially insofar as the subjects under discussion, who were themselves of the highest standard, may not always have been able to find teachers of sufficient merit.

The Great Composers were therefore upheld as exemplary for according with the righteous notion of using one's talents to the full, in that they were presented as never, at any time in their lives, having wasted the gifts that had been bestowed upon them. Indeed, Crowest cited the constant study undertaken by Beethoven in order to bring his abilities to fruition as the reason, insofar as one could be identified, for his greatness:

> There is no inexplicable secret in the vast scope and character of Beethoven's muse, nor is it difficult to account for its remarkable ascendancy over the minds of men. Beethoven was a great artist and a tremendous worker... That he was a born genius with [a] wonderful wealth of ideas and creative faculties is admitted, but these would not have made him the greatest of the great composers save for other gifts which he exercised and developed to the full.[45]

These figures were therefore appropriated to indicate the heights to which ordinary people could rise if they were dedicated and industrious in pursuit of their aims, and to demonstrate how they should ideally lead their lives. (More commonplace explanations for subjects' productivity, such as the need for money and the demands of employment, were inevitably sidelined.) Hadden, for example, indicated why Haydn might have succeeded where others did not in writing that he 'toiled upwards in the night, while less industrious mortals snored'.[46] It seemed especially important for the biographers to establish their protagonists' unremitting labour in the case of such crowning achievements as Handel's *Messiah*, Mozart's *The Marriage of Figaro*, Beethoven's *Missa Solemnis* and Wagner's project to build the Bayreuth Festival Theatre (Festspielhaus).[47] The industry of the Great Composers relative to the lay person also meant that the former could undertake many activities simultaneously – composition, performance, teaching, and so forth – and achieve much in the course of their lives, without affecting either the quality of their work or the meticulousness with which it was carried out.

Strength through Suffering

Success did not come easily to the Great Composers, despite their phenomenal industry, for they were seen to have encountered many obstacles, throughout their lives, which stood in the way of their accomplishments. According to the Master Musicians biographers, a great life was characterised precisely by such obstructions, and by the exemplary strength its subject exhibited in facing, and ultimately resolving, them. Crowest and Lidgey both claimed that the only respite from such turmoil came with death, thereby demonstrating the extent to which their subjects' lives were perceived to have been troubled, as well as their commitment to their vocation; the latter wrote that '[Wagner's] whole existence was one long struggle; even the day of his death was clouded by disillusion.'[48] Following the above analysis, it should come as no surprise that composers met such barriers from childhood, thus establishing early in the biography the ability to transcend boundaries that lesser subjects might have found insurmountable. Such hindrances included familial opposition to their early study of music (Bach, Handel) or to their vocation (Schubert, Schumann), and education being either generally unavailable (Tchaikovsky) or restricted (Brahms). One common theme was the poverty that composers experienced (and overcame) both during their formative years and throughout their life, which demonstrated how, in exemplary fashion, they sacrificed quality of life in pursuit of their art. Such situations typically required them to undertake jobs well below their calling (as with Bach, Wagner and the young Brahms), in order to make possible their ultimate achievements by sustaining them while they engaged in the indefatigable study that offered the only path to true genius. Moreover, the trope of the subject's rise to fame despite humble beginnings, and continued poverty, served to divorce any perceived connection between artistic success, and social status or wealth as potential short cuts thereto. This point may also be situated within the context of late Victorian and Edwardian England, in which professional musicians typically did not have roots in the highest echelons of society, and indeed it was problematic for people from these classes to pursue a career in music.[49]

Composers' ability to overcome adversity was linked not only to their determination to succeed but also to their greatness, which was frequently portrayed as related to the obstructions encountered, or even their direct cause, in accordance with the popular conception of genius as sufficiently ahead of its time as to be misunderstood by the masses. Had they not been such Great Men, it was supposed, their determination to succeed would surely have been challenged, and they would have abandoned the paths for which they were destined. Lidgey, drawing on the stories that originate in Wagner's own autobiographical writings and their interpretations, stated that though most would have been discouraged after so many setbacks, the opposite was true for his exemplary subject: 'the reverses and disappointments [Wagner] experienced served but to strengthen his character, and to enable him to face without flinching the far greater trials that lay before him. . . . far from being discouraged, he was spurred on to redoubled energy.'[50]

In other volumes of the series, the suffering experienced by subjects as a result of such hindrances was seen to enhance not merely their determination, but also their creative prowess, by actively furthering their genius. Handel, for example, turned to oratorio following the failure of his operatic enterprises, rather than give in altogether; as Williams wrote, he was 'not to be beaten'.[51] In several instances, composers' misfortunes were presented as either the direct cause of attempts to improve themselves in their chosen direction, or as precluding them from other, potentially distracting activities. Patterson suggested that Schumann's celebrated maiming of his hand 'must be regarded as fortunate', despite its obvious tragedy, since he was thereafter forced to dedicate himself to composition.[52] Crowest even suggested that Beethoven's deafness was the necessary condition for the composer's true greatness, writing that 'for the first time in Beethoven's great career we witness the matured strength of the giant composer asserting itself in a character and degree which, but for the awful calamity that had settled upon him, might never have been demonstrated'.[53] Indeed, the rhetoric that a genius must also possess a compensatory deficiency by way of counterbalance is a common explanatory strategy in life-writing, and receives abundant exemplification in musical biography, as later instances will confirm.

Love and Marriage: The Woman as Muse

The Master Musicians authors recognised a time in their subjects' lives at which love was inevitable, and the social expectation of marriage was sufficiently pronounced as to warrant caution over those subjects who remained single, following Mozart's famous remark that 'a bachelor lives only half a life'.[54] In observing that Handel was 'twice nearly married', but that on both occasions his vocation presented a difficulty, Williams drew on a frequently-encountered strategy by which to explain the absence of a spouse, namely the choosing of a life of art over one of marriage.[55] Another familiar ploy is found in the volumes on Chopin and Tchaikovsky, where claims are made that both these subjects felt an enduring love for their mother, over and above 'ordinary filial devotion', which therefore precluded relationships with women of their own generation.[56] This point also arose from the popular construction of Clara Schumann as Brahms's surrogate mother. It was a view to which Erb evidently subscribed, writing that 'in every way their relations were practically those of mother and son'.[57] But even if the ultimate outcome was not marriage (or even a relationship), the Great Composers were portrayed as being ideally suited to being in love, precisely because of their musicality. Moreover, according to the biographers, their creative prowess was actually enhanced by being in this state of mind. Hadden proposed that Chopin's romantic interests might be found inscribed in his music, a claim that assumes an added significance given that attempts to relate life and music so explicitly were rare in the Master Musicians volumes, which sought deliberately to segregate the two.[58]

The most important of the composers' unions prove to be those in which love and music are directly aligned: the woman in question is herself musical, and the protagonist's affection for her is presented as having arisen through their shared art. This condition resulted in a bond perceived to be stronger and more beneficial, as in Tchaikovsky's love for Désirée Artôt, or that of Mozart for Aloysia Weber.[59] In an extension of the androcentric model explored above, various instances involved the portrayal of specific women as inspiring a composer to greater feats of creativity through the love that connected them. This notion, which I shall term the 'muse paradigm', received its fullest flowering in the exploration of the relationship between Schumann and his celebrated musical beloved, the pianist and composer Clara Wieck.[60] Patterson presented their bond as having arisen through music itself, 'rather through spiritual communion than by personal intercourse'.[61] Correspondingly, their love was seen as strong, deep-rooted, and able to overcome the many troubles they encountered, not least the fierce opposition to their marriage on the part of Clara's father. In claiming that '[a] more ideal union could scarcely be imagined than that of a creative and an executive artist, both of the first rank', the biographer upheld the exemplary musical *and* matrimonial dynamic between the composer and his devoted wife, while relegating the function of the latter to the passive reproduction of her husband's creations, thereby marginalising Clara's own compositional ability.[62] Patterson's observation that 'the opening years of Schumann's married life mark the most active, as the most varied, period of his musical output and editorial labours' exemplifies her portrayal of Clara not just as the person with whom Schumann attained happiness, but also as the inspiration for the greatest fruits of his genius.[63] The view partly originated with Schumann himself, who once wrote to Clara that '[y]ou complement me as a composer, just as I do you. Each of your ideas comes from my soul, just as I owe all of my music to you.'[64] Patterson thus constructed the pair as artistically inseparable, as Clara was seen to have brought her husband's musicality to completion. This point is evidenced by the metaphorical description of her as 'a right hand to her husband', which phraseology recalled the injury that ended the composer's own performing career.[65]

The muse paradigm also operated in the negative. Lidgey drew upon the notion to justify both Wagner's unsuccessful marriage to Wilhelmina (Minna) Planer and his subsequent union with Cosima von Bülow. Since the former wife 'had not the power to understand her husband's genius', it became necessary for him to seek an alternative muse in someone 'who could understand and sympathize with him'; that Cosima was herself the daughter of another Great Composer, Liszt, serves to reinforce the paradigm.[66] The unsuccessful outcomes of two other marriages, those of Tchaikovsky to Antonina Ivanovna Milyukova and Haydn to Anna Maria Keller, were also seen as inevitable precisely because the women involved could not function as vessels for their composers' genius – and, moreover, actively obstructed their creativity. The biographers of both composers drew upon their subjects' own testimonies by way of illustration, specifically, Tchaikovsky's reference to 'his inability to work in [his wife's] presence' and Haydn's oft-quoted remark that 'it did not matter to [his spouse] whether he were a cobbler or an artist.'[67]

Particular females also came into view at crucial junctures in the texts as signifiers of the genius of the composers with whom they were associated. Examples include the surprise appearance of Clara Schumann at the first performance of Brahms's *Ein deutsches Requiem*,[68] and the fact that Tchaikovsky believed he was writing his Fourth Symphony for his benefactor Nadezhda von Meck.[69] According to Erb, *Ein deutsches Requiem* 'ranked among the loftiest music ever given to the world', following which Brahms had 'reached his full growth. The struggle for acknowledgement was over, the victory won'.[70] Similarly, Evans wrote that Tchaikovsky's Fourth Symphony – the work inextricably associated with von Meck's patronage, which enabled the composer to devote himself to his art – represented 'the passing from the creation of merely good musicianly symphonies to that of works to which unquestionably the term 'great' must be applied'.[71] The fact that Clara Schumann and von Meck were relatively invisible characters within these biographies sets in relief the significance of their sudden rise to prominence in connection with two works of profound importance to the developing genius of their attendant composers.

Crowest's biographers were similarly preoccupied with the importance of the family. Certain composers were upheld for their idealised domestic relationships, especially in cases in which their loved ones were themselves significantly musical, or when (as with Bach and Schumann) works were composed expressly for their benefit.[72] Williams noted that '[t]he clan feeling was very strong' in the Bach family, and Breakspeare observed the 'loving regard' Mozart always held for the musical members of his immediate family, namely his father and sister.[73] Patterson's romanticisation of Schumann's union with his wife Clara was reflected in her description of the composer's fondness for and devotion to their children, and Stratton similarly argued that Mendelssohn's exemplary familial relations showed his character 'at its best'.[74] In cases where it was not possible to explore relationships between composers and their close dependent family – if they did not have a successful marriage or had no children – the biographers found it necessary to look further afield in the demonstration of exemplary domesticity. Beethoven and Brahms, for example, were presented as having instead cared for other families – the former adopted his nephew following the death of his brother, while the latter supported Schumann's family from the time of that composer's last illness[75] – as well as overseeing their own households upon the deaths of their fathers, thus underlining Victorian notions of the domestic patriarchy.[76]

Death as Apotheosis

The well-known fact that several Great Composers met with an early death offered another instance of the biographical rhetoric of the genius possessing physical deficiency by way of balance. The Master Musicians biographers revelled in the tragedy of the premature demise of certain subjects, especially when they had both died unusually young *and* been exceptionally productive, using their gifts to the full in the short time that was available to them. Their creative prowess, which was seen to have become stronger as a direct result of misfortunes experienced in the course of their life, was also presented as having been ultimately responsible for their untimely deaths: in their relentless efforts to bring their genius to fruition, they correspondingly exhausted themselves. Although they were portrayed as being unusually resilient in terms of the strains they suffered – their labours and industry, and their fight against opposition – they were, fundamentally, only mortal. The concept received fullest application with Mendelssohn and Schumann, who engaged in a variety of activities in addition to composition – one as performer and conductor, the other as writer and editor – which took their toll on their (relatively frail) physical frames. Stratton wrote that

> With less call upon his vital powers, Mendelssohn might have lived longer; but it was in the blood, this unceasing energy and devouring passion for work, and the spark of life burnt itself out by the time middle age was reached. . . . whether he knew it or not, [Mendelssohn] was broken and worn, at thirty-seven.[77]

Drawing on the Romantic ideal of the genius as androgyne, the inspiration that brought about composers' acts of creation – which, as we have seen, was aligned in musical biography with the feminine – was considered to have progressively exhausted their masculine bodies. In pursuit of this point, the biographers of both Schumann and Mendelssohn invoked a metaphor with clear Freudian overtones, that of the sword 'wear[ing] out the scabbard before its time' by its overuse.[78] That their texts provide two of the most developed examples of the muse paradigm – the case of Mendelssohn is to be discussed presently – further reinforces the notion.

Composers' early deaths were linked not just to their greatness, but also to the fruits of this genius in terms of the extent of their corresponding activities and output, which served to resolve the tension over certain subjects having lived longer than others. Hadden justified Haydn's claim to greatness, despite his relative longevity, by reference to his 'sane, sound and, on the whole, fortunate existence'.[79] Moreover, he demonstrated his subject to have taken full advantage of the length of his life, by developing his genius in new and important directions even in his advanced years. And whether short-lived or not, composers were portrayed as having kept active until the bitter end, in testimony to their unwavering commitment to their art. Seemingly ignoring both their own suffering and the troubles unfolding around them, they remained entirely focussed on music and on their studies. Breakspeare, for example, wrote that in Mozart's final year, 'the composer would appear to have determinedly put aside. . . his worldly anxieties, and to have pursued his art with all the greater intensity and concentration of thought.'[80]

The emphasis placed by the biographers on the hard work undertaken by composers unceasingly from childhood to death, in accordance with the Protestant work ethic, led to their genius being charted as having evolved progressively throughout their lives.[81] This model, which I term the 'paradigm of continual development', was of major consequence for the opportunities it afforded to relate biographical and stylistic histories, as we shall later see, and to demonstrate that composers had indeed brought their gifts perfectly to fruition. The latter point yields the implication that the last year (or period) of composers' lives was that in which they necessarily enjoyed their fullest success or produced their greatest music, especially since many (including Mozart and Brahms) were presented as instinctively knowing that death was imminent. Duncan, for example, claimed that

The year 1828, Schubert's last, saw him at the height of his powers... There is but little record of Schubert's doings in [this year], apart from composition, which so fully engrossed him. He perhaps found himself driven to it by the inner consciousness that he was as yet undelivered of his best message to his fellow-men, or it may be that the creeping shadows of that long night which was so soon to close in on his labours spurred him on to his most strenuous endeavours.[82]

Despite the tragedy of composers' illnesses and premature deaths (not to mention the paradigm of continual development), the biographers were adamant that had they lived longer, their powers would not have developed further. This notion enabled them to conclude their account of their subjects' lives when they were at their peak, and served to prepare the reader for this outcome in that having reached the zenith of the protagonist's powers, the sole episode that remained to be recounted was that of the death. The only real resistance to the paradigms concerning subjects' development and ultimate demise occurs in the volume on Chopin. Hadden not only claimed that this subject, unlike other Great Composers, 'presents no such study of evolution', but also suggested that a longer life 'would have strengthened and expanded his genius' – actually contradicting himself in these two statements.[83] His partial rejection of the otherwise standard life-shapes of the Master Musicians series aided his construction of Chopin as standing apart from its other subjects, which idea receives ample voice elsewhere in the monograph and indeed served to justify the composer's inclusion within the set.

Death and the Maiden: The Woman as Muse (bis)

We have seen above that specific women, invariably loved ones of some description, made appearances at defining moments of the life story, as signifiers of subjects' creativity. In view of the connections between the height of protagonists' genius and their death, it is unsurprising that these otherwise marginal females also resurfaced towards the end of the lives of their associated composers. Just as the exertions of their manifold musical endeavours were portrayed as having brought about death, their female muses were similarly seen to have contributed to their demise. One such case is provided by Mendelssohn, whose musically-talented sister Fanny (herself a composer) was cast in the role of vessel for his genius.[84] Stratton described the pair as 'bound by the ties of art as well as blood', implying a strong and special union consistent with the muse paradigm.[85] He noted that Mendelssohn was profoundly affected by her passing, which was presented as directly precipitating his final, greatest period of creation, prior to his own demise just a few months (and pages) later.[86] Moreover, Stratton, citing as his source Lampadius's early German-language biography of Mendelssohn, stated that the composer's own death was directly caused by the shock at learning of that of his sister – thus making explicit the connection between the demise of the muse and that of an associated composer.[87]

Scarcely had he arrived at Frankfort, when – all too abruptly – [Mendelssohn] received the news of his sister Fanny's death. With a shriek he feel senseless to the ground. His own death was directly caused by this sad event, for his physician stated that there was a rupture of a blood-vessel in the head at the moment of this sudden shock.[88]

Similarly, Erb concurred with Brahms's own belief that his final illness was caused by his anxiety to attend Clara Schumann's funeral, and speculated that its severity was related to the fact of her death.

On 20th May 1896 came what proved to be Brahms's death-blow: Clara Schumann passed away[.] When he received the news he hastened at once to Frankfort to be present at the funeral, and it was to 'a fit of anger' at missing a train…that he attributed the illness which eventually proved fatal. This was an affection [cancer] of the liver… Undoubtedly the shock of Clara Schumann's death had much to do both with bringing it on and with its fatal issue.[89]

This standard plot is inverted in the cases of Tchaikovsky and Chopin. According to Evans, Tchaikovsky was extraordinarily pained by the decline in the attention paid to him towards the end of his life by Nadezhda von Meck. Her financial backing of the composer ceased, as did the correspondence between them. Evans wrote that his thoughts were of her in his final days, for '[o]n his death-bed, even in the height of fever, the name of Nadezhda Filaretovna was perpetually on his lips.'[90] Though von Meck outlived Tchaikovsky, she had faded from his life and so precipitated his passing; and Evans's observation that she herself died very shortly after receiving news of Tchaikovsky's departure suggests that the composer's death brought about that of his muse, rather than the other way around. Chopin's associated females and his demise were discussed with greater unease. Hadden, despite his endeavours to resist standard biographical paradigms, evidently subscribed to the correlations between association with an artistic partner, inspiration derived therefrom, and ultimate passing. Though he appeared strongly to reject the popularised connection between Chopin's own end and that of his relationship with the novelist George Sand, he nevertheless acknowledged the link between the two events that had been suggested by earlier (Continental) biographers such as Wilhelm von Lenz.[91] However, Sand posed a challenge to the muse paradigm, since she was herself a creative genius rather than a mere executant. This issue was resolved in Hadden's volume by reversing the couple's gender roles, thereby continuing a trend which was well established by the time of writing and which had originated, insofar as biography is concerned, with Franz Liszt's French-language life of Chopin.[92] Of the composer's Polonaises, for example, Hadden wrote that '[t]he Chopin of the popular ideal – the feverish, feminine Chopin of a thousand drawing-rooms – is here; but there is here also a Chopin of the masculine gender, who puts into these energetic rhythms a vigour and a boldness that must arouse the sleepiest indifference.'[93] This view preserved the heterosexuality of Chopin's relationship to Sand at the same time as allowing the former creative artist to function, androgynously, as his own vessel.

Religion as Artistic Motive

The Master Musicians biographers aimed to provide not only an outline of composers' lives, but also a more general assessment of their character. They were particularly preoccupied with matters of religion, which issue merits further discussion for its intersection with themes discussed elsewhere in the present article. While the point no doubt reflects their own faith, since many held church posts as organist or choir director, alternative origins may be found in the beliefs overtly held by a number of the subjects themselves. Notably, Bach and Haydn were both devout Christians, who habitually signed their scores – even those of secular works – with religious phrases such as 'Soli Deo Gloria' ('Glory be to God alone'). The musical genius exhibited by the Great Composers was considered to be a divine gift that had been bestowed upon them, reflective of a higher calling. They were therefore viewed as having worked in the service of God, both in furthering their abilities and in their general activities. These premises allowed the biographers to claim some degree of religious intent and motivation for composers who were not themselves practising Christians, especially in terms of their sacred output, which was correspondingly given an added significance. Observing the lack of knowledge surrounding Schubert's beliefs, for example, Duncan looked to his works as evidence, claiming that '[c]ertainly the Masses breathe forth a piety and deep feeling which none but a devout man could offer'.[94] The paradigm of continual development is again invoked, as several authors commented upon the fact of their subjects having turned to the composition of religious works late in their lives. This point further demonstrated the relative greatness accorded to sacred music in comparison to its secular counterpart; Schumann himself wrote that 'a musician's highest aim is to apply his power to religious music'.[95]

By reinforcing righteous Christian virtues, the biographers also extrapolated their subjects' moral beliefs from the exemplary way in which they conducted their lives. Patterson, for example, claimed that in selflessly promoting contemporaries above himself in his music criticism, Schumann 'put in practice one of the noblest of Christian precepts.'[96] Additional justification for those composers who were not overtly religious came from subscription to the anti-Marian view that considered too strict an adherence to doctrine to be negative. Hadden, citing Liszt's testimony that Chopin 'held his faith without calling attention to it', described the composer as 'refreshingly like the normal sensible man, who shrinks from being too closely catechized' – and it is deeply ironic that the life of a Catholic composer, as written by a biographer who subsequently took minor orders in the Catholic Church, should be appropriated in Protestant England to anti-Roman ends.[97] Drawing on the same notion, Lidgey justified Wagner's attacks on Christianity as being essentially directed toward hypocrisy and dogma.[98]

3. ENGLISH APPROPRIATION AND DISCIPLINARY BIASES

The original twelve volumes of the Master Musicians series represented an attempt to establish a musical-historical canon through a set of paradigms that drew heavily on the prevalent ideologies of the interpretative communities for which they were originally written. But since the biographies so strongly reflected late Victorian ideals, not to mention the (often uneasy) reception of their subjects in turn-of-the-century England, they quickly became dated. This point was abundantly apparent by the time of Eric Blom's revisions to the originals in the 1930s. Blom was more concerned with the emendation of matters of fact and prose style than with updating the views and interpretations expressed by the original biographers, arguing that '[i]t is not an editor's duty to interfere with an author's opinions, as distinct from... statements of fact'.[99] For this reason, the reviewers of the revised volumes repeatedly condemned the archaic portrayal of the subjects they offered, and even the outmoded form of biography they embodied: one critic complained of 'thirty-year-old opinions lying cheek by jowl with lately acquired wisdom which disproves them'.[100] Blom's own description of one such monograph as 'something of a period-piece, a relic of an age still capable of a romantic outlook' would seem to have wider application.[101]

However, the original biographies had not only been tailored to the readership of a specific time, but also that of a particular geographical place. Although published simultaneously in America, and presumably also distributed to the various colonies and dominions of the British Empire, the texts were evidently written primarily for readers situated in Britain itself, consistent with the nationalities and places of activity of its authors.[102] But this endeavour did not merely take the form of discussion of the reception enjoyed by composers and their works in that country. Indeed, certain reviewers, especially those of the staunchly English *The Musical Times*, felt that the volumes did not meet expectations in this respect. One made the general claim that 'the value of the series... would be increased... were [it] to contain an appendix giving dates, places, and conductors of first performances of the composers' works in England.'[103] Instead, the Master Musicians biographies were made relevant to Britain, notably England, in ways that focussed more immediately on subjects' lives, rather than on the subsequent history of their music.[104]

Though none of the twelve protagonists of the original series were of English descent, there were nevertheless important correspondences to be drawn between these composers and England itself. The country was presented as having afforded them opportunities and support, even when they had been neglected by their native land. Crowest remarked that the London Philharmonic Society provided the dying Beethoven with the financial assistance unforthcoming from sources closer to home.[105] Lidgey noted that England 'show[ed] great interest' in his subject by holding a Wagner Festival comprising a series of concerts in 1877, thereby rescuing this scheme at a time when the composer's career was otherwise at a low point owing to the financial failure of the Bayreuth Theatre project.[106]

Such offers were portrayed as arising as a direct result of the nation's recognition of the genius of these figures, which could even take place when no actual contact existed between the two. Duncan acknowledged that Schubert, who never visited England, was nonetheless known there by the time of his death; that his music was published and performed in the country thereafter; and most importantly, that English scholars (notably the celebrated biographer George Grove) made substantial contributions to his rediscovery.[107] Patterson referred to Schumann's strong, albeit unrealised, 'hankering' for England; her observation that on leaving Vienna in 1839, the composer 'thought seriously of crossing the water to settle permanently in England', further indicated that the country was one of the most alluring places for a Great Composer.[108]

Such identification of musical genius on the part of the English was presented as occurring in advance of similar recognition received elsewhere. Evans claimed that the fact that Tchaikovsky's music met with greater success in England than all countries apart from his own offered 'a convincing refutation of the charge. . . that we are an unmusical nation', as compared with France – a country repeatedly chided within the Master Musicians volumes for its musical philistinism, based on the poor reception accorded to such figures as Mendelssohn and Wagner – and even Germany.[109] Stratton similarly demonstrated that England, rather than Germany, was the first country to provide Mendelssohn's music with public exposure 'in a manner worthy of his genius'.[110] Moreover, he explicitly suggested that the composer would not have achieved such success had it not been for England, 'the scene of Mendelssohn's greatest triumphs'.[111] Hadden's version of this notion was more extended: Haydn's two journeys to England represent his only excursions abroad, and he was received warmly, his greatness abundantly recognised. Unlike Mendelssohn, Haydn did not visit England until his later years, and the country was therefore portrayed as having provided him with additional possibilities for bringing his genius to fruition, according to the paradigm of continual development. Indeed, Hadden asserted that the limitations placed on the composer in his feudal service in Austria and Hungary actually prevented him reaching the highest levels of creation, which he attained only in the more liberating climate of England's more advanced economy:

. . . Haydn's genius blossomed so luxuriantly [in England] as to place him with almost amazing suddenness among the very first of composers. There is hardly anything more certain than this, that if he had not come to London he would not have stood where he stands to-day. . . . the narrow limits of the Esterházy audience and the numbing routine of the performances were against his rising to the top heights of his genius.[112]

Hadden also suggested that the fact that England did not at the time possess native creative genius in music of Haydn's calibre was the very reason for the country's recognition and fervent support of such greatness in foreigners.[113] The dearth of English Great Composers in the canonical period encompassed by the Master Musicians series was an issue addressed principally in the biography of Handel, the subject whose connections to the country were the strongest. Of course, Handel differed from the other composers under discussion in that rather than merely visiting England, he lived there for most of his adult life, and indeed took British citizenship in 1727. Nevertheless, his foreign origins could not be denied, and as comparison of the articles on Handel and Mendelssohn in Grove's *Dictionary* reveals, the biographical rhetoric by which the naturalised composer was claimed for England was not so far removed from that for an indisputably German subject.[114] Williams, however, invoked the figure of Handel in one additional respect, situating him between Purcell and the emergent English Musical Renaissance in order to explain the apparent break in the country's musical tradition.[115] Specifically, he argued that his subject was so great that his 'overpowering grandeur and strength. . . struck a blow at native English productivity, from which it only began to recover in the latter half of the nineteenth century'.[116] In claiming that the English school of composition was 'nipped in the bud by Handel' owing to this inescapable and far-reaching influence, Williams attempted to justify the aridity of the country's musical scene for some time thereafter.[117]

Through their authors' endeavours to make their subjects relevant to a late Victorian readership, then, the Master Musicians biographies represent to some extent an appropriation of the Great Composers for England by virtue of their connections thereto. The same was true of their music, for the ultimate aim of the series, as I have shown above, was to promote its subjects' output to the target communities.[118] Certain works were upheld for having been written specifically for England, such as Haydn's 'London' Symphonies – which epitomise the composer's vast output in the genre he is universally recognised as having established – as well as his late English-language choral works *The Creation* and *The Seasons*, which similarly rank among his greatest music. In other instances, significant musical corpuses were justified by reference to existing English traditions. Breakspeare attempted to explain the apparent inanity of

Mozart's comic operas, as perceived from a late nineteenth-century English perspective, through analogy to that of Shakespearian clowns and Gilbert and Sullivan operetta.[119] He also provided a lengthy comparison of the standard texts used in the composer's Latin Masses with the liturgy of the Anglican Church – which he noted was largely identical, excepting the different language – in order that anti-Roman feeling might not discourage the listener.[120] Evans observed that in Tchaikovsky's Russia, ballet music was on a par with opera in terms of quality and corresponding reception, unlike that heard at the time in England.[121] And Duncan, by way of resolving the difficulty surrounding the absence of explicit associations with the country in the case of Schubert, appropriated his song-settings to translated texts by native poets including Scott and Shakespeare.[122]

Although the Master Musicians authors collectively followed formats that consciously separated life and works, there were nevertheless many points of intersection between biographical paradigms and those at work in discussions of the music.[123] The traditional pairing of Haydn and Mozart in musical biography, for example, hinged on the contrast between a genius that evolved slowly and uneventfully across a long, stable life and one that developed at a phenomenal rate from prodigious childhood to premature death. We have already seen that the paradigm of continual development functioned at the biographical level to aid the construction of subjects as exemplary by revealing endless hard work as the only laudable means by which to achieve success and to bring one's gifts to fruition. But the notion was similarly invaluable, especially given the biographers' practice of discussing their subjects' works by genre, as a strategy by which to chart stylistic evolution according to a teleological model. In addition to fostering the historical unilinearity upon which biography is ontologically dependent, the paradigm allowed the authors to explain the relative greatness of specific works to their target non-specialist readership without resorting to technical language, through relating them to the stage of life at which they were composed.

An added emphasis was correspondingly given to subjects' later output, and to their final works in particular, as reflecting the fullest flowering of their genius, especially when they served to reinforce two of the biographers' other preoccupations, namely correspondences to England (a point already considered with respect to Haydn) and matters of religion. Handel's move from (secular, Italian) opera to (sacred, English) oratorio not only marked a late change of direction in his career, but also led to the fullest realisation of his genius, resulting in the celebrated *Messiah* which, in the words of Williams, was 'a household word with all English people, whether music-lovers or not'.[124] Likewise, Mendelssohn's oratorio *Elijah* – his last great composition and, according to Stratton, his 'crowning effort' – was written for England and represented the 'greatest glory' of the Birmingham Musical Festival, which gave its premiere in 1846.[125] The Requiems of Mozart and Schumann were both late works (and Brahms's *Ein deutsches Requiem*, though early, was a turning-point in his career). Mozart's remained unfinished at his death – an obvious potential problem when privileging an artist's final output – and an elaborate mythology quickly emerged surrounding the work and its mysterious commission, fuelled by the composer's conviction that he was writing the piece for himself.[126] Practitioners of musical biography have amply exploited the irony that several last works were either on themes of death – most explicitly in the aforementioned Requiems, and in Schubert's melancholic song cycle *Winterreise* – or connected thereto, especially when (as with Mozart) the composer believed that death was impending.[127] A performance of *The Creation*, Haydn's last major sacred work, provided the setting of the composer's final appearance in public, frequently embellished in biographies as a *faux* death scene;[128] and the reception of Tchaikovsky's enigmatic Sixth Symphony is inextricably tied to his untimely demise.[129]

The issue of religion was also important to the paradigm of continual development for another reason, for it was related to Protestantism in terms of the work ethic. The notion would have been essentially contradicted by many Marian Continental texts of the later 1800s, which privileged more immediately-inspired compositional genius;[130] and, as recent studies by Linda Colley and David Hempton have shown, the Protestant religion was a key agent in the establishment and enforcement of distinctly British identities (as against those of the Continent) in the eighteenth as well as the nineteenth century.[131] But the paradigm is not only significant to the present study for the fact that it may be read as reflecting Victorian values by virtue of its religious affinity. It also received pronounced application within musical biography, especially given its implicit relation to the obstructions that composers were portrayed as having endured, without respite, throughout their lives, and which correspondingly strengthened their artistic powers. This biographical trajectory departs from standard nineteenth-century life-shapes, in which subjects were presented as having encountered an initial struggle in early adulthood following which they attained their ultimate aims, leading to a sustained period of success and distinction. As Paula Backscheider has written, many biographies follow the stereotypical plan of 'youth

[a]s a preparatory period, early and middle adulthood induction and struggle to attain specific, individual goals, and mature adulthood and old age as full achievement and later consolidation and appreciation of success.'[132] The trials faced by the protagonists of musical biography were therefore much more marked and prolonged than for those in other disciplines (and other tropes, such as the prodigious childhood and the premature death, similarly did not accord with traditional models). It was as though the practice of grafting the lives of foreigners onto the existing Victorian mould, as abundantly demonstrated in the above analysis, required biographers to overstate the case for the validity of the Great Composers as subjects.

For the figures at the heart of the great canons of classical music were, of course, predominantly Germanic; and although English biography had previously circumvented this potential problem by emphasising either native composers or those currently in fashion in the country, the Master Musicians series necessarily considered those of wider historical importance – hence the need to construct associations with England via other means. The former trends date back to the origins of modern music history and biography in this country: John Mainwaring's 1760 volume on the naturalised Handel is understood to have been the first full-length composer biography in any language;[133] the classic early histories by John Hawkins and Charles Burney possess a strong English bias;[134] and John Sainsbury's watershed biographical dictionary (1825) claimed as its *raison d'être* the perceived inadequacy of Continental counterparts in the treatment of British musicians.[135] In the late nineteenth and early twentieth centuries, English biography fostered national personages in such centrally canonical works as the *Dictionary of National Biography* and the 'English Men of Letters' series,[136] and this movement was similarly discernible in the field of music in publications including Grove's monumental *Dictionary*.[137] Even amongst the original Master Musicians authors themselves, Crowest had written extensively on British music and musicians;[138] Hadden's 1887 monographs of Handel and Mendelssohn were conceived as the earliest volumes in a projected but unrealised set of 'Biographies of Great Composers'; Evans was later to produce a celebrated series of articles on British composers in *The Musical Times* (1919-20); and most strikingly, Stratton's co-authored *British Musical Biography* claimed that '[a] country is musical only by the music it produces for itself, not by what it takes from others.'[139] The same tendency to commemorate national heroes through biography may be seen in other countries at the time: in France, for example, the renowned 'Les musiciens célèbres' series included volumes on such figures as Hérold, Boïeldieu and Félicien David, alongside those of broader historical value,[140] and French scholars had worked in their own ways to defend their country's musical reputation in light of complaints such as those of Mendelssohn.[141] The absence of English protagonists amongst the greatest subjects for musical biography – a problem unknown to biographers of British novelists, painters and playwrights – therefore presented a substantial difficulty for a venture such as the Master Musicians series, written not only in a distinctly Victorian vein, but also within a general environment of increased nationalist feeling and contemporaneous with the emergent English Musical Renaissance.[142]

No doubt partly for this reason, musical biography frequently drew on the discipline of literature – which was not only conveniently mainstream, but also possessed a much stronger English tradition – in investigating the genius exhibited by its subjects in areas other than composition. The Master Musicians series incorporated discussion of the multitude of prose writings of Wagner and the music criticism of Schumann – both of which were portrayed as having strengthened their respective compositional activities – as well as the correspondence of Mendelssohn and others.[143] The importance accorded to composer's words, rather than their music, in the context of biography had associated implications for discussions of the works: literary creations could be examined with relative ease through the medium of narrative in the way that purely musical counterparts could not, even when accompanied by music examples. Bearing in mind the audience of non-specialists for whom the series was written, works that incorporated extra-musical elements could be discussed in literary terms and thereby made more accessible to the general reader; hence the space devoted to the music dramas of Wagner (in addition to his writings), the operas of Mozart, and the operas and ballets of Tchaikovsky, exploration of which proceeded largely by way of plot summary.[144] An added irony presents itself in that nineteenth-century musical aesthetics idealised the purity of 'absolute music', which was ostensibly free from the external reference of texts and plots; thus the works considered the greatest of all by virtue of their autonomy were, by the same token, also more difficult to discuss within the context of (and canonise through) biography written for a general readership.

The traditional predication of music history on a small number of Great Composers – a top-down conception that lends itself perfectly to biography, especially when volumes are collected into series – meant that there existed much less room for minor figures in its canons relative to those of a discipline such as literature.[145] Correspondingly, hegemonies have been more strongly enforced in music than elsewhere, as exemplified by the relative invisibility of women among composers. By the end of the nineteenth century if not before, the presence of female creative genius in literature could not be ignored – indeed, biography had begun to celebrate such figures as George Sand, Jane Austen, George Eliot, and the Brontë sisters – and yet, women remained inadmissible to musical canons internationally.[146] The point was reinforced in biography through the establishment of the muse paradigm, which effectively denied female composers, such as Clara Schumann, the potential for musical creation.[147] At the same time, it functioned as a signifier denoting the relative greatness of individual works, and its associated biographical tropes additionally underlined the domination of society by the patriarchy, through their emphasis on such issues as marriage and domestic propriety. Significantly, the only notable resistance to these notions in the Master Musicians series, found in the volume on Chopin, was brought about by the prominence in the composer's biography of a female creative genius. I have already noted Hadden's separation of this subject from the other Great Composers of the set, based on the biographer's departures from standard life-paradigms, and it is surely no coincidence that Chopin – one of only two non-Germanic subjects out of the original twelve – was similarly detached in terms of his musical output, having composed small-scale works for piano almost exclusively. Hadden, following the opinion of the writer on music Sir Henry Hadow, anachronistically constructed Chopin as having 'approached our Western key system from the outside and never [having] wholly assimilated himself', which legitimised his situation within musical canons in that he 'struck out on his own path' rather than conforming completely.[148]

In attempting to establish just such a canon, rather than merely writing about those composers of more immediate interest to the reading public, it became even more important for the Master Musicians authors to construct texts that explicated the relevance of their subjects to their intended audiences. Perhaps it is true of all biographical endeavours, especially when the historical significance of their protagonists is not firmly recognised at the time of writing, that they represent an appropriation of those figures and their works for the wider community. But in the case of the Master Musicians series, this practice of appropriation additionally responded to the problems surrounding both the apparent infertility of England's own musical tradition and the consequent contention that the country was ignorant in such matters. Indeed, it seems likely that the strength of connections to England,

and continued popularity in that country, provided much of the reason for the relative greatness accorded to such figures as Handel, Mendelssohn, Haydn and perhaps also Tchaikovsky within the series and its correspondent canon, if not also influencing the order in which its constituent volumes were issued.[149] Moreover, by demonstrating that England was sufficiently culturally-sensitive to have recognised musical greatness in specific individuals, as well as to have nurtured their genius when other nations would not, the biographies served to promote the image of a surrogate national tradition in which foreign composers would flourish. The project embodied by the Master Musicians series may therefore be read not only within the context of late Victorian sensibilities, but also against the backdrop of the emergent revitalisation of music as a truly English institution.

ABSTRACT

Musical biography proliferated in England in the hagiographical climate of the later nineteenth century, partly as an outcome of the rise of the aesthetic of the idolised Great Composer and the corresponding emergence of musical canons (whose constituency was, however, by no means certain at this time). This article presents a theoretically-enriched demonstration of the paradigms through which its late Victorian authors attempted to canonise their subjects, focussing on three interrelated thematic issues that are of especial importance to musical biography as compared with that of other disciplines: the relative invisibility of women, the absence of national heroes, and the scope for discussion of the works. My investigation proceeds via an analytical case study of the metabiography of the Master Musicians series (London: Dent, 1899-1906), whose original twelve volumes together represent one of the earliest significant attempts in England to establish and maintain a musical-historical canon through a unified set of full-length composer monographs.

In determining the relevance of their subjects to the interpretative communities for whom they were writing, the Master Musicians authors appealed heavily to the prevalent values of the day, for their volumes quickly became discernible as period pieces. They typically offer a teleological charting of their protagonists' creative genius, from mere talent exhibited in their (often prodigious) childhood to death at the height of their compositional powers, which are brought to fruition – in accordance with the Protestant work ethic – only through industrious and unremitting labours throughout their self-disciplined career. The representation of specific women as muse to their attendant composer, capable only of inspiring or realising (but not exhibiting) musical genius, and their corresponding rhetorical function as signifiers of subjects' productivity and developing creativity, enforced the androcentricity of musical canon as well as the patriarchal hegemony of contemporary society.

The Master Musicians biographers also foregrounded any connections that could be drawn with England, thus to an extent appropriating the Great Composers and their music for that nation, counterbalancing its relative dearth of native genius. This endeavour served to demonstrate the country's cultural awareness, and its capability (over and above Continental counterparts) to recognise and support greatness in music, against the backdrop of the emergent English Musical Renaissance and a general environment of nationalism. The resulting biographical paradigms had profound implications not only for the membership of the proposed canon but also for discussions of the music itself, employing such factors as continual creative development, female inspiration and connections to England as markers of greatness within discursive contexts where life and works were consciously separated and technical descriptions kept to a minimum for the benefit of the non-specialist readership.

NOTES

This article is drawn from my doctoral thesis 'Rewriting Composers' Lives: Critical Historiography and Musical Biography' (Royal Holloway, University of London), two chapters of which are dedicated to analysis of the original twelve volumes of the Master Musicians series, in terms of the paradigms of musical biography they exemplify through their treatment of both the life and the works of their subjects. An earlier version of this article was delivered as a paper at the Institute of Historical Research, London, on 18 November 2002, as part of the 'Music in Britain' series. My thanks to the members and conveners of that seminar for a valuable discussion, to Katharine Ellis and Matthew Mills for many helpful comments on preliminary drafts of the present article, and to the Arts and Humanities Research Board for providing financial support to enable me to pursue this research.

1 On the rise of the creative genius in music in the nineteenth century, see Jim Samson, 'The great composer', in *The Cambridge History of Nineteenth-Century Music*, edited by Jim Samson (Cambridge: Cambridge University Press, 2002), pp. 259–284.

2 Joseph Kerman, 'A Few Canonic Variations', *Critical Inquiry*, 10 (1983), 107–25, reprinted in idem, *Write All These Down: Essays on Music* (Berkeley: University of California Press, 1994), pp. 33–50; William Weber, 'The History of Musical Canon',

in *Rethinking Music*, edited by Nicholas Cook and Mark Everist (Oxford: Oxford University Press, 1999), pp. 336–55. See also *Disciplining Music: Musicology and Its Canons*, edited by Katherine Bergeron and Philip V. Bohlman (Chicago: University of Chicago Press, 1992).

3 *A Dictionary of Music and Musicians (A. D. 1450–1889) by Eminent Writers*, edited by George Grove, 4 vols., with an Appendix by J. A. Fuller Maitland (London: Macmillan, 1879–90).

4 The twelve volumes of the original Master Musicians series, edited by Frederick J. Crowest, are as follows: Frederick J. Crowest, *Beethoven* (London: Dent, 1899); Charles A. Lidgey, *Wagner* (London: Dent, 1899); C. F. Abdy Williams, *Bach* (London: Dent, 1900, rev./1934); Stephen S. Stratton, *Mendelssohn* (London: Dent, 1901, rev./1934); C. F. Abdy Williams, *Handel* (London: Dent, 1901, rev./1935); Eustace J. Breakspeare, *Mozart* (London: Dent, 1902); J. Cuthbert Hadden, *Haydn* (London: Dent, 1902, rev./1934); idem, *Chopin* (London: Dent, 1903, rev./1934); Annie W. Patterson, *Schumann* (London: Dent, 1903, rev./1934); Edmondstoune Duncan, *Schubert* (London: Dent, 1905, rev./1934); J. Lawrence Erb, *Brahms* (London: Dent, 1905, rev./1934); Edwin Evans, *Tchaikovsky* (London: Dent, 1906, rev./1935). Significantly, both this venture and Grove's *Dictionary of Music and Musicians* have continued, in some guise, to the present time, and remain fundamental to the discipline of music today.

5 Where available, the 1930s revised editions of the Master Musicians volumes (see n. 4) have been used for the purposes of citation in the present article. The original texts have, however, been consulted to ensure that they are not at variance, and any discrepancies over and above trivial points of prose style or punctuation have been separately noted.

6 The one full-length (and largely historical) study on the subject that has appeared to date is Hans Lenneberg's *Witnesses and Scholars: Studies in Musical Biography* (New York: Gordon and Breach, 1988). See also Maynard Solomon's article 'Thoughts on Biography', *19th Century Music*, 5/3 (Spring 1982), 268–76, reprinted in *Beethoven Essays* (Cambridge, Massachusetts: Harvard University Press, 1988), pp. 101–15. The Royal Musical Association recently held its 37th Annual Conference on the subject of 'The Theory and Practice of Musical Biography' (King's College London, 19–21 October 2001).

7 The watershed study of the various agents through which women have historically been excluded from musical canon (though without extended critical discussion of the specific role played by biographies) is Marcia J. Citron's *Gender and the Musical Canon* (Cambridge: Cambridge University Press, 1993).

8 The former publishing house did not assume the name by which it is now better known, J. M. Dent & Sons, until 1909.

9 F. Crowest, *The Great Tone-Poets: Being Short Memoirs of the Greater Musical Composers* (London: Bentley, 1874); Frederick J. Crowest, *Cherubini* (London: Sampson Low, 1890), in the 'Great Musicians' series (see n.19); idem, *Verdi: Man and Musician: His Biography with Especial Reference to his English Experiences* (London: Milne, 1897).

10 James D. Brown and Stephen S. Stratton, *British Musical Biography: A Dictionary of Musical Artists, Authors and Composers, born in Britain and its Colonies* (Birmingham: Stratton, 1897; reprinted, New York: Da Capo, 1971).

11 J. Cuthbert Hadden, *George Frederick Handel* (London: Allen, 1888); idem, *Mendelssohn* (London: Allen, 1888). Hadden's other biographical publications include *George Thomson: The Friend of Burns: His Life & Correspondence* (London: Nimmo, 1898); *Thomas Campbell* (Edinburgh: Oliphant Anderson & Ferrier, [1899]), in the 'Famous Scots' series; and *Prince Charles Edward: His Life, Times, and Fight for the Crown* (London: Pitman, 1913).

12 Amongst Williams's most important scholarly publications are *A Short Historical Account of the Degrees in Music at Oxford and Cambridge. With a Chronological List of Graduates in that Faculty from the Year 1643* (London: Novello, [1893]), *The Rhythm of Modern Music* (London: Macmillan, 1909), and *The Aristoxenian Theory of Musical Rhythm* (Cambridge: Cambridge University Press, 1911).

13 The biographical information in this paragraph is taken from Brown and Stratton, *British Musical Biography* and various other sources. For citations of the original volumes referenced above, see n. 4.

14 On the early history of the business, see J. M. Dent and Hugh R. Dent, *The House of Dent 1888-1938, being The Memoirs of J. M. Dent with Additional Chapters Covering the last 16 years by Hugh R. Dent* (London: Dent, 1938). Dent's Everyman Library series, which was initiated in 1904 under the editorship of Ernest Percival Rhys, quickly ran to hundreds of volumes of literary classics, selling for just one shilling each.

15 The Master Musicians volumes sold for 3s. 6d. each, a comparable price to many works of fiction at the time, and cheap for biography, especially given that these books were bound in cloth and contained printed music as well as text.

16 On the activities of Britain's communities of lay readers and their responses to the texts they perused, see Jonathan Rose, *The Intellectual Life of the British Working Classes* (New Haven: Yale University Press, 2001).

17 Crowest, *Beethoven*, p. v.

18 Citations for the revised volumes are given in n. 4 above; those for the biographies newly written are as follows: Marion M. Scott, *Beethoven* (London: Dent, 1934); Eric Blom, *Mozart* (London: Dent, 1935); Robert L. Jacobs, *Wagner* (London: Dent, 1935). By the time of the revival of the series, most of the original biographers had passed away, with the exception of Erb – who was called upon to approve Blom's emendations to his volume – and Evans.

19 Edited by Francis Hueffer, the Great Musicians series (London: Sampson Low, 1881-90) included the following monographs: Sir Julius Benedict, *Weber* (1881); William H. Cummings, *Purcell* (1881); H. Sutherland Edwards, *Rossini and His School* (1881); H. F. Frost, *Schubert* (1881); Francis Hueffer, *Richard Wagner* (1881); W[illia]m Alex[ander] Barrett, *English Church Composers* (1882); Reginald Lane Poole, *Sebastian Bach* (1882); F. Gehring, *Mozart* (1883); Mrs Julian Marshall [Florence Ashton Marshall], *Handel* (1883); J. A. Fuller Maitland, *Schumann* (1884); W. S. Rockstro, *Mendelssohn* (1884); Pauline D. Townsend, *Joseph Haydn* (1884); Frederick J. Crowest, *Cherubini* (1890); H. A. Rudall, *Beethoven* (1890).

20 As far as I have been able to ascertain, no relevant archival materials have survived. The J. M. Dent & Sons archives, held at the Manuscripts Department of the Library of the University of North Carolina at Chapel Hill, contain no documentation on the original Master Musicians series, nor was any such material moved to Oxford University Press on its recent purchase of the series from Dent.

21 See, for example, Crowest, *Beethoven*, pp. 29–30; Lidgey, *Wagner*, pp. 19, 116; Patterson, *Schumann*, pp. 112, 146. Handel's wealth – a result of the phenomenal success of his Italian operas in England – was however considered acceptable, not least because he donated substantial earnings to charitable and musical causes, and ultimately turned away from this 'popular' genre.

22 Musical biography reflected this growing interest in Tchaikovsky through the publication of a number of English-language volumes at around this time, notably Rosa Newmarch's *Tchaikovsky: His Life and Works* (London: Richards, 1900) and her edited translation of Modeste Tchaikovsky's *Zhizn' P. I. Chaykovskovo* (Moscow: Jurgenson, 1900-2) as *The Life and Letters of Peter Ilyich Tchaikovsky* (London: Lane, 1906).

23 Erb, *Brahms*, p. 116.

24 Many of the original Master Musicians biographies followed a tripartite structure comprising sections on the composer's life, character and works, with the latter incorporating assessments of other activities (in the musical domain and elsewhere) undertaken by the subject.

25 Williams's volume on Handel, for example, contained only limited discussion of the music, as the author observed that there already existed three 'exhaustive treatises. . . full of details and discussions of the greatest interest and value to the student who wishes to go deeply into the works of the great composer'. Williams, *Handel*, p. v.

26 See Evans, *Tchaikovsky*, pp. 182–4.

27 See Blom's preface in Duncan, *Schubert*, pp. vii–viii. Notably, many of the quotations of themes from Schubert's last two symphonies (the 'Unfinished' and the 'Great' C major Symphony) were not included in the revised monograph.

28 Even the shortest-lived volumes of the series survived for over thirty years in their original form, without either being superseded or achieving the status of dated classic, which is somewhat unusual for biography. Evans's *Tchaikovsky* was revised in 1935 and again in 1966; Hadden's *Chopin* was reprinted by AMS Press of New York in 1977, and is still available today.

29 Of course, the childhood of some of the more precocious Great Composers, notably Mozart, may be more appealing to the reader, as well as better documented, than that of biographical subjects in other disciplines.

30 Hadden, *Haydn*, p. 4.

31 On the musical families of Bach and Mozart see, for example, Karl Geiringer and Irene Geiringer, *The Bach Family: Seven Generations of Creative Genius* (London: Allen & Unwin, 1954) and Ruth Halliwell, *The Mozart Family: Four Lives in a Social Context* (Oxford: Clarendon, 1998).

32 See Stratton, *Mendelssohn*, pp. 1, 25 (see further, below, n. 77). On genius in the Mendelssohn family from Moses to Felix, see also Herbert Kupferberg, *The Mendelssohns: Three Generations of Genius* (London: Allen, 1972).

33 Patterson, *Schumann*, p. 3.

34 Stratton, *Mendelssohn*, p. 7. The point is made more emphatically in the original text, which reads 'simply wonderful' (p. 8) instead of just 'wonderful'.

35 Williams, *Bach*, p. 19. Williams gave concise biographies of Bach's distant male relations (*ibid.*, pp. 5–15) and of his sons (*ibid.*, pp. 15–20), yet cast his daughters aside without due consideration of the historical factors that limited their possibilities for development in the field of music. The original volume was

even more cutting in its treatment of the females of the family: 'The eight daughters of [Bach] showed none of the musical talent of their brothers' (p. 18).

36 Hadden, *Haydn*, p. 4.

37 Hadden, *Haydn*, p. 4; the author, however, continued by acknowledging that this view did not hold in the case of Haydn. The origin of the 'popular idea' to which Hadden referred is not stated.

38 Evans, *Tchaikovsky*, p. 1.

39 Such was the scepticism that the young Mozart provoked that he was repeatedly subjected to musical experiments designed to put his phenomenal abilities to the test, notably by Daines Barrington. See Breakspeare, *Mozart*, pp. 15–16; Barrington, *Philosophical Transactions of the Royal Society*, 9 (1770), 54–64, reprinted in Otto Erich Deutsch, *Mozart: die Dokumente seines Lebens* (Kassel: Bärenreiter, 1961), translated by Eric Blom, Peter Branscombe and Jeremy Noble as *Mozart: A Documentary Biography* (London: Black, 1965), pp. 95–100.

40 See Hadden, *Haydn*, p. 6.

41 Crowest, *Beethoven*, p. 7.

42 See Hadden, *Chopin*, p. 51; Patterson, *Schumann*, p. 8.

43 Erb, *Brahms*, p. 5; Evans, *Tchaikovsky*, p. 3.

44 Williams, *Handel*, p. 152; Crowest, *Beethoven*, p. 120.

45 Crowest, *Beethoven*, pp. 119–20. Crowest's description of Beethoven as a 'born genius', which contradicts the notion of Great Composers as initially talented and only subsequently attaining genius, is explicable in the tension surrounding Beethoven's slow development as a composer relative to more prodigious figures such as Mozart and Schubert.

46 Hadden, *Haydn*, p. 14.

47 See Williams, *Handel*, p. 189; Breakspeare, *Mozart*, p. 168; Crowest, *Beethoven*, pp. 28–9; Lidgey, *Wagner*, pp. 62–5.

48 Lidgey, *Wagner*, p. 77; compare to Crowest, *Beethoven*, p. 52.

49 On this point see Cyril Ehrlich, *The Music Profession in Britain since the Eighteenth Century: A Social History* (Oxford: Clarendon, 1985).

50 Lidgey, *Wagner*, pp. 16, 31–2. Of Wagner's various autobiographical writings, the most important is *Mein Leben*, which was dictated to his wife intermittently in the years 1865–80 and published privately, entering the public domain only in 1911. Richard Wagner, *Mein Leben*, 2 vols. (Munich: Bruckmann, 1911), translated as *My Life*, 2 vols. (London: Constable, 1911).

51 Williams, *Handel*, p. 124.

52 Patterson, *Schumann*, p. 16. Around the age of twenty, Schumann had used a mechanical device in order to strengthen his fingers and thereby improve his piano-playing, but the result was permanent injury to his right hand. See further, Peter F. Ostwald, 'Florestan, Eusebius, Clara, and Schumann's Right Hand', *19th Century Music*, 4/1 (Summer 1980), 17–31.

53 Crowest, *Beethoven*, pp. 16–7.

54 '[E]in lediger Mensch lebt…nur halb' ('[a] bachelor…is only half alive'; the above quotation uses the translated form typically found in nineteenth-century biography). Mozart to his father, 15 December 1781, *Mozart: Briefe und Aufzeichnungen*, edited by Wilhelm A. Bauer, Otto Erich Deutsch, and Joseph Heinz Eibl, 7 vols. (Kassel: Bärenreiter, 1962-75), III, 181; *The Letters of*

Mozart and his Family, edited and translated by Emily Anderson, 3 vols. (London: Macmillan, 1938; third edition, revised by Stanley Sadie and Fiona Smart, 1985), I, 783.

55 Williams, *Handel*, p. 165.

56 Evans, *Tchaikovsky*, p. 5; compare to Hadden, *Chopin*, p. 5. We shall presently see that Tchaikovsky did in fact take a wife, though the marriage was extremely short-lived.

57 Erb, *Brahms*, p. 21. The exact nature of Brahms's association with Clara Schumann – the wife of his late friend – represents dangerous biographical territory. On their relationship see, for example, Nancy B. Reich, 'Clara Schumann and Johannes Brahms', in *Clara Schumann: The Artist and the Woman*, second edition (Ithaca: Cornell University Press, 2001), pp. 169–89.

58 See Hadden, *Chopin*, pp. 39–40.

59 See Evans, *Tchaikovsky*, pp. 26–31; Breakspeare, *Mozart*, pp. 51–6. Both women were singers who took husbands shortly after the episode involving their associated composer – indeed, in the case of Tchaikovsky, Désirée Artôt's marriage precluded further involvement with her. Mozart was ultimately to marry Aloysia Weber's sister Constanze.

60 There is a certain irony in the fact that the androcentric muse paradigm should receive its fullest exegesis in the one volume of the original twelve written by a woman. Patterson's sensitivity to the importance of women to Schumann biography is exemplified by the inclusion in her monograph of dedicated sections on Clara (Patterson, *Schumann*, pp. 100–7) and on other females associated with the composer (*ibid.*, pp. 87–99). The fact that apparently the only way to explore such characters in detail, and to enhance their role in the life story, was to invoke this paradigm perhaps offers an indication of its stranglehold within musical biography.

61 Patterson, *Schumann*, p. 29. The quotation refers to the fact that Clara Wieck was on tour at this point in the biography, so personal contact with Schumann was literally absent as their relationship was necessarily epistolary.

62 Patterson, *Schumann*, p. 42.

63 Patterson, *Schumann*, p. 42.

64 'Du vervollständigst mich als Componisten, wie ich Dich. Jeder Deiner Gedanken kömmt aus meiner Seele, wie ich ja meine ganze Musik Dir zu verdanken habe.' Robert Schumann to Clara Wieck, 10 July 1839, *Clara und Robert Schumann Briefwechsel*, edited by Eva Weissweiler and Susanna Ludwig, 3 vols. (Frankfurt: Stroemfeld, 1984-2001), II, 629, translated by Hildegard Fritsch and Ronald L. Crawford as *The Complete Correspondence of Clara and Robert Schumann*, 3 vols. (New York: Lang, 1994-2002), II, 307. Schumann's output offers various demonstrations of the point: his piano piece *Impromptus*, Op. 5 is a set of variations on a theme by Clara; his song-cycle *Myrthen*, Op. 25 is dedicated to her; and his set of songs, *Zwölf Gedichte aus 'Liebesfrühling'*, Op. 37 was written jointly with her.

65 Patterson, *Schumann*, p. 105. This point is made explicit in the original volume, which included the word 'literally' (p. 124) immediately prior to the quotation as given above.

66 Lidgey, *Wagner*, pp. 21–2, 57. The irony here is that Wagner's second marriage was hardly exemplary, as Cosima had left her existing husband Hans von Bülow,

a strong friend of Wagner, for him. Lidgey was clearly anxious not to be detained by the matter (see *ibid.*, p. 57).

67 Evans, *Tchaikovsky*, p. 40; Hadden, *Haydn*, p. 33. The latter comment was made by Haydn to G. A. Griesinger and recorded in his *Biographische Notizen über Joseph Haydn* (Leipzig: Breitkopf und Härtel, 1810), p. 15, translated with introduction and notes by Vernon Gotwals as 'Biographical Notes Concerning Joseph Haydn' in *Joseph Haydn: Eighteenth-Century Gentleman and Genius* (Madison: University of Wisconsin Press, 1963), pp. 3–66, at p. 16. On Tchaikovsky's perceived difficulty in engaging in work during his brief period with his wife see, for example, Tchaikovsky to von Meck, 28 July 1877, *'To my best friend': Correspondence between Tchaikovsky and Nadezhda von Meck, 1876-1878*, translated by Galina von Meck, edited by Edward Garden and Nigel Gotteri, with an Introduction by Edward Garden (Oxford: Clarendon, 1993), p. 30.

68 See Erb, *Brahms*, p. 41. Clara Schumann had told Brahms that she would not be present at the event, but when the composer conveyed his dismay at this fact to a friend, Albert Dietrich, he contacted Clara and she was persuaded to attend.

69 See Evans, *Tchaikovsky*, pp. 112–3. As Evans observed, Tchaikovsky frequently referred to the work in such terms in letters to von Meck; see *Correspondence between Tchaikovsky and Nadezhda von Meck* (cited above, n. 67), *passim*. The score famously carries the dedication 'To my best Friend'.

70 Erb, *Brahms*, p. 45.

71 Evans, *Tchaikovsky*, p. 112.

72 Notably, J. S. Bach wrote two *Clavierbüchlein* volumes for his wife Anna Magdalena and one for his son Wilhelm Friedemann, for whom he also composed his six Trio Sonatas, BWV 525-30; and Schumann wrote his *Drei Clavier-Sonaten für die Jugend*, Op. 118 for his daughters, in addition to those pieces for Clara cited above (see n. 64).

73 Williams, *Bach*, p. 20; Breakspeare, *Mozart*, p. 246.

74 See Patterson, *Schumann*, p. 107; Stratton, *Mendelssohn*, p. 138.

75 See Crowest, *Beethoven*, pp. 80–2; Erb, *Brahms*, p. 18. In fact, Beethoven's relationship with his nephew, like that of Brahms and Clara Schumann (for which, see n. 57), is a hazardous area of his biography. See, for example, Maynard Solomon, 'Beethoven and his Nephew: A Reappraisal', in *Beethoven Studies*, vol. 2, edited by Alan Tyson (Oxford: Oxford University Press, 1977), pp. 138–71.

76 See Crowest, *Beethoven*, p. 54; Erb, *Brahms*, p. 90.

77 Stratton, *Mendelssohn*, pp. 25, 124. The reference to Mendelssohn's work ethic being 'in the blood' recalls his grandfather Moses; the original text has 'ripe manhood' (p. 32) instead of 'middle age'.

78 Patterson, *Schumann*, p. 81; compare to Stratton, *Mendelssohn*, p. 116.

79 Hadden, *Haydn*, p. 1.

80 Breakspeare, *Mozart*, p. 83.

81 See, for example, Crowest, *Beethoven*, p. 121; Breakspeare, *Mozart*, p. 93; Hadden, *Haydn*, p. 154.

82 Duncan, *Schubert*, pp. 60, 61. The first sentence of this quotation is phrased differently in the original biography: 'With the dawn of our composer's last year (1828), his powers are discovered at their best' (p. 67).

83 Hadden, *Chopin*, pp. 177, 2.

84 On the musical relationship between Felix and Fanny Mendelssohn, and the eclipsing of the latter by the former, see Marcia J. Citron, 'Fanny Mendelssohn Hensel: Musician in Her Brother's Shadow', in *The Female Autograph: Theory and Practice of Autobiography from the Tenth to the Twentieth Century*, edited by Domna C. Stanton (Chicago: University of Chicago Press, 1984), 152–9.

85 Stratton, *Mendelssohn*, p. 139.

86 Mendelssohn's last major work was the String Quartet in F minor, Op. 80, written at this time as a Requiem to his departed sister; his final song, 'Vergangen ist der lichte Tag', is also associated with her.

87 Lampadius wrote as follows: 'Auf die erste Kunde von Fannys Tode soll Mendelssohn einen lauten Schrei ausgestoßen haben. Es war aber nicht blos ein geistiger Schmerz, sondern auch ein physischer, der ihn so heftig ergriff. Wie der Nerv seiner geistigen Verbindung mit der Schwester durch diesen plötzlichen Todesfall abgerissen wurde, so zersprang nach der Ansicht des Arztes in diesem Momente heftiger Gemüthsbewegung vielleicht auch in seinem Kopfe ein kleines Blutgefäß... Mittelbar war also in der That der Tod der Schwester auch die Ursache seines frühen Scheidens'. ('The first news of Fanny's death drew a loud shriek from Mendelssohn. Nor was this all. His physician declared that his own death, which followed soon, was caused by the rupture of a blood-vessel in the head, at the moment of this sudden shock... The death of the sister was thus the cause of the death of the brother.') W. A. Lampadius, *Felix Mendelssohn-Bartholdy: Ein Denkmal für seine Freunde* (Leipzig: Hinrichs'sche, 1848), p. 187, edited and translated by William Leonhard Gage as *Life of Felix Mendelssohn-Bartholdy* (New York: Leypoldt, 1865), p. 150.

88 Stratton, *Mendelssohn*, p. 129.

89 Erb, *Brahms*, p. 73.

90 Evans, *Tchaikovsky*, pp. 50–1.

91 Hadden, *Chopin*, p. 106. Lenz wrote of Sand that '*Chopin* war verblendet, von vornherein eingenommen für die Giftpflanze... Chopin starb an Seelenkummer und Betrübniss, nicht an Schwindsucht' ('Chopin was dazzled and blinded from the first for the poisonous plant... Chopin did not die of consumption. He died of a broken heart'). W. von Lenz, 'Chopin', in *Die grossen Pianoforte-Virtuosen unserer Zeit aus persönlicher Bekanntschaft: Liszt – Chopin – Tausig – Henselt* (Berlin: Behr, 1872), pp. 19–50, at pp. 38, 48 (italics in original), translated as Wilhelm von Lenz, 'Frédéric Chopin', in *The Great Piano Virtuosos Of Our Time*, edited by Philip Reder (London: Kahn & Averill, 1983), pp. 27–58, at pp. 45, 56.

92 F. Liszt, *F. Chopin* (Paris: Escudier, 1852), translated by John Broadhouse as *Life of Chopin*, second edition (London: Reeves, 1912). On Chopin and his gendered music, and critical response thereto, see Jeffrey Kallberg, *Chopin at the Boundaries: Sex, History, and Musical Genre* (Cambridge, Massachusetts: Harvard University Press, 1996).

93 Hadden, Chopin, p. 192.

94 Duncan, *Schubert*, p. 74. In the original volume (p. 85), the word 'good' is used in place of 'devout'; nevertheless, as the quotation appeared within the context of a discussion of religion, its sense is faithfully rendered in the form in which it is given above.

95 'Der geistlicher Musik die Kraft zuzuwenden bleibt ja wohl das höchste Ziel des Künstlers'. Schumann to Lieutenant Strackerjan, 13 January 1851, *Robert Schumann's Briefe*, edited by F. Gustav Jansen (Leipzig: Breitkopf & Härtel, 1886), p. 281; translation as quoted in Patterson, *Schumann*, p. 173.

96 Patterson, *Schumann*, p. 127; the original text (p. 150) contains the word 'maxims' instead of 'precepts'. Schumann founded the *Neue Zeitschrift für Musik* (initially, the *Neue Leipziger Zeitschrift für Musik*) in 1834, as a forum in which contemporary composers and their music might be discussed without prejudice. His early recognition of such composers as Berlioz, Chopin and Brahms is well-known, but he only rarely wrote about his own works.

97 Hadden, *Chopin*, p. 152. On Chopin's religion, Liszt offered the following: 'Sincèrement religieux, et attaché au catholicisme, Chopin n'abordait jamait ce sujet, gardant ses croyances sans les témoigner par aucun apparat. On pouvait longtemps le connaître sans avoir de notions exactes sur ses idées à cet égard.' ('Chopin was sincerely religious and attached to Catholicism, but he held his faith without calling attention to it, and never touched upon this subject. It was possible to be acquainted with him a long time without knowing what were his religious views.') Liszt, *F. Chopin*, p. 114; Liszt, translated by Broadhouse, *Life of Chopin*, pp. 137–8.

98 See Lidgey, *Wagner*, p. 90. The composer's writings on religion include his famous essay 'Religion und Kunst', *Bayreuther Blätter*, October 1880, translated and edited by William Ashton Ellis as 'Religion and Art' in *Richard Wagner's Prose Works*, 8 vols. (London: Kegan Paul, 1892-99), VI, 211–52.

99 Hadden, *Chopin*, p. 187, n. 1 (inserted editorially); see also Blom's preface in Duncan, *Schubert*, p. vii.

100 W. Glock, *Music & Letters*, 16/2 (March 1935), 147, in the context of a review of four of the revised Master Musicians volumes (those on Schumann, Chopin, Mendelssohn and Schubert).

101 Blom's preface in Patterson, *Schumann*, p. xii. Blom made this assessment in the context of observing Patterson's assimilation of Clara Schumann's views on her husband, which assumes an added irony given the extent of the development of the muse paradigm therein, according to the present reading (see n. 60).

102 The majority of the Master Musicians biographers were English and worked in their native country, predominantly in London, though Stratton and Breakspeare were based in Birmingham, and Williams in Bradfield. Hadden, who was Scottish, was active in Edinburgh; Patterson was Irish, though of French Huguenot ancestry; and Erb spent his life in America.

103 *The Musical Times*, 48/767 (1 January 1907), 33. See further the more specific comments found in the review of Williams's *Bach* (1900) in *The Musical Times*, 41/687 (1 May 1900), 316, and that of Patterson's *Schumann* (1903), in *The Musical Times*, 44/724 (1 June 1903), 401.

104 In addition to exploring Chopin's time in England, Hadden presented some previously-unknown information concerning the composer's visit to Scotland in 1848. See Hadden, *Chopin*, pp. 117–27. The author's preoccupation with Scotland – his own country of origin – is demonstrated even more strongly in his biographies of non-musical subjects (for citations, see n. 11).

105 See Crowest, *Beethoven*, pp. 41–2. Crowest also excerpted Ferdinand Hiller's account of the composer's death, where it is written that '[s]peaking of the noble behaviour of the Philharmonic Society, and praising the English people, [Beethoven] said that as soon as he got well he should go to London and compose a grand symphonic overture for his friends, the English'. Hiller, *Monthly Musical Record*, 1 June 1874, quoted in Crowest, *Beethoven*, p. 43.

106 Lidgey, *Wagner*, p. 69. Ironically, in so doing, England nearly did Wagner a disservice; the demand for such a series had been considerably overestimated and its projected scope had to be dramatically reduced, so the financial gain for the composer was much less than anticipated.

107 See Duncan, *Schubert*, pp. 111–5. Grove famously wrote an extensive essay on the composer for inclusion in his *Dictionary* ; G[rove], 'Schubert, Franz Peter', in idem, *Dictionary of Music and Musicians*, III, 319–82, reprinted, together with his two other major contributions to that publication, as George Grove, *Beethoven – Schubert – Mendelssohn* (London: Macmillan, 1951). On the significance of Grove's article on Schubert to the composer's inclusion within musical canon, see David Gramit, 'Constructing a Victorian Schubert: Music, Biography, and Cultural Values', *19th Century Music*, 17/1 (Summer 1993), 65–78.

108 Patterson, *Schumann*, pp. 51, 34.

109 Evans, *Tchaikovsky*, p. 104.

110 Stratton, *Mendelssohn*, p. 45.

111 Stratton, *Mendelssohn*, p. 20.

112 Hadden, *Haydn*, pp. 116, 155.

113 See Hadden, *Haydn*, pp. 66–7.

114 Compare J[ulian] M[arshall], 'Handel, George Frederick', in Grove, *Dictionary of Music and Musicians*, I, 647–57, at p. 652 and [George] G[rove], 'Mendelssohn, Jakob Ludwig Felix', in *ibid.*, II, 253–310, at p. 293 (subsequently reprinted; see n. 107).

115 Williams, *Handel*, pp. 205–8; the original text, written before the English Musical Renaissance had truly blossomed, is longer and more speculative (pp. 233–8).

116 Williams, *Handel*, p. 206.

117 Williams, *Handel*, p. 207. In fairness to the biographer, he continued by acknowledging that '. . . there are doubtless many who will say that even if Handel had not appeared, or had remained in Germany, we should have had no great school of English composers during the eighteenth and part of the nineteenth centuries. It is after all doubtful whether the English composers who succeeded Handel. . . would have been sufficiently in earnest to carry on Purcell's work.' Nevertheless, the present point stands.

118 Indeed, modern biographical theorists are generally agreed that biography ultimately functions to elucidate the work of the subject through exploration of the life.

119 See Breakspeare, *Mozart*, pp. 211–2.

120 See Breakspeare, *Mozart*, pp. 139–41.

121 See Evans, *Tchaikovsky*, p. 96.

122 See Duncan, *Schubert*, pp. 130–5, on Schubert's settings of poems by British writers, and on English translations of the texts of his songs originally written in German.

123 The scope of this article precludes in-depth discussion of the paradigms that arise from discussions of the music – as distinct from those primarily connected to composers' lives – in the Master Musicians volumes. However, some preliminary analysis is offered above.

124 Williams, *Handel*, p. 190; see *ibid.*, pp. 185–91, on this work.

125 Stratton, *Mendelssohn*, pp. 160, 120; on *Elijah*, see *ibid.*, pp. 157–60. This connection to Birmingham held personal significance for the biographer, who settled in the city just twenty years later.

126 On Mozart's Requiem, see Breakspeare, *Mozart*, pp. 144–55.

127 See, for example, Patterson, *Schumann*, p. 173; Duncan, *Schubert*, p. 67.

128 See Hadden, *Haydn*, pp. 134–5. Biographical descriptions of this episode are based on early accounts including that of Carpani, who was an eyewitness to the event. See Giuseppe Carpani, *Le Haydine, ovvero Lettere su la vita e le opere del celebre maestro Giuseppe Haydn* (Milan: Buccinelli, 1812), pp. 242–5, translated (via a French adaptation) by Robert Brewin as 'Letters on the Celebrated Composer Haydn' in *The Life of Haydn, in a Series of Letters Written at Vienna. Followed by The Life of Mozart, with Observations on Metastasio, and on the Present State of Music in France and Italy* (London: Murray, 1817), pp. 1–332, at pp. 309–11.

129 See Evans, *Tchaikovsky*, pp. 122–3.

130 See, for example, Katharine Ellis, *Music Criticism in Nineteenth-Century France: La Revue et Gazette musicale de Paris, 1834-1880* (Cambridge: Cambridge University Press, 1995).

131 Linda Colley, *Britons: Forging the Nation 1707-1837* (New Haven: Yale University Press, 1992); David Hempton, *Religion and political culture in Britain and Ireland: From the Glorious Revolution to the decline of empire* (Cambridge: Cambridge University Press, 1996).

132 Paula R. Backscheider, *Reflections on Biography* (Oxford: Oxford University Press, 1999), p. 103.

133 John Mainwaring, *Memoirs of the Life of the Late George Frederic Handel* (London: Dodsley, 1760).

134 Sir John Hawkins, *A General History of the Science and Practice of Music*, 5 vols. (London: Payne, 1776); Charles Burney, *A General History of Music, from the Earliest Ages to the Present Period*, 4 vols. (London: Author, 1776-89).

135 See the Preface to [John S. Sainsbury], *A Dictionary of Musicians From the Earliest Times*, 2 vols. (London: Sainsbury, 1825; reprinted, New York: Da Capo, 1966), I, i–iii. Henry George Farmer has more recently demonstrated this claim to have been unjustified; Farmer, 'British Musicians a Century Ago', *Music & Letters*, 12/4 (October 1931), 384–92, reprinted with revisions in Sainsbury, *A Dictionary of Musicians From the Earliest Times* (1966 edition), I, vii–xvi.

136 *Dictionary of National Biography*, edited by Sir Leslie Stephen and Sir Sidney Lee, 68 vols. (London: Smith, Elder, 1885–1900); 'English Men of Letters' series, edited by John Morley, 68 vols. (London: Macmillan, 1878-1919).

137 In his editorial preface, Grove wrote that '[i]n an English dictionary it has been thought right to treat English music and musicians with special care, and to give their biographies and achievements with some minuteness of detail.' Grove, Preface, in idem, *Dictionary of Music and Musicians*, I, v–vi, at p. vi.

138 Frederick J. Crowest, *Phases of Musical England* (London: Remington, 1881); idem, *A Catechism of Musical History and Biography. With Especial Reference to English Music and Musicians* (London: Reeves, [1883]); idem, *The Dictionary of British Musicians: From the Earliest Times to the Present* (London: Jarrold, 1895); idem, *The Story of British Music (From the Earliest Times to the Tudor Period)* (London: Bentley, 1896).

139 Brown and Stratton, *British Musical Biography*, Preface, page unnumbered.

140 Published by Henri Laurens of Paris, the earliest volumes of the 'Les musiciens célèbres' series appeared in 1905 under the editorship of Élie Poirée. Over twenty monographs were brought out in the following six years, including the following: P.-L. Hillemacher, *Gounod* (1905); Arthur Pougin, *Hérold* (1906); Camile Bellaigue, *Mozart* (1907); Henri de Curzon, *Grétry* (1907); Élie Poirée, *Chopin* (1907); Paul de Stœcklin, *Mendelssohn* (1907); Lucien Augé de Lassus, *Boïeldieu* (1908); L.-A. Bourgault-Ducoudray, *Schubert* (1908); Lionel de la Laurencie, *Rameau* (1908); Arthur Coquard, *Berlioz* (1909); René Brancour, *Félicien David* (1910); Henri Prunières, *Lully* (1910); Henry Gauthier-Villars, *Bizet* (1911); Vincent d'Indy, *Beethoven* (1911); Charles Malherbe, *Auber* (1911).

141 See, for example, Adolphe Jullien, 'Mendelssohn à Paris', in *Airs variés: Histoire, critique, biographie musicales et dramatiques* (Paris: Charpentier, 1877), pp. 65–136.

142 From the point of view of the Master Musicians series, the figure who laid the strongest claim to being an English Great Composer was surely Purcell; on the expansion of the set in the 1930s, a biography by Jack Westrup on this subject was soon included. Another addition was a monograph on Elgar (whose career was very much in its infancy at the time of production of the original series), a decision no doubt influenced by his recent death and the opportunity presented by the availability of its author, William Reed, a good friend of the composer. J. A. Westrup, *Purcell* (London: Dent, 1937); W. H. Reed, *Elgar* (London: Dent, 1939).

143 See Lidgey, *Wagner*, pp. 95–143; Patterson, *Schumann*, pp. 135–48; Stratton, *Mendelssohn*, pp. 17, 149. For collected editions of the literature referenced above see, respectively, the following: Richard Wagner, *Gesammelte Schriften und Dichtungen*, 10 vols. (Leipzig: Fritzsch, 1871–83), edited and translated by William Ashton Ellis as *Richard Wagner's Prose Works*, 8 vols. (see n. 98); Robert Schumann, *Gesammelte Schriften über Musik und Musiker*, 4 vols. (Leipzig: Wigand, 1854), edited and translated by Fanny Raymond Ritter as *Music and Musicians: Essays and Criticism*, 2 vols. (London: Reeves, 1877–80); Felix Mendelssohn-Bartholdy, *Briefe aus den Jahren 1833 bis 1847*, edited by Paul Mendelssohn-Bartholdy and Carl Mendelssohn-Bartholdy (Leipzig: Mendelssohn, 1863), translated by Lady [Grace] Wallace as *Letters from 1833 to 1847* (London: Longmans, 1863).

144 Lidgey's biography contained eight chapters on Wagner's stage works (Lidgey, *Wagner*, pp. 144–244), as well as two summarising his major literary writings (*ibid.*, pp. 95–143); Breakspeare devoted a substantial portion of his monograph to Mozart's major operas (Breakspeare, *Mozart*, pp. 155–210); and Evans's volume included sections on Tchaikovsky's operas (Evans, *Tchaikovsky*, pp. 57–92) and ballets (*ibid.*, pp. 96–103).

145 I argue this point in my article 'When a Woman Speaks the Truth About Her Body': Ethel Smyth, Virginia Woolf and the Challenges of Lesbian Auto/biography', *Music & Letters*, 85/3 (forthcoming, August 2004).

146 See, for example, Jane Spencer, *The Rise of the Woman Novelist: From Aphra Behn to Jane Austen* (Oxford: Blackwell, 1986). Biographies of female writers that emerged in nineteenth-century England include Mrs [Elizabeth] Gaskell's canonical *The Life of Charlotte Brontë*, 2 vols. (London: Smith, Elder, 1857).

147 While subscribing to the muse paradigm, Patterson explored the compositional activities of Clara Schumann in as much detail as she apparently felt able (see Patterson, *Schumann*, pp. 31, 102). She did not, however, have the benefit of Berthold Litzmann's extensive biography *Clara Schumann: ein Künsterleben nach Tagebüchern und Briefen*, 3 vols. (Leipzig: Breitkopf & Härtel, 1902–8), abridged and translated by Grace E. Hadow as *Clara Schumann: An artist's life based on material found in diaries and letters*, with a preface by W. H. Hadow, 2 vols. (London: Macmillan, 1913).

148 Hadden, *Chopin*, pp. 179, 177. Hadow had written in an essay on Chopin that '[w]e hardly think of him as marking a stage in the general course and progress of artistic History, but, rather, as standing aside from it, unconscious of his relation to the world, preoccupied with the fairyland of his own creations.' W. H. Hadow, 'Frederick Chopin', *Studies in Modern Music*, 2 vols. (London: Seeley, 1893–5), II, 77–170, at p. 169.

149 The earliest volumes of the series intertwined the composers at the very heart of music's great classical canons (Beethoven, Wagner, Bach, Mozart) with those possessing significant English connections (Handel, Mendelssohn, Haydn). The biographies of those figures whose position therein was more tenuous (notably Schubert, Brahms, and Tchaikovsky) followed later.

PART II
Literature and translations

Comparative Criticism **XXV**, p. 205.   © 2004 Edinburgh University Press
Printed in the United Kingdom

Winners of the BCLA/BCLT 2002 Translation Competition

OPEN COMPETITION

First Prize

Mike Mottram, for his translation from the Latin of George Herbert, *Latin Poems*.

Second Prize

Timothy Adès, for his translation from the French of Robert Desnos, *Against the Grain*.

Third Prize (Joint)

Anamaria Crowe Serrano and Riccardo Duranti, for their translation from the Italian of Valerio Magrelli, *Instructions on How to Read a Newspaper*.

and

Kathryn Woodham, for her translation from the German of Herta Müller, *The Big Black Axle*.

Commendations

Wendy Griswold, for her translation from the Spanish of Julio Cortázar, *The Southern Expressway*.

Anna-Marjatta Milsom, for her translation from the Spanish of Lydia Cabrera, *The Roads on the Island Closed and Opened Again*.

Christopher Pilling, for his translation from the French of Maurice Carême, *Defying Fate*.

Comparative Criticism XXV, pp. 207–228. © 2004 Edinburgh University Press
Printed in the United Kingdom

Introduction to *Against the Grain* by Robert Desnos

KATHARINE CONLEY

Robert Desnos was born on the fourth of July 1900 in Paris and died in the newly liberated concentration camp of Terezin outside of Prague on June 8th 1945. He grew up in the medieval streets of central Paris, between the Tour Saint-Jacques, where Nicolas Flamel was reputed to have conducted alchemical experiments in the fourteenth century, and the present-day Pompidou Center. His father had a poultry stand in the huge Halles market nearby, now the site of a metro station. He wrote his first poem at age fifteen. A year earlier he spent a summer month in England just before the outbreak of World War I, which helped him to get his first job as a translator of pharmaceutical 'prospectuses', resulting in the selection of *Prospectus* for the title of his first, posthumously published collection of poems. He spent his military service in Morocco and met the young Paris Dadaists André Breton and Louis Aragon while on leave, in 1921. Upon his return to Paris in 1922, he walked into a starring role in the surrealist movement.

When Breton decided to conduct automatic experiments in his apartment in September 1922, Desnos emerged as the most talented of the group for oracular poetic pronouncements while in a self-induced trance, during what became known as the 'period of sleeps'. Borrowing an alter-ego invented by Marcel Duchamp in New York, 'Rrose Sélavy' (which sounds like 'eros is life' in French), Desnos began to pronounce remarkable one-line word-game poems. One hundred and fifty of these were later published under the title 'Rrose Sélavy', including one in English, 'From Everest mountain I am falling down to your feet for ever, Mrs Everling', in homage to Francis Picabia's companion, Germaine Everling. Duchamp had already begun to use English expressions to make visual jokes. His 'readymade' *Why not Sneeze, Rrose Sélavy*, for example, is a bird cage containing 'sugar cubes' made of marble with a thermometer sticking out of it, and turns on the English phrase 'to catch a cold'. Using a similar technique, Desnos makes an implicit verbal joke that underlines the explicit poetic line. The phrase 'head over heels' floats just beneath the surface of his short poem implying rather humorously that not only does he imagine falling chivalrously at the lady's feet, but that he has fallen as precipitously in love with her as a fall from the top of Mount Everest might suggest.

Breton defined 'surrealism' during that autumn of 1922 as a word that he and his friends had come to understand as designating 'a certain psychic automatism which corresponds fairly well with the dream state'. He identified Desnos as 'the most advanced of us all'. In the first *Manifesto of Surrealism* published two years later, Breton declared: 'Robert Desnos *speaks surrealist* at will'. However, in 1930, with his 'Third Manifesto of Surrealism', Desnos broke with Breton, who had scathingly repudiated him in the *Second Manifesto of Surrealism*. In the 'Third Manifesto' Desnos claimed that surrealism had fallen into the public domain and that he, who was 'entitled to talk about surrealism', declared that for true surrealists— by implication those who no longer followed Breton—there was only 'one reality, unique, whole, open to everyone'.

The same year that Desnos broke with Bretonian surrealism he published his first collection of poems with Gallimard, *Corps et biens*, which included the 'Rrose Sélavy' poems from 1922. This volume also contained the surrealist love poems for which he is best known, including the seven poems entitled 'To the Mysterious One', (initially published in 1926 in *The Surrealist Revolution*), featuring his most famous poem 'I have dreamed of you so much you are losing your reality'. These poems, and those of the following collection, *The Shadows*, chronicled his unrequited love for the singer Yvonne George, who died as a result of her drug addiction in April 1930, not long after he had met and begun his love affair with Youki Foujita, who became his life companion.

During the 1930s Desnos had a successful career as a journalist and as a pioneer on the radio. He invented shows, wrote advertising jingles that resembled the word-game 'Rrose Sélavy' poems he had invented during the 'period of sleeps', planned multiple radio concerts featuring American jazz, and, in 1938, he created his most surrealistic show, 'The Key of Dreams', for which he interpreted the listeners's dreams on the air. In 1939 he was mobilized in France's so-called 'phony war' against Germany that lasted from the German invasion of Poland in September to the armistice Marshall Philippe Pétain signed with Hitler in June 1940. When Pétain dissolved the French Republic and created the Vichy state,

Desnos abandoned radio work for print journalism and poetry because the radio had become a propaganda instrument for the government.

Throughout the Occupation until his arrest by the Gestapo for 'acts of Resistance' in February 1944, Desnos specialized in writing double-edged pieces that barely escaped censure and were aimed at those Parisians who never relinquished hope for an Allied victory and the restoration of the republic. Desnos became active in the Resistance in the summer of 1942, about the time of the huge round-up of Parisian Jews during which almost 13,000 people were arrested and deported, including 4000 children. He used his position as a journalist to pass information to his Resistance cell, 'Agir' ('To Act'); he photographed documents in secret; and he made false identity papers for Jews and others who needed them. Desnos's poetry, however, constituted his most durable participation in the Resistance.

Ironically, Desnos published prolifically during the war, at a time when one could be arrested for ideas expressed in print. These publications included a volume of poetry and a novel with Gallimard, *Fortunes* and *Le Vin est tiré* in 1942 and 1943 and then, in addition to his subsequently famous poems for children, the *Trente chantefables pour les enfants sages à chanter sur n'importe quel air*, thirty stories to be sung by good children to any tune they like, two volumes of poetry published semi-legally by the young Robert J. Godet in 1943 and 1944, *Etat de veille*, state of vigil, and the present volume *Against the Grain* (*Contrée*). These books were semi-legal in the sense that they were available in bookstores but never registered with the German propaganda office as was required by law during the Occupation. He also published several poems pseudonymously in the completely clandestine press, including sonnets in slang that mocked Hitler, Pétain, and Vichy Prime Minister Pierre Laval, as well as three poems in the two editions of *L'Honneur des poètes*, the honour of poets, released by the newly formed underground press, the Editions de Minuit, in 1943 and 1944.

Against the Grain resonates with Desnos's passion for France, yet his desire for liberation from fascism and Vichy's racist policies had to be expressed with his gift for indirection and suggestion already present in his 'Rrose Sélavy' automatic poems. In *Against the Grain* the French landscape contrasts with the same bucolic landscape present visually around Paris in the form of Vichy propaganda posters. His France runs literally 'against the grain' of Pétain's France. Under Pétain the slogan of the French Republic, 'Liberty, Equality, Fraternity', was replaced with the new slogan of the Vichy state, 'Work, Family, Country', thus substituting moralizing, prudish, hierarchical values and the image of a mythical homeland for the egalitarian values of the republic. Vichy propaganda idealized rural, agricultural France populated by a docile, acquiescent peasantry. The landscape of Desnos's 'country' is equally agrarian but in his 'country' 'The Vintage' is dominated by the cultivation of grapes, that intoxicating fruit that yields wine, one of the products most identified with France. This 'Vintage' has the potential to subvert the moralizing propaganda of the harvests in Vichy propaganda, because it harks back to an older, freer France, with a democratic heritage. The god of wine, Bacchus, is directly invoked in 'The Beach', a poem which emphasizes France's greco/gallo-roman past, and also its current vulnerability with the reference to 'Corinth', the once wealthy Greek trading port that, like France in 1940, lost its influence to powerful, conquering neighbors.

Desnos's 'country' strives to reassure its troubled people. In 'The Voice' the land calls out words of encouragement in muffled tones, suggesting that France is only truly alive clandestinely and that those who hear her voice can participate in hastening the return of *la belle saison*. This secretive yet optimistic voice contrasts sharply with the voice of Pétain on the radio airwaves encouraging French citizens to collaborate with the occupying German forces and harmonizes instead with Charles de Gaulle's call for resistance to Pétain's policies, broadcast from London only four days after the German army's victorious entry into Paris.

Desnos's *contrée*—a word which also suggests 'to position oneself against'—is a country whose contested borders are emphasized in such poems as the opening 'Waterfall' and 'The Beach'. When he was writing these poems, France had been divided into the Occupied and Non-occupied zones; by the time *Against the Grain* was published in the spring of 1944, all of France had become occupied and Desnos was leaving the transit camp of Compiègne for a trajectory that led him across the border through Auschwitz, Buchenwald, Flossenburg, Flöha, and, finally, Terezin, on May 8th 1945, the day it was liberated by the Soviet army. France's borders were closely monitored by both German–French police and the groups of clandestine warriors of the armed Resistance known as the *maquis*. These clandestine French patriots traverse Desnos's 'country' in the guise of anonymous men bearing secret messages. They are acutely aware of the dangers they face in a 'Countryside' that is redolent with flowers but where a single spark carries the risk of destroying what it illuminates.

Most poignantly, the love expressed in these poems is for a country that must work 'against the grain' of its desire for peace after the devastation of World War I and fight for the liberties lost the day that Marshall Pétain signed the armistice with Hitler. Skilfully Desnos interweaves romantic love through this patriotic love for an egalitarian France. The book opens with the dedication 'For Youki', his companion, and then turns to the first sonnet, 'The Waterfall', which is addressed in an apostrophe to an unnamed 'you'. With this device, Desnos confuses the identity of his beloved French woman with that of his beloved French land—identified only syntactically in the poem as the Countryside itself, guarded by two password-bearing hikers, stealthily making their way through the beautiful yet potentially dangerous countryside.

Another way in which Desnos diguises patriotic love as romantic love is through the sonnet form itself. Popular during the French Renaissance and representative of French patriotism in the sixteenth-century, when poets such as Pierre de Ronsard and Joaquim du Bellay decided to write in French instead of Latin, the sonnet form was most often used for love poems. Like Ronsard and Du Bellay, Desnos writes poems of love that use the metaphor of the hunt in such poems as 'The Waterfall' in the shape of the hunted Resistance fighters. Like them he celebrates the beauty and history of the French language in opposition to a potentially more dominant language which, in his case, is German rather than Latin. In all of these poems the longing and love expressed can indeed refer to the love of an individual man for a woman. The 'return of the archer' in 'The Waterfall' hints at the hope that the Archer in the shape of Cupid might return to the French 'Countryside' in the near future and distract those archer-warriors with the simpler pleasures of sensual love.

The poems of *Against the Grain* are everyday poems in the sense that there are twenty-four poems for the twenty-four hours of the day, plus an 'Epitaph' in conclusion. With their fixed forms they express the multiple constraints imposed on resistant French citizens throughout the Occupation, forced to withhold their words, songs, truths, and secrets until they rot, as Desnos explains with bitter frustration in 'The Alarm Clock'. Already in his 'Afterword' to *Etat de veille*, published by Godet in 1943, Desnos had written: 'it is not poetry which must be free, it is the poet'. In his 'Epitaph' he insists that he managed to maintain his freedom:

> Among the slaves in face-masks, I was free.
> I've lived today, and nonetheless been free.

He maintained his freedom because underneath the clandestine 'coat' of poetry he succeeded in expressing the forbidden emotions and beliefs to which he persisted in clinging and for which he lost his life.

Desnos was at once surrealist and patriotic throughout his life. At the start of his career he was the most visibly surrealist of the entire group. At the end, he was also the most visible patriot—the other former and active surrealists survived, either through the luck of having escaped arrest, like Aragon, or through self-imposed exile in New York, like Breton. At the same time, while the surrealists were against the governmental policies that had led to World War I, they were consistently patriotic in their faith in the egalitarian principles of the French republic. One of their first political acts as a group was to anticipate postcolonial France by writing a tract in sympathy with the Berber rebels of the Moroccan Rif who sought independence from France in the early 1920s.

Desnos remained surrealist until the end of his life, according to his own principles of Desnosian surrealism. In his final letter to Youki he invokes one of his 'Rrose Sélavy' poems from 1922: 'Aside from everything else, I find refuge in poetry. It is truly the horse that runs over the mountains that Rrose Sélavy talks about in one of her poems and which, for me, is completely justified'. He was referring to his own poem published under the title 'Rrose Sélavy' in 1922 which translates roughly as the following: 'Despite her prisoner's uniform Rrose Sélavy keeps a mount capable of flying over mountains'. He himself is Rrose Sélavy here, representative of his very first surrealist identity, and poetry his mount. To go back to his own statement about freedom, poetry, and the poet, it is clear that in his imagination and in these, his most constrained poems, Desnos succeeded in remaining free. Thus he inspired others in their love for the pleasures and ideals so dear to him and, for him, exemplary of France—loyalty, friendship, wine, sensual love, the struggle for freedom, and the abundant countryside of his native *contrée*.

Against the Grain by Robert Desnos

TRANSLATED BY TIMOTHY ADÈS

Translator's Note

AGAINST THE GRAIN is a translation of CONTRÉE, the sequence of poems, published in 1944, by the Resistant and former Surrealist, Robert Desnos, 1900-45. This note draws on the learned work of Mme Marie-Claire Dumas and Dr Katharine Conley.

ROBERT DESNOS (both s's are sounded) was born in Paris on 4 July 1900, the son of a licensed poultry and game dealer at the Halles Market. Much of his poetry, beside its other merits, shows enormous talent in rhyme and metre, alliteration and wordplay. Early on he worked as a journalist and also joined the Surrealists, whose leader, Breton, in 1924 proclaimed him their 'prophet', mainly for composing two hundred elaborate and witty spoonerisms while asleep, or hypnotised, on behalf of Duchamp's alter ego, Rrose Sélavy. Already a journalist, he wrote a surrealist novel, Liberty or Love. Siramour *and* Les Nuits Blanches *were inspired by Lucie Badoud (Youki Foujita), his long-term love. He moved on into radio, with* Fantômas, *and wrote poems for children, and musical or cinematic lyrics. He joined the Popular Front and the war-time Resistance, writing some of his strongest and most beautiful poetry in this period, until he was arrested. He died of typhus, a victim of the death-camps, on 8 June 1945, never having seen Contrée in print.*

Some of the poems had been published or quoted as early as 1942. 'It's an odd experience for me', Desnos wrote to Paul Eluard that year. 'I'm feeling my way forward, but the images, words and rhymes come to me like the details of a key to open a lock. Everything must be useful and essential for the poem to work, everything must be there to finish it and nothing else. I wonder why they come out so easily as sonnets. I believe more and more that automatic writing and speech are only the elementary stages of poetic initiation... I dream of poems which could not be other than they are: for which a different outcome could not be imagined. Something as implacable as the resolution of an equation'.

The title Contrée denotes both the various places visited in each poem (because it can mean something like Back Country) and the effect of 'countering', more or less by stealth, an enemy whose defeat is proclaimed: 'I have wished your death and there is nothing that can delay it'. The allusions multiply. Here is denunciation: 'on a yellow poster the word in black letters, plague;' the voice

*declaring 'the beautiful season is near;' and the poet's anticipatory epitaph, his
refusal to give in: 'I lived intact, but I was prey'. Classic in form, and drawing
on mythology, the poems were able to pass the censor; and their philosophy of
human destiny puts into a wider context various topical allusions which those
in the know could understand.* Two of these translations have appeared in
In Other Words.

CONTRÉE – AGAINST THE GRAIN

THE WATERFALL

What arrow split the sky and pierced the rock?
Vibrant, it spreads its peacock tail and flaunts
Its blurry shaft and sleek unblemished flights,
The way the midnight comet finds its mark.

The flesh is opened. For the blood to rise,
While lips suppress the murmurs and the cries,
A finger bids time stop, pre-occupies
The witness who records it with his eyes.

Silence? And yet we know the passwords well.
We strayed from our camp-fires, we sentinels:
Drifting from shady corners we can smell
Salt surf aromas, honeysuckle smells.

Dawn bursts on far-off depths; a sunbeam limns
Upon the waves, at last, a sketch that leads
Back the returning archer and his hymns:
A rainbow, with its quiver full of reeds.

THE RIVER

I walked to where the river can be crossed –
A jutting point: from bank to bank I passed.
Its shadow and reflection merge their hue;
Laundresses turn the stream a soapy blue.

I trudged the ford, that sings to suit its mood,
Strewn underfoot with stars and bits of rock.

I headed for the greensward and the wood
Where the wind shivered in its flimsy frock.

I swam, I got across, clothed better in
That water than in my own flesh and skin.
A night has passed. Now, sky has married dawn.

And see, my eyes and limbs are faltering,
It's bright, I'm thirsty, looking for the spring
Whose song regales the middle of a lawn.

THE SLOPE

Behind this slope the valley is in shade.
Odours of burning wood and grass pervade
The bare expanse, crag after fire-flecked crag;
The loud voice of a child, a barking dog.

The child is being murdered. Rending cries;
Barking, no use. A doom is on this dell.
Nothing is real but this hot iron smell
That lulls us, gets us drunk, and reds our eyes.

Dawn may return and sunlight may refresh;
But all in vain: the barking and the yells
Pierce the thick night, the cinders and the ash
That fill our hearts and burn inside our skulls.

THE ROAD

Hereabouts there is a road
Where I hear the cars go by,
The wind, and the uncertain plod
Of a heavy entity,
Coming, going, with a sigh,
Stumbling on the stones, and I
Hear it beg and plead and die.
Is it guttersnipe or god?

Heavily one hand he raises
To the meadow of his hair,

He delineates caresses,
Clamps the nervous fingers there.
Then his other parts all rush
Helter-skelter to the moon
And the sun gilds with its brush
The big beast of the lagoon.

Is it Hercules? Or Atlas?
Striding on across the plain
Falls full-length, no cry of pain,
Winded in the solar plexus.
Blotting out the countryside
He obliterates the place,
Not a single mountainside,
Not a pathway, not a trace.

Less real than mirror-images
The man who would be disappears,
Dictator of the centuries,
The winds, the nights, the days, the years.

THE CEMETERY

Under these three trees, nowhere else, is my burial-place.
I pluck from them spring's first and earliest leaves
Between a marble column and a granite base.

I pluck from them spring's first and earliest leaves,
But other leaves shall grow thick on the fortunate rotting
Of this corpse that may have ten thousand years to live.

But other leaves shall grow thick on the fortunate rotting
But other leaves shall grow black
From the pens of those with adventures to tell in writing.

But other leaves shall grow black
With an ink more liquid than blood and the water of fountains:
Neglected testaments, words lost across the mountains.

With an ink more liquid than blood and the water of fountains
Can I protect my memory from forgetting
As a cuttlefish spends its blood and breath, retreating?

Can I protect my memory from forgetting?

THE CLEARING

This empty plinth with tall trees shaded round
Bears the unseen load of a marble ghost
That tramples, kicks, exerts a downward thrust,
Driving it daily deeper in the ground.

Or else, on leaving for a fatal feast,
The Commandant consigned it to be wrecked,
As a small stone, across the tide-line tossed,
Meets its own bull's-eye that the waves reflect.

But I should hear, beside the pond, at least,
The fanfare Don Giovanni blows, inviting...
Yes, now I hear it, on the echoes riding.
Beneath my feet I feel the ground emoting.

THE CAVE

Here is the entrance in the rock, the start:
Here, the world's tumult sleeps and comes apart.
Beyond this point, the sun and moon depart:
Dark downward passage to the planet's heart.

Eurydice walked here, you see her trail,
These are her footprints, but the traces fail,
The phrase breaks off, the vow achieves release,
The horseman jibs at the *cheval-de-frise*.

These other steps diverge, which Orpheus made,
It's bright, and the eclipse has had its hour,
Giving us back our haunted house of shade.

Where thorns and roses weave a bramble-bower,
The mænad sleeps in the forbidden glade.
A cloud above is like an open flower.

THE MEMORY

Lucky to be overdue,
Strolling down each avenue,
At your window I saw you,
Caught you wearing *rien du tout*;
To another I was true.

Yes, my heart already loved
Voices very far removed.
Shadows of black night had daubed
The big statue's pale eyes, carved
At the crossroads where I roved.

In the street the breeze blew fair
From Passy or Pépinière:
I was passing, I know where,
And I chanced to find you bare,
Blot of white on soft night air.

Fallen leaf of seasons past,
Phantom and nocturnal ghost,
Pennants proud for daybreak hoist,
With what future were you faced,
In our capital hard-pressed?

Paris, pressed to live and flame,
Stolid, fired up all the same
By the nights that quickly came,
Like the night you had no shame,
Propped against your window-frame.

THE PROPHECY

From a Paris square a fountain so clear shall spring
That virgins' blood and glacier streams

Beside it shall seem opaque.
The stars shall emerge in a swarm from their distant hives
And mass to admire themselves in its waters near the Tour St-Jacques.

From a Paris square a fountain so clear shall spring
That from daybreak onward the bathers will tiptoe forth.
St Opportune and her laundresses will be godmothers
And its waters shall run south, coming out of the north.

A great red chestnut-tree is in bloom in the square
Where the fountain will run, in the future.
Perhaps in my later years
I shall hear its murmur;

So sweet is this clear fountain's melody
That already it bathes my eyes and heart with its waters.
It will be the Seine's most beautiful tributary,
The surest token of spring-times to come, their birds and their flowers.

THE DESTINY

I have wished your death and there is nothing that can delay it.
At the very moment of your greatest pain
I have seen you covered in pus and sweat
And everything in you was cruel and insane.

Listen. That day from the hills of Bicêtre a great big cloud
Climbed up behind the Val-de-Grâce and its Dome.
A child had just been born and it cried aloud,
In the Rue Saint-Jacques, in a low-built home.

From now on nothing can save you from shame and pain
For my wish had the taste of things that materialise.
Already imperceptible physical signs, in your heart and your brain,
Warn you it's time you were saying your goodbyes.

It would be pointless for you to weep in repentance
Pointless to have an attitude fine and noble,
Because your only future is non-existence
And your name will not live in the sayings of the people.

The cloud passed the Val-de-Grâce and Saint-Sulpice,
Was reflected for long in the Seine before resolving
Into a storm. I watched from a tall white building,
There were great caged birds, its thunder was their release.

THE HARVEST

It's incredible to credit
One's alive, existing, real.
It's incredible to credit
One's the late, defunct and dead. It
Is incredible to credit
And least credible of all
Is to credit, you'll recall,
One is dream, unbodied soul.

Lovely roses passed away,
Lovely roses, scented flowers,
Trembling since the break of day,
Now disclosed to midnight hours,
Your prolonged and rapid doom
Measures up to our decades
Though you reach the sitting-room
Even as your colour fades.

They were frail, our deities,
They were little nobodies,
Living in a little street,
Managing to make ends meet.
Greater is our own fortune,
Darker is our destiny.
We do not desire the moon,
We are not afraid to die.

Trussed by our five senses, this
Universe is shrunk in size.
Goodbye, dream and loveliness!
You shall be my sacrifice
To a world not limitless.

THE SIESTA

Ten thousand decades of my noonday sleep
Endure a second's-breadth or even less.
I rise from dreams unquestioned and most deep
To my reality of world and flesh.

Here in my mouth again I find that taste,
Long-vanished names, kisses of tender greeting:
Don't know my name, or if my heart is beating
In the sure present or the ashen past.

Volcanoes, burst from memory's depths, and boil
Drown me in lava, for my mind is slack.
Burn the old screeds, turn permanently black
The mirror that is bitten by the foil.

THE CITY

Jostling the crowds and running down the roads,
Gripped in full sun, he's suffering, afraid;
It's danger, death, disaster he forebodes,
Twisting his tracks to flee an unknown shade,

The fate of one who drifts and dreams along,
Strays into dream and joins the phantom throng,
Purloins their coat, supplanting them in lands
Where matter yields to warm caressing hands.

This whole world issues from his bony crown.
He coops it, cloaks it, tricks it and constrains,
He has to halt, give way to passing trains
Of creatures born in bodies tumbling down.

Suns mourning, yearning; nauseous memory;
Wellsprings resurgent, echoing fogs' refrain:
You are mere scum and scouring. I would fain
Be born each day beneath a brand-new sky.

THE HOUSE

Freer and fiercer than an angel, wind
Has blown around the house its triple horn.
An angel? One from prison, on the run,
Coming downstairs, though shadows tease its mind,

Driving it back, their curious canvases
Hanging the far horizon's wires with suns,
More glow-worms too than gather on the lawn,
Or in the sheltering darkness of the barn.

As it comes down, its foot chinks on the stair
Like crystal glassware on the cellar floor.
It's near the hallway, it will soon be there.

Night's funnel is beyond the open door.
Listening, I sense it walk, and leave, and fly
Into peninsulas of broken sky.

THE COUNTRYSIDE

I dreamed of loving. Still I love, but now
Love is no more that rose and lilac spray
Whose perfume filled the woods where each pathway
Led on directly to the blazing glow.

I dreamed of loving. Still I love, but now
Love's not that storm whose lightning kindled high
Towers, unhorsed, unhinged, and fleetingly
Would set the parting of the ways aglow.

Love is the flint my footstep sparks at night,
The word no lexicon can render right,
Foam of the sea, the cloud across the sky.

Old age makes all things fixed and luminous:
Knots are unravelled, streets anonymous;
Set in our ways, the countryside and I.

THE SUMMER NIGHT

Roses go rambling up. Your dress is torn,
Snagging the bush with scraps of misty morn.
Perfumes from other days, another clime,
Blend, as you walk, with lilac and with thyme.

You move towards the wood, whose boundaries
Open a path that's loud with distant cries.
Fires of midsummer in the vale die back;
The night, so short, has soon strayed off the track.

Fine-bosomed girl, no light shines in your gaze.
I've seen your sisters. You are not the first
To run through fields and gardens and be lost.

You scrambled through the hedge and, as you passed,
The bramble-bushes scratched your thigh and face;
New songs were heard; the sky turned pale at last.

THE PLAGUE

In the road a footstep echoes. The bell has only one
clapper. Where's he going, the walker, coming
slowly nearer and briefly stopping? Now he's outside
the house. I hear him breathing behind the door.

I see the sky through the glass. I see the sky where the
stars run on the rooftops. It's the great
Bear or Betelgeuse, it's Venus the white-bellied, it's
Diana unfastening her tunic near a fountain of light.

Never did moons or suns run so far from the
earth, never was the night air so dense and so
heavy. I lean on my door which resists . . .

It opens at last, it swings and knocks against the
wall. And while the footstep moves away I decipher
on a yellow poster the word in black letters, 'Plague'.

THE NYMPH ALCESTIS

Two fountains kiss, and on the midnight hour
You're born, Alcestis. Here's your cosmic dower:
Reflections, fireflies, distant lights, the seven
Torches of Ursa Major, up in heaven.

It's dark; the starting signal bids you run;
You don't suspect that night must soon disperse,
Give way, when birds are singing, and the sun
Spreads gold along the peaks with open purse.

I know that dawn and morning will resume.
I've seen them, you will see them, I know well:
Their rhythmic dance excites my heart to swell.

But, nymph, your sister's born in noonday light:
How shall I tell her of the coming gloom,
Return of dusk, of silence, and of night?

THE VOICE

A voice, a voice coming from so far away
That it no longer rings in the ears,
A voice, like a drumbeat, muffled
Reaches us even so, distinctly.
Though it seems to issue from a tomb
It speaks only of summer and spring,
It fills the body with joy,
It kindles a smile on the lips.

I'm listening. It's only a human voice
Coming across the din of life and of battles,
The crash of thunder and the babble of talk.

What about you? Don't you hear it?
It says 'The pain will be short-lived'
It says 'The beautiful season is near'.

Don't you hear it?

THE VINTAGE

The fallow deer are gone, culled in the fall,
While in the city that the flute-song made
The games are finished and the laurels fade,
And names of champions rub off the wall.

The escort climbs the street of sepulture.
Below the bluffs, the soldiers rot in heaps;
The earth, blood-sodden, sweats and froths and weeps,
Drowning the victors in a rich manure.

Wine, in your casks, unscathed! Your colours will
Transmute our lips until we lie at last
Beneath the earth, at one with palace bells

That chimed with the cicada's canticles,
Stilled now, like flutes and cymbals long since past.
Today the thunder and the wind are still.

THE EQUINOX

Cocks crow repeatedly. Beneath grey skies
The equinox rolls out its barrel-train
And trundles from the North Sea to the Seine
Through all the smells, the lightning and the cries.

The martyred corpse of Bishop Denis lies
Bleeding with grapes of Argenteuil, Suresnes.
Chariots haul queens and heroes on a chain.
Each temple crumbles to its roots and dies,

And yet just now a midnight rainbow shone,
Spanning the valley, to entice the moon.
Day broke; thick vapours hid the world away.

Can it be truly called a day, this day
That drags love, life and Paris in the mire?
Yes: in the fog, a spark flares into fire.

THE BEACH

On the beach, the sea whitens in the shadows.
A fig-tree quivers with the weight of birds.
A certain man has breathed one word of words;
His hearer moves away among the cedars.

It's time to go and conquer. Bacchus girds.
Meetings depress him; like a brook that mutters,
Space skewers him. Night's over. Is it day?
Put out the party bonfires, anyway.

A country of fresh streams and trackless wood
Lets a man feel his veins, his coursing blood.
He knows this land and people, knows their sound,
Well-versed in the aromas of the ground.

On the beach, he who gave the secret sign
Lies with a dagger sticking in his spine.
Along the mole his voice, still waterborne,
Repeats the word from which his grief was born.

That word is Corinth, copiously said,
And the earth groans with lassitude and dread.

THE ASYLUM

The one whom his own belly's rage betrays,
Many times humbled when his nights glow pale,
Humbles himself, submits, and joins the strays
In the asylum, as one takes the veil.

May I stay free and healthy in my thinking
Like an unfailing sextant in a storm,
Take refuge in my heart, my hand, my home,
And gaze on man and beast with eye unblinking.

Virtue, mere word, you've set me free to pass:
You've opened up the view, torn down the drapes,
Bent to my prayers the hoped-for Val-de-Grâce,

Where the sage wakens and the hero sleeps.
Grant that the city soon enjoys their presence:
The wise man's dream, the warrior's vital essence.

THE AWAKENING

Listen: the noise of wheels on cobbled streets.
It's late. Get up. Noon blasts its foghorn trump,
Keen to go through the lock-gates. Sleep recedes:
The world of dreams takes flesh and flaunts its pomp.

It's late. Get up. The bath-tap's on, and splashing.
This body that the night has soiled needs washing.
This body starved of victory needs feeding.
This body needs a thorough soak, then clothing.

When we have scrubbed these hands of inky stains,
When we have brushed these teeth that hold decaying
Words, like boats rotting on their anchor-chains,
Words of a song, a true or secret saying.

It's late. Get up. The clarion in the street
Summons you: 'This is real life. This is it'.
The table's laid, and you are hungry: eat.
The horse is being bridled: fix the bit.

Think, though, of those who neither speak nor hear,
Having been murdered as the day dawned clear.

THE EPITAPH

I've lived today, and since antiquity
Been dead. I lived intact, but I was prey.
Man's nobler side was jailed and put away;
Among the slaves in face-masks, I was free.

I've lived today, and nonetheless been free.
I watched the river and the earth and sky

Turn round me, and they kept their harmony;
Honey and birds, a seasonal supply.

How did you use these gifts, you there alive?
Would you want back the days I spent in toil?
Was it for others that you tilled the soil
To harvest? Did you make my city thrive?

Don't fear me, you who live: I'm dead and gone:
Not soul nor body, nothing lingers on.

Comparative Criticism XXV, pp. 229–245. © 2004 Edinburgh University Press
Printed in the United Kingdom

Latin poems by George Herbert

TRANSLATED BY MIKE MOTTRAM

TWO OCCASIONAL POEMS

[*For the wedding of the Elector Palatine and the Princess Elizabeth*]

Dawn calls, the wedding bed is in the hall,
Each star puts out its light reluctantly.
Rise Earth, fling wide the flowers you warmed all
Winter; you, thawing waters, lead the dance;
Air, sound the trumpet; and fire, while the sun
Still lingers, burn bright in the muted lamps.
You, Prince of Germany and here, come on
And gladden heaven with your countenance.
Those looks you wore in council or in war
Discard, and shine now in your lady's eyes.
Eliza, with rare loveliness appear,
Jewel of our Isles, and Indies of our North:
Take in the whole world with your happy gaze
So all men wonder at the cloudless day.
May risen Phoebus now no brighter blaze
Than you, nor evening blush more beautifully.

On the Death of the Incomparable Francis Bacon

As you lie groaning, wasted with disease,
As your lost last days stagger in a maze,
It comes to me what fate foresaw and meant:
That with the month of April you should die,
That flowers' tears and nightingales' complaints
Could lead your learning's lonely obsequies.

TWO OCCASIONAL POEMS

[*For the wedding of the Elector Palatine and the Princess Elizabeth*]

En Aurora vocat, lectus genialis in aula est,
    Invitoque fugit singula stella pede:
Exere terra caput, servatos projice flores,
    Flumina caelestem ducite lenta chorum:
Tuque aer inflato tubam, dum plurimus ignis
    Incendat tacitas, sole morante, faces:
Interea precede Comes Germano-britanne
    Et coelum vultus exhilarato tui,
Nec qua consuleres, populumve ad bella vocares,
    Hac facie dominae conspiciare tuae:
Et tu gemma etiam Britonum, Septentrionum
    India, non solitum profer Eliza decus:
Perstringas homines vultu, miretur ut orbis
    Hos oculos laetos, hunc sine nube diem:
Sic non Phobeus jam plus te splendeat ortus
    Nec plus te rubeat vesper, Eliza, precor.

In obitum incomparabilis Francisci Vicecomitis Sancti Albani,
Baronis Verulamii

Dum longi lentique gemis sub pondere morbi
    Atque haeret dubio tabida vita pede,
Quid voluit prudens Fatum, jam sentio tandem:
    Constat, *Aprile* uno te potuisse mori:
Ut Flos hinc lacrimis, illinc Philomela querelis,
    Deducant linguae funera sola tuae.

FROM A PASSION IN TATTERS

III [*On his blood and sweat*]

Your blood exultant in its own expense for sin
Can barely keep the merest droplet in.

IV *On his Side Pierced*

Christ, where the steel has torn your side apart
I hope it made a pathway for my heart.

XI *On the Good Thief*

A superthief, you stole a-plenty from the rest,
And now up close you've stolen in Christ's breast.

XV *On the Bowing of the Head: John 19.30*

Foxes have holes, and birds a nest:
All things have beds to lay them in,
Yet Christ no friend to take him in,
But on a cross his only rest.

XVI *On the Eclipse of the Sun*

Are you then faint, you who fill up the sky,
    Lord of the kindly dancing light,
Unlocking heaven, bringing a bright world out
    With dawn, and hiding it at night?
But now you're tired. And our spendthrift master
    Has left his store provisionless;
And that bright spangle which he would not keep,
    He would not have his kin possess.
Let the houseboys flounder in the same dark
    Our lord has made for his own eyes.
And yet do not by any means despair:
    Our failing lord again will rise,
Those empty stores be stocked with richer beams
    And we washed over in their shining streams.

FROM **PASSIO DISCERPTA**

III *In sudorem sanguineum*

Sic tuus effundi gestat pro crimine sanguis,
    Ut nequeat paulo se cohibere domi.

IV *In latus perfossum*

Christe, ubi tam duro pates in te semita ferro,
    Spero meo cordi posse patere viam.

XI *In pium Latronem*

O nimium latro! reliquis furatus abunde,
    Nunc etiam Christum callidus aggrederis.

XV *Inclinato capite. Joh. 19*

Vulpibus antra feris, nidique volucribus adsunt,
    Quodque suum novit stroma, cubile suum.
Qui tamen excipiat, Christus caret hospite: tantum
    In cruce suspendens, unde reclinet, habet.

XVI *Ad Solem deficientem*

Quid hoc? et ipse deficis, caeli gigas,
    Almi choragus luminis?
Tu promis orbem mane, condis vesperi,
    Mundi fidelis claviger:
At nunc fatiscis. Nempe Dominus aedium
    Prodegit integrum penu,
Quamque ipse lucis tesseram sibi negat,
    Negat familiae suae.
Carere discat verna, quo summus caret
    Paterfamilias luminis.
Tu vero mentem neutiquam despondeas,
    Resurget occumbens Herus:
Tunc instruetur lautius radiis penu,
    Tibi supererunt et mihi.

FROM **THE GROVE**

V *On the Holy Scriptures*

What breath is it mastering me, what heat
Melting my bowels? What is it has deranged
The meditations of my deepest heart?
That other evening sitting at the door
Did I perhaps gulp down some shooting star
And is it - restless in this vile new home -
Already pondering its prompt return?

Did I suck honey and take in the bee
Have I swallowed the builder with the comb?
No, neither bees or stars have stung me through
But, Holy Scripture, it was surely you
Paced through my heart's close-hidden places
And you who tested all its cul-de-sacs,
The lanes and wynds of fading appetite.
How well how wisely you perambulate
These twisting and entangled alleys.
The power that built the city knows its ways.

XII *The Storm with Christ Sleeping*

The sea runs high with you asleep. But when you wake
   The waves nod off. You have them well in check.

XV *Martha and Mary*

'Now Christ has come, quick with your brooms,
Shake out the sheets, make the hearth bright,
Scrub and polish through all the rooms,
Spare the lamps, make the house a light.
Sluggards! Here's something needs a duster'.
'Your heart. All else is clean, dear sister'.

XVIII [*On the Proud Man*]

We are all of one mould, sons of the earth:
Valleys of plenty or mountains of dearth.

XXIV *On the Angels*

How unlike ours the perfect intellect
Of angels: ours limited by nature
To beg the senses what they know.
Until our seeing lights unseal the door
Until our mills have ground the grist to flour
We work away most times to no effect.
Far off, removed from us, the rivers flow

Of all or anything that we might know.
What in ourselves we are, we should not guess
Unless we had it by appearances.
Angels need no such circuit to their sea:
They are rushed in upon by what they know;
By windows open always to the air
Of what they are they're painlessly apprised,
Themselves at once the grinding and the grist.

XXIX *Reasonable Sacrifice*

Altars and men are built both from the sod,
Alive in man, and in the altar dead;
Such noxious origins, by Christ once wed,
Make man the living altar of his God.

XXXV *To the Lord*

Beauty and sweets, and a hundred Hyblas,
   My heart's summit, and my soul's war and peace:
Grant me, each time I ask, full sight of you,
   And in your eyes, my life, so let me die.
So let me die. If meeting you is life,
   Why must I stay, and pray without relief?
But let me see; if you escape my gaze,
   Can you who healed the blind think I have eyes?
I'm blind, I swear; if I may not swear so,
   Prevent my wrong with the full sight of you.

FROM LUCUS

V *In Sacras Scripturas*

Heu, quis spiritus, igneusque turbo
Regnat visceribus, measque uersat
Imo pectore cogitationes?
Nunquid pro foribus sedendo nuper
Stellam vespere suxerim uolantem,
Haec autem hospitio latere turpi

Prorsus nescia, cogitat recessum?
Nunquid mel comedens, apem comedi
Ipsa cum domina domum uorando?
Imo, me nec apes, nec astra pungunt:
Sacratissima Charta, tu fuisti
Quae cordis latebras sinusque caecos
Atque omnes peragrata es angiportus
Et flexus fugientis appetitus.
Ah, quam docta perambulare calles
Maeandrosque plicasque, quam perita es!
Quae vis condidit, ipsa novit aedes.

XII *Tempestas Christo dormiente*

Cum dormis, surgit pelagus: cim, Christe, resurgis,
    Dormitat pelagus: quam bene frena tenes.

XV *Martha: Maria*

Christus adest: crebris aedes percurrite scopis,
    Excutite aulaea, et luceat igne focus.
Omnia purgentur, niteat mihi tota supellex,
    Parcite luminibus, sitque lucerna domus:
O cessatrices! eccum puluisculus illic!
    Corde tuo forsan, caetera munda, SOROR.

XVIII [*In Superbum*]

Unusquisque hominum, Terra est; et filius arui.
    Dic mihi, mons sterilis, uallis an uber eris?

XXIX Λογικη θυσια

Ararumque hominumque ortum si mente pererres,
    Cespes uiuus, homo; mortuus, ara fuit:
Quae divisa nocent, Christi per foedus, in unum
    Conueniunt; et homo uiua fit ara Dei.

XXIV *In angelos*

Intellectus adultus angelorum
Haud nostro similis, cui necesse,
Ut dentur species, rogare sensum:
Et ni lumina ianuam resignent,
Et nostrae tribuant molae farinam,
Saepe ex se nihil otiosa cudit.
A nobis etenim procul remoti
Labuntur fluuii scientiarum:
Si non per species, nequimus ipsi,
Quid ipsi sumus, assequi putando.
Non tantum est iter Angelis ad undas,
Nullo circuitu scienda pungunt,
Illis perpetuae patent fenestrae,
Se per se facili modo, scientes,
Atque ipsi sibi sunt mola et farina.

XXXV *Ad Dominum*

Christe, decus, dulcedo, et centum circiter Hyblae,
    Cordis apex, animae pugnique paxque meae,
Quin, sine, te cernam; quoties iam dixero, cernam;
    Immoriarque oculis, O mea vita, tuis.
Si licet, immoriar: vel si tua visio vita est,
    Cur sine te, votis immoriturus, ago?
Ah, cernam; tu, qui caecos sanare solebas,
    Cum te non videam, mene videre putas?
Non video, certum est jurare; aut si hoc vetuisti,
    Praevenias vultu non facienda tuo.

FROM **TO MY MOTHER'S MEMORY**

IV

    Why scribble when I should be still?
Wet with the dew of everlasting happiness
    My mother tends (no little plot)
An Eden where the cold North blasts are powerless.

But my own Heavens are now
The beauty and the obligations of her name;
    And while I watch these (as I do)
At night, I join the stars and leave the body's frame.
    And then I urge my special star
And then I strain my fingers busily to write,
    Dear mother, your last eulogy,
By day or night I write, both equal in your light.
    Into this world you brought me:
Now leaving it, you bring me to another.
    Wherefore these twofold verses sound
Double for you, who were twice to me a mother.

V

You gardens, you who once made your mistress happy,
Should wither now you have made beautiful her bier
And you are free to die; look how your loveliness
Is thick with thorns, and desperate for a gardener's shears.
They smell of loam and death, the flowers. Your lady's dead,
And sours the roots grow by her grave; and they the roses.
The violets bend their dark heads, heavy, to the earth,
As if they showed which way their mistress' new home lies.
Gardens no more, but dormitory of the dead,
Each bank is like a pillow for its absent lady.
Now you have done, so perish all. Nor ever let
A bud or leaf look now to her for remedy.
Let them shrink to their roots in the graves they grew from
(God gives his children gratis a last resting place).
Die, or rather live until the dew at evening
Weep some sad drops and grant us mourners here some grace.

VII

Pale she looks, my mother's ghost, and bloodless.
What made me happy once has turned to mist,
A mimicry of you, a lying likeness,
Air, not food, for a disappointed child,
Only a cloud, heavy with rain not milk,

Mocking my weeping, grey like rain, and cold.
You leave? My Juno was not cloud like this,
Slow, as if she never saw an April dawn,
Pale, as if she lay in wavering ash.
Rather she looked a saint, at home in heaven:
As Astraea when she resolved to quit
Her wasteland fens, or on her ancient throne
The kindly Themis poised with her true scales.
Appear again like this, with such a dream
I'll live what time is left me, my years I'll
Hitch, unmurmuring, to your star alone.
My wasted days and my aborted effort,
Pale as I am from books, I'll not complain.
For hopes unrealised and dreams grown old,
I'll blame the barren world. It can have back
Its lying comets and its stars grown cold.
I have a hut in the country, with twice
Five timbers beamed, and a small garden plot
Of narrow paths with flowers overfleeced,
Such as wise gardeners love, where plants set close
Make one perfume, and the untrodden beds
A single posy grown, a nest of spice.
Here we will live, and daily feast on scents
The herbs give out. So come to me as when
I loved you best: and do not come so faint
When I recall so clear. The differing
Would divide us, make the flowers dizzy,
And with the garden blossom, our growing
Gladnesses suffer their own withering.

VIII

Gladly I follow the strait path of truth,
    And shun the broad highway of vice:
But evil stars corrupted my good faith
    And mixed my wine with bitterness.
I bustle now and murmur and make threats:
    Enraged against the sun and moon.
But then a friendly presence takes my coat

And whispers in my ear a sound:
This is the drink your Lord drank long ago.
I taste the wine, I let it flow.

IX

Mother, lay by your hymns and read these lines
Sent by an anxious son. It is like song
For the new sainted dead to hear home news:
Where once you loved, abides your care in heaven.
Two clouds created by our flowing eyes
Darken the kindly days. We are all tears.
Our navy's readied for great enterprise,
But weeping is our only real business.
The ships are still in port and blame the wind:
But had they wanted rain we could have wept it.
Tilly is on the Dane, France gone to sea;
And still we weep. Tears are our only coin.
The days run slow, Time's busy cogs and wheels
Falter in all this watery excess.
I would have written more (for what is praise
To me, or what delight, not shared with you),
But while my lines give tears a part to play,
The ink grows faint from their transparency.

X

Travellers have till now complained
Of rain-soaked gloomy skies
With little cause, of dreary wind,
Of slithery British soil.
But now, since you are dead my dear,
Well might they curse and spit aside
The soaking and contagious air.
Fields, city, court are all in black,
England, the homelands of the Scots;
And Wales, millennia old, shakes
Lest the ancestral tears she weeps
Should join your obsequies too late.

No corner of the sky is clear,
The sea around has drowned the air.

FROM **MEMORIAE MATRIS SACRUM**

IV

   Quid nugor calamo favens?
Mater perpetuis uvida gaudiis,
   Horto pro tenui colit
Edenem Boreae flatibus inuium.
   Quin caeli mihi sunt mei,
Materni decus, et debita nominis,
   Dumque his invigilo frequens
Stellarum socius, pellibus exuor.
   Quare sphaeram egomet meam
Connixus, digitis impiger urgeo:
   Te, Mater, celebrans diu,
Noctu te celebrans luminis aemulo.
   Per te nascor in hunc globum
Exemploque tuo nascor in alterum:
   Bis tu mater eras mihi,
Ut currat paribus gloria tibiis.

V

Horti, deliciae Dominae, marcescite tandem;
   Ornastis capulum, nec superesse licet.
Ecce decus uestrum spinis horrescit, acuta
   Cultricem reuocans anxietate manum:
Terram et funus olent flores: Dominaeque cadauer
   Contiguas stirpes afflat, eaeque rosas.
In terram uiolae capite inclinantur opaco,
   Quaeque domus Dominae sit, gravitate docent.
Quare haud uos hortos, sed coemeteria dico,
   Dum torus absentem quisque reponit heram.
Euge, perite omnes; nec posthac exeat ulla
   Quaesitum Dominam gemma vel herba suam.
Cuncta ad radices redeant, tumulosque paternos;
   (Nempe sepulcra satis numen inempta dedit.)

Occidite; aut sane tantisper uiuite, donec
   Vespere ros maestis funus honestet aquis.

VII

Pallida materni Genii atque exsanguis imago,
In nebulas similesque tui res gaudia nunquid
Mutata? et pro matre mihi phantasma dolosum
Uberaque aerea hiscentem fallentia natum?
Vae nubi pluuia grauidae, non lacte, measque
Ridenti lacrimas quibus unis concolor unda est.
Quin fugias? mea non fuerat tam nubila Iuno,
Tam segnis facies aurorae nescia uernae,
Tam languens genitrix cineri supposta fugaci:
Verum augusta parens, sanctum os caeloque locandum,
Quale paludosos iamiam lictura recessus
Praetulit Astraea, aut solio Themis alma uetusto
Pensilis, atque acri dirimens examine lites.
Hunc uultum ostendas, et tecum, nobile spectrum,
Quod superest uitae, insumam: Solisque iugales
Ipse tuae solum adnectam, sine murmure, tensae.
Nec querar ingratos, studiis dum tabidus insto,
Effluxisse dies, suffocatamve Minervam,
Aut spes productas, barbataque somnia vertam
In uitium mundo sterili, cui cedo cometas
Ipse suos tanquam digno pallentiaque astra.
Est mihi bis quinis laqueata domuncula tignis
Rure; brevisque hortus, cuius cum uellere florum
Luctatur spatium, qualem tamen eligit aequi
Judicii dominus, flores ut iunctius halent
Stipati, rudibusque uolis imperuius hortus
Sit quasi fasciculus crescens, et nidus odorum.
Hic ego tuque erimus, uariae suffitibus herbae
Quotidie pasti: tantum verum indue vultum
Affectusque mei similem; nec languida misce
Ora meae memori menti: ne dispare cultu
Pugnaces, teneros florum turbemus odores,
Atque inter reliquos horti crescentia foetus
Nostra etiam paribus marcescant gaudia fatis.

VIII

Paruam piamque dum lubenter semitam
    Grandi reaeque praefero,
Carpsit malignum sidus hanc modestiam
    Vinumque felle miscuit.
Hinc fremere totus et minari gestio
    Ipsis seuerus orbibus;
Tandem prehensa comiter lacernula
    Susurrat aure quispiam,
Haec fuerat olim potio Domini tui.
    Gusto proboque dolium.

IX

Hoc, Genitrix, scriptum proles tibi sedula mittit.
    Siste parum cantus, dum legis ista, tuos.
Nosse sui quid agant, quaedam est quoque musica sanctis
    Quaeque olim fuerat cura, manere potest.
Nos misere flemus, solesque obducimus almos
    Occiduis, tanquam duplice nube, genis.
Interea classem magnis Rex instruit ausis:
    Nos autem flemus: res ea sola tuis.
Ecce solutura est, ventos causata morantes:
    Sin pluviam, fletus suppeditasset aquas.
Tillius incumbit Dano Gallusque marinis,
    Nos flendo: haec nostrum tessera sola ducum.
Sic aeuum exigitur tardum, dum praepetis anni
    Mille rotae nimiis impediuntur aquis.
Plura tibi missurus eram (nam quae mihi laurus,
    Quod nectar, nisi cum te celebrare diem?)
Sed partem in scriptis etiam dum lacrima poscit,
    Diluit oppositas candidus humor aquas.

X

Nempe huc usque notos tenebricosos
Et maestum nimio madore caelum
Tellurisque Britannicae saliuam

Iniuste satis arguit uiator.
At te commoriente, magna mater,
Recte, quem trahit, aerem repellit
Cum probro madidum, reumque difflat.
Nam te nunc ager, urbs, et aula plorant:
Te nunc Anglia, Scotiaeque binae,
Quin te Cambria peruetusta deflet,
Deducens lacrimas prioris aevi
Ne serae meritis tuis venirent.
Non est angulus uspiam serenus,
Nec cingit mare, nunc inundat omnes.

FROM **POEMS IN ANSWER**

V *On the Metre*

When to so many measures verse could dance
Why single out effeminate sapphics?
Did the packed heroic line not entrance
Your musing mood? Or could elegiacs
Not have wept for you, or quick iambics
Stung? The one weeping measure would have served
Your brainsick turn, the other well bespeaks
The straight road you walk while the vulgar swerved.
But you sent heroes and healers packing,
And work away to woo the frail fair sex
In unarmed measures, while blandly taking
Their tender ears with sweeter tetrastichs.

XXXV *Scotland: An Exhortation to Peace*

You Scotsmen shiver under the icy Bear,
So why your unchecked flames of zeal?
Is it contrariness that feeds the fire,
As when numb hands are scalded by a chill?
Or as coal burns keener in deep winter,
Is it the cold provokes your calentures?
Put out those flaming torches, for they kill
(The sea's at hand, it rolls its waters close,

And for a surer cure, there Christ's blood flows
Down from above, yet nearer and more sweet)
And if a fresh stray breeze the fire renews
The world will shatter early in the heat.

XL *To God*

Once you Great God have blessed
With your quiet dew my inky hand
    I am not sad and sleepless
To no end, nor sore at my fingers' ends
    With chewing of my nails,
Nor does my pen droop. Now I am well:
    A rich and active vein
Of versing has baptised my mood.
    To its dykes indifferent
A Nile spills out its amiable flood.
    O sweetest Breath who plant
In me these holy groans. From you,
    The Dove, what I write pours,
And if I please the graciousness is yours.

FROM **MUSAE RESPONSORIAE**

V *In metri genus*

Cur, ubi tot ludat numeris antiqua poesis,
    Sola tibi Sappho, feminaque una placet?
Cur tibi tam facile non arrisere poetae
    Heroum grandi carmina fulta pede?
Cur non lugentes Elegi? non acer Iambus?
    Commotos animos rectius ista decent.
Scilicet hoc vobis proprium, qui purius itis,
    Et populi spurcas creditis esse vias:
Vos ducibus missis, missis doctoribus, omnes
    Femineum blanda fallitis arte genus:
Nunc etiam teneras quo versus gratior aures
    Mulceat, imbelles complacuere modi.

XXXV *Ad Scotiam. Protrepticon ad Pacem*

Scotia quae frigente iaces porrecta sub Arcto,
   Cur adeo immodica relligione cales?
Anne tuas flammas ipsa antiperistasis auget
   Ut niue torpentes incaluere manus?
Aut ut pruna gelu summo mordacius urit,
   Sic acuunt zelum frigora tanta tuum?
Quin nocuas extingue faces, precor: unda propinqua est
   Et tibi vicinas porrigit aequor aquas:
Aut potius Christi sanguis demissus ab alto
   Vicinusque magis nobiliorque fluit:
Ne, si flamma nouis adolescat mota flabellis,
   Ante diem uestro mundus ab igne ruat.

XL *Ad Deum*

   Quem tu, summe Deus, semel
Scribentem placido rore beaueris,
   Illum non labor irritus
Exercet miserum; non dolor unguium
   Morsus increpat anxios.
Non maeret calamus; non queritur caput.
   Sed fecunda poeseωs
Vis, et vena sacris regnat in artubus;
   Qualis nescius aggerum
Exundat fluuio Nilus amabili.
   O dulcissime Spiritus
Sanctos qui gemitus mentibus inseris
   A te turture defluos
Quod scribo, et placeo, si placeo, tuum est.

PART III

Essay reviews

Comparative Criticism **XXV**, pp. 249–254. © 2004 Edinburgh University Press
Printed in the United Kingdom

A Mind-body problem. On *Cambridge Scientific Minds*

SCOTT MANDELBROTE

During the past decade, Cambridge University Press has issued a series of books that attempt to capture some aspect of the distinctive contribution made by the denizens of its academic parent to intellectual life and human culture.* Essays have been written on individuals and their influence in establishing particular Cambridge styles of academic enquiry; on Cambridge women, including the X-ray crystallographer Rosalind Franklin whose work at King's College, London, pushed Watson and Crick along the correct path in their analysis of the structure of DNA, and on the contributions that Cambridge University has made to particular fields or methods of research.[1] Something of the intended audience for these books can be guessed from the fact that they concern themselves principally with the last 150 years and that they treat the distinctively Cantabrigian contribution to British, or rather Soviet, espionage in the 1940s on an equal footing with lasting moments of scientific or literary discovery. Prompted by such populist gestures, one might be permitted to wonder whether consideration of the achievements of Cambridge men and women in politics, sport, literature, or the visual and the performing arts might not be more likely to sell the brand to the voyeurs and navel-gazers who must between them constitute the market for these books.

In this sense, the editors of *Cambridge Scientific Minds* have picked a version of the formula that is more likely to deliver a winner, bearing in mind the continued success of popular science in the bookshops.[2] Given the inclusion of an exiguous, almost vacuous chapter on Stephen Hawking, by one of the two editors, Simon Mitton, it seems a fair bet to assume that the emulation of this phenomenon was indeed the purpose of the book. Certainly, the tone is unashamedly triumphalist: this is not the place to go

* Peter Harman and Simon Mitton (eds), *Cambridge Scientific Minds* (Cambridge University Press, 2002) is under review here.

for any reflection on the institutional attitude of Cambridge University to science or scientific invention. At a moment when that University is proposing to seize an increased share of the royalties and other financial benefits 'spun off' by individuals on its payroll, yet is busy doing deals with outside businesses interested in exploiting its scientific training and know-how that may well compromise the future exercise of academic freedom, this silence is perhaps a little too tactful. In due course, may we look forward to essays on the theme of *Cambridge Fat Cats*?

Historians of universities, of science, and of scientists have usually been rather more receptive to the importance of intellectual setting, friendship, and interaction in the making of ideas than the authors of the essays in this book succeed in being. That is particularly puzzling, given that this is meant to be a work that considers, in the words of Peter Harman's introduction, 'Is there indeed a specifically Cantabrigian scientific culture?' This is certainly a question worth asking, and deserved to be raised on page 1 of the book. By page 343, the reader can be quite sure that the contributors have not themselves thought to answer it. For example, this book will not tell you anything about the demographic growth of scientific disciplines at Cambridge in the nineteenth or twentieth centuries. Remarkably, it includes no chapter on the eighteenth-century, during which the University for the first time assimilated a new body of scientific knowledge into its curriculum and pioneered a system of competitive examination, admittedly based on a rather old-fashioned view of the subject, in the Mathematical Tripos.[3] The influence on the Tripos on generations of Cambridge scientists is apparent in the lives of Whewell, Sedgwick, and Babbage that are included here, but the peculiar nature of its learning and the background in natural theology that was also provided for Cambridge scientists in the Newtonian tradition are largely neglected. Characteristics of late eighteenth- and early nineteenth-century Cambridge (and, to a lesser extent, British) science thus appear as curiosities in the careers of a pioneering philosopher of science, a liberal geologist, and the inventor of computing.

In practice, Richard Yeo's account of Whewell and David Oldroyd's brief life of Sedgwick are nevertheless among the better chapters in the collection. Simon Schaffer's study of James Clerk Maxwell does make a serious attempt to consider the setting for Maxwell's Cambridge triumphs as well as the relative shortcomings of mid-nineteenth-century Cambridge physics when compared to that of French or German institutions. Nevertheless, Schaffer is caught out to some extent by the problem that floors most of the contributors completely: how to describe the life and scientific career of an individual or group of individuals and to assess their Cambridge career as a part of a broader pattern of achievement for a general audience in the narrow scope of fifteen pages. The editors were surely wise to include potted biographies of the subjects of each chapter. It is unfortunate that the reader will often find them more informative as well as more succinct than the chapters themselves.

Too little thought has gone into deciding who should be classed as a 'Cambridge Scientific Mind' and why they qualified as such. Thus, there can be no doubt that A. N. Whitehead, Bertrand Russell, G. H. Hardy, J. E. Littlewood, and Mary Cartwright (the only woman to be included in this collection) all contributed much to the mathematical reputation of Cambridge. Russell's career was linked to the creation of a particular Cambridge style of philosophy and of an intellectual ethos, deriving in part from it, that had wide-reaching and not always positive consequences in English intellectual life during the first half of the twentieth century.[4] It is harder, however, to make the case that the mathematics of Whitehead and Russell, or even that of Hardy and Littlewood, played much of a role in the scientific practice of twentieth-century Cambridge.[5] Indeed, it would appear to be the case that whereas all of the nineteenth-century scientific figures discussed in this book (from Whewell to J. J. Thomson) spent at least part of their studies on the Mathematical Tripos, and that some of them were active in its reformation, none of the twentieth-century scientists considered here were trained in that school. Moreover, Russell's great *Principia Mathematica* was published after his association with Trinity College, Cambridge, and thus with the University, had ended. One might suggest that the achievements of Cambridge science are such that they do not need padding out by the inclusion of those whose science was mostly practised outside that University. Yet many of those described here, for example William Gilbert (the subject of a superb essay by Stephen Pumfrey), William Harvey, or Lord Kelvin, should be considered at least as much London, Paduan, Oxonian, or Glaswegian minds as Cambridge ones.

Given the achievements of recent writing on the history of scientific education and the broad range of styles available to scientific biographers, it is surprising to find most of the essays in this collection stuck in one of two ruts.[6] Many essays constitute brief trials in the old-fashioned genre of life and works, in which the inevitability of the subject's choices and achievements tends to be assumed (for example, the accounts of Newton; Babbage; Sherrington, Adrian and Dale; Eddington, and Dirac). Others are memoirs of the author's own scientific career. These are sometimes engaging (Antony Hewish's account of the discovery of pulsars) but usually rather flat (for example, the uncharacteristically dull piece by Max Perutz, on the very important topic of molecular biology in Cambridge during the 1950s and 1960s, which is recycled from *Cambridge Minds*). Although there are some more sprightly pieces, notably Harmke Kamminga's account of the diminutive Frederick Gowland ('Hoppy') Hopkins and his battles with the University over the creation of a department of biochemistry, most of the essays in *Cambridge Scientific Minds* ignore the impact of place and style on the formation of scientific ideas and practices. There is nothing here to set beside Simon Schaffer's magical account of Newton's experimental practice or Geoffrey Cantor's insightful analysis of Faraday's manipulation of the public and private spaces of the Royal Institution.[7]

This leads to a sense of frustration: are Cambridge scientific minds not somehow connected to scientific bodies, their needs and their foibles? Might it not be useful, for example, to know that Dirac, to whose 'aristocratic sense of physics' during his forty-six year tenure of the Lucasian chair Helge Kragh refers, lived in one of those huge houses in South Cambridge that were once the preserve of the professoriate, one reception room of which ('the post room') he gave over to decades of unopened mail?[8] Anecdotal information of this kind can be extremely revealing; it would also have provided relief from the reverential tone of most of the essays in this book. The serious implications of some anecdotes that are told in the book are largely missed. Thus, the accounts of the instruments built at the Cavendish Laboratory or of the arrays constructed by Hewish suggest both the inventiveness and the relative poverty of British science, even after the bonanza produced by the Second World War. Cambridge science has not, by and large, been 'big science'. It has, however, been remarkably successful, both in terms of discoveries and of recognition given by others in the profession.

Part of the reason for this may have been the sense of scientific community made possible by the nature of departments and Colleges in mid-twentieth-century Cambridge. This is hinted at in some of Hewish's remarks, where he describes how he considered and eventually rejected the hypothesis that the scintillations detected by his radio arrays were the product of alien broadcasts. It is also familiar from the many accounts of the competitive friendship of Watson and Crick (and their exclusion of Franklin). Community and competition have perhaps been essential elements in the creation of a Cambridge scientific culture that has produced as many as 70 Nobel Prize winners. They may also help to explain the importance of Cambridge scientists, above all Joseph Needham, in movements to consider the social and historical meaning and relevance of science.[9]

One of the implied assumptions of *Cambridge Scientific Minds* is that the University's excellence in science has a continuous history (apart from the eighteenth century) and, presumably, a glorious future. By failing to consider the circumstances and relationships that have helped to create scientific achievement at Cambridge, the authors reduce their subjects to being objects of curiosity, rather like the fine buildings and strange inhabitants of Cambridge as they are viewed by tourists in the summer. Yet the idea of continuity that underpins this collection of essays is not itself uncontroversial. Alternative histories could and should be written. They might stress the exceptionalism of early modern scientific discovery, or the routinisation of science in the eighteenth-century university.[10] Equally, they might note the importance of the overlap between kinship, sociability, and professionalisation in nineteenth-century science, not least in the careers of Darwin, Kelvin, and Stokes described by Peter J. Bowler and David B. Wilson in their chapters in this book. They might reflect on the creation of an aristocracy of science in the early twentieth century and the paternalist culture of improvement associated with it, both in laboratory practice and attitudes to society as a whole.[11] They would register the decline in status, prestige, and ambition in late twentieth-century Cambridge and British science that cannot be obscured by the temporary celebrity of Stephen Hawking. Above all, they would recognise that scientific achievement, whatever it may owe to luck or circumstance, is due to the ability of human minds to be captivated by strange and difficult things, by the material that popular science writing, by definition, leaves out of the equation.

But all of this might be too difficult for the voyeurs and too troubling for the navel-gazers. Some of it might even disturb the Vice-Chancellor who gives his imprimatur to this book. Nevertheless, such considerations ought to have been part of the answer to Peter Harman's opening question about Cantabrigian scientific culture and are the essence of good biographical writing in the history of science. Taking them into account might have given life and body to *Cambridge Scientific Minds*.

Peterhouse, Cambridge and
All Souls College, Oxford

NOTES

1 Richard Mason (ed.), *Cambridge Minds* (Cambridge University Press, 1994); Edward Shils and Carmen Blacker (eds), *Cambridge Women* (Cambridge University Press, 1996); Sarah J. Ormrod (ed.), *Cambridge Contributions* (Cambridge University Press, 1998).

2 For reflections on this phenomenon, see David Philip Miller, 'The "Sobel Effect"', *Metascience*, 11 (2002), 185–200; David Oldroyd, 'Fossils in the Airport Lounge', *Metascience*, 12 (2003), 25–36.

3 John Gascoigne, *Cambridge in the Age of the Enlightenment* (Cambridge University Press, 1989), pp. 270–99.

4 Ray Monk, 'The Effects of a Broken Home: Bertrand Russell and Cambridge', in Mason (ed.), *Cambridge Minds*, pp. 1–19; Peter Stansky, *On or About December 1910* (Cambridge, MA: Harvard University Press, 1996).

5 See Jeremy Gray, 'Mathematics at Cambridge and Beyond', in Mason (ed.), *Cambridge Minds*, pp. 86–99.

6 For example, Jack Morrell, *Science at Oxford, 1914–1939* (Oxford: Clarendon Press, 1997); Michael Shortland and Richard Yeo (eds), *Telling Lives in Science* (Cambridge University Press, 1996).

7 Simon Schaffer, 'Glass Works: Newton's Prisms and the Uses of Experiment', in David Gooding, Trevor Pinch, Simon Schaffer (eds), *The Uses of Experiment* (Cambridge University Press, 1989), pp. 67–104; Geoffrey Cantor, *Michael Faraday: Sandemanian and Scientist* (Basingstoke: Macmillan, 1991), pp. 110–18.

8 I owe this information to Professor Chris Calladine.

9 Ulf Larsson (ed.), *Cultures of Creativity* (Canton, MA: Science History Publications, 2001), pp. 194–9.

10 This position has been argued by Richard S. Westfall, 'Isaac Newton in Cambridge: The Restoration University and Scientific Creativity', in Perez Zagorin (ed.), *Culture and Politics from Puritanism to the Enlightenment* (Berkeley: University of California Press, 1980), pp. 135–64. For a contrary view, which gives more weight to the importance of friendship and collaboration and takes into account botanising and collecting, as well as experiment, see Charles E. Raven, *John Ray: Naturalist*, 2nd edition (Cambridge University Press, 1986), pp. 21–141. It is astonishing that *Cambridge Scientific Minds* contains no consideration of the biological sciences whatsoever; for a different perspective, see S.M. Walters, *The Shaping of Cambridge Botany* (Cambridge University Press, 1981).

11 See Gary Werskey, *The Visible College* (London: Allen Lane, 1978), especially pp. 19–43.

Comparative Criticism XXV, pp. 255–265.   © 2004 Edinburgh University Press
Printed in the United Kingdom

Composing and decomposing the corpus of William Beckford: French and English Beckford

ELINOR SHAFFER

The publication of the volume of *Vathek with the Episodes* constitutes a landmark, for the minor classic *Vathek* (1786) has never before in English appeared with the Episodes Beckford intended to include, the tales of the damned waiting in the anteroom to hell. The tale of the manuscript and the misadventures that have dogged it are worthy of a romancer: Beckford wrote the novel in French (like many of his works), and handed it to his translator, the Rev. Samuel Henley, without the Episodes, which were not yet quite finished; Henley pirated the work, publishing his English translation without permission in 1786, and without the Episodes, claiming that the work was translated from the Arabic, and supplying his own notes on the Oriental references. Beckford was understandably infuriated and hastened to publish his own, original French version in Lausanne, still without the Episodes, dated 1787. Later that year he published an amended version of the main text in Paris. Although Beckford never altogether gave up on publishing them, they remained a rumour

---

*A review of *Beckford: Vathek et ses épisodes*, ed. Didier Girard (Paris: Jose Corti *Domaine romantique*, 2003);

Beckford: L'Esplendente et autres contes inédits, ed. Didier Girard (Paris: José Corti *Domaine Romantique*, 2003);

William Beckford, *Vathek with the Episodes of Vathek*, ed. Kenneth Graham (Calgary: Broadview Literary Texts, 2001);

Timothy Mowl, *William Beckford: Composing for Mozart* (John Murray, 1998);

William Beckford 1760-1844: An Eye for the Magnificent. Catalogue of an Exhibition at the Bard Graduate Center for Studies in the Decorative Arts, Design and Culture, New York October 18, 2001-January 6, 2002 and the Dulwich Picture Gallery, London, February 5-April 14, 2002 (New York: The Bard Graduate Center, 2001)

until 1912, when they were published in French and English, edited by Beckford's first biographer, Lewis Melville, in a translation by T. Marzials—but without the rest of *Vathek* (which on its own had had thirty-three editions by the turn of the century).

Vathek with the *Episodes* appeared in French, edited by Guy Chapman, in 1929. There have been a number of later editions in several languages, but in English *Vathek with the Episodes* has never before appeared. Roger Lonsdale in the standard Oxford edition of *Vathek* (1970) refers to them briefly, and gives their titles in a footnote, but does not describe their content. The present Editor, Kenneth Graham, a senior Beckford scholar, has himself in the past opposed publishing them together, on the grounds that it might bring *Vathek* 's well-established position into dispute. It is good that he has changed his mind and at last placed the whole work before the English-language audience.

Not only the piracy of *Vathek*, but other unforeseen events stood in the way of publication of the Episodes. A scandal had broken over Beckford in 1784, relating to a young friend, William Courtenay, then sixteen, with whom he was accused (by the boy's uncle, a political enemy) of having had illicit relations, and he had left the country for Switzerland in 1785. Precipitated into publication by the piracy, and fearing further damage to his reputation, he may have hesitated to publish the Episodes, the first of which, *Histoire des deux princes amis, Alasi & Firouz* is a moving and terrifying tale of an obsession with a boy of thirteen; the second, a story of the innocent yet sensual love of a brother and sister, Zulkais and Kalilah; the third, a grosser tale of Prince Barkiarokh. In the Lausanne edition a fourth tale was mentioned, but without supplying the name of the main character. Moreover, the ending of *Zulkais and Kalilah* has since been 'lost', but there is reason to believe that it existed in manuscript into the twentieth century, for there is a report of its ending. In addition, both Graham and Girard include *Histoire du prince Alasi et de la princesse Firouzkah,* the softened or bowdlerized version of *Prince Alasi,* which Beckford appears to have rewritten in order to make it more palatable, probably in the 1830's, as he again considered publishing the Episodes and had fair copies made. In this version, the second prince (Firouz) is revealed as a woman (Firouzkah), which greatly weakens the impact of the tale. Graham and Girard agree in viewing this as a later and inferior variant, not 'travesti' but 'travestissement'. Girard in addition argues that this order of the tales is incorrect, and that in line with the genre of the 'suite' of tales *Barkariokh* constitutes a change of tone, a grotesque and humorous interlude, and should occupy the second position, while the affecting tale of Zulkais and Kalilah should be the third. The 'lost' ending, which if the report is to be credited, involves an enactment of the sexual nature of their feelings in a spectacular setting within a pyramid, may have been thought a too shocking finale to the three tales. Both editors rightly hold that the *Episodes* were not intended to stand on their own, but must be restored to their original place as tales of the damned in the hell to which Vathek too comes. This would occasion a reassessment of the novel as a whole in its eighteenth-century context and thus begin to establish its place in the twenty-first century.

These two volumes edited by Didier Girard make nine volumes devoted to the works of William Beckford (1760-1844) from José Corti, a small French publisher specializing in Romantic texts. The first appeared as long ago as 1986, a translation of Beckford's Portuguese journals (discovered only in the 1950's), by the veteran Beckford scholar and translator, Roger Kann; the second, also by Kann, a translation of Beckford's travels in Italy, *Dreams, Waking Thoughts and Incidents*, superbly titled *Voyage d'un rêveur éveillé*. The third was by the *éminence grise* of French Beckford scholarship, André Parreaux, who in 1960 wrote the best and most substantial work on Beckford to date, never translated into English, and in Corti's series translated Beckford's last published work, often considered his best, his description of his journeys to the exquisite Portuguese monasteries of Alcobaça and Batalha (1835). The fourth was again by Kann, a translation of Beckford's brilliant essay, written when he was seventeen, his first publication, *Biographical Memoirs of Extraordinary Painters*, again improved in translation as *Vies authentiques de peintres imaginaires*. The four most recent volumes have been edited by Didier Girard, together with his critical essay on Beckford of 1993. Girard's volumes continue the work of the distinguished French Beckfordians, bringing over from manuscript and printed text two volumes that Beckford himself wrote in French: the *Suite de contes arabes* (1992), and one Arabian tale, 'Histoire du prince Ahmed' (1993); and now, in the present volumes, *L'Esplendente et autres contes inédits*, bringing five tales that Beckford wrote in English into French (translations provided by Sophie Mondiès and Christophe Sagnet) and two he wrote in French, *Histoire de Kebal* and *Histoire de Mazin*; and, finally, the French *Vathek*.

In this volume of *Vathek et ses Episodes* it is especially welcome that Girard in addition to his meticulous text reprints Mallarmé's Preface to *Vathek* of 1876, which established Beckford's reputation in France, where he has ever since been more highly valued than in England. Girard also includes a Note on orthography and a *postface*, 'Totem: A la mémoire d'un manuscrit', a title which half conceals a useful introductory essay.

The text that the editor is giving us is, strikingly, that of the Lausanne edition of 1787, the first French text, and the first authorized by Beckford: *Vathec* (in the French spelling). Girard makes a strong claim for this text as the original, and as the one that Mallarmé read and championed, and the one that Byron prized. It has sometimes been considered inferior to the Paris text, because of the 'Anglicisms' in the text, which were largely removed in the Paris text. Girard argues that these have been exaggerated (often by critics who were unfamiliar with eighteenth-century usage in French or English). More important is that this text is closer to Beckford's original, which had already been changed in the translation, perhaps to give colour to Henley's claim to have translated it from the Arabic. As Borges wittily said, 'The original is unfaithful to the translation', highlighting the fact that Beckford's English readers have never read the original.

Girard argues further that Beckford had begun by writing a philo-sophical tale, a *conte philosophique*, and had ended with a *conte exotique*. Girard earlier put the case in his book *William Beckford, terroriste au palais de la raison* (Corti 1993) for a Beckford whose allegiances were initially closer to the Enlightenment than to Romantic Orientalism, whereas recent interpretations have moved Beckford closer to Romanticism, in line with the general tendency for the capacious and dominant Romantic movement to absorb what used to be called 'pre-Romantic' writers. Mallarmé, whose brilliant preface is a work of art in its own right, presents a subtle picture, supplying the historical parameters in which *Vathek* is indeed a French work, a summation of the *conte morale* (and *immorale*) that had been brought to a high pitch in France since the translation of the *Arabian Nights* by Galland in 1700, that is, a 'travesti' of Oriental style. Mallarmé is excited by the book as a missing link, a jewel in the crown of French literature (so for him too 'Anglicisms' are beside the point); there is a shock of recognition when he compares it to the only work that could challenge it in the nineteenth century, Flaubert's *St Julien*. This is high praise indeed; and it is illuminating of both works (as well as of other works briefly mentioned as reference points, Flaubert's *Salammbô*, his novel of the destroyed civilization of Carthage, Merimée's tales, and earlier, Sébastien Mercier, who it was rumoured may have been instrumental in publishing the Paris edition). It is not merely the exotic settings that bring Beckford and Flaubert together but the strange, charged yet dreamlike atmosphere, fervid, sensual, with a streak of cruelty, that in *St Julien* characterizes the Christian crusader, in *Vathek* the Muslim Caliph. The union of

Enlightenment irony at the expense of religions (all of which were held to be Oriental in origin and nature) with the masterly deployment of Oriental motifs and décor is characteristic of the genre. Mallarmé recreates his own excitement as he searched in libraries and bookstalls for the few extant copies of *Vathec* in France—the lost masterpiece of French literature. His biographical information is sparse, and sometimes inaccurate, but this only adds to the effect of discovery of a lost work, an unknown master.

These *contes* are compelling in themselves, as well as throwing light on *Vathek* and the *Episodes*, and on the adaptation of the French *conte* in England. Girard's organization of them into two mixed volumes does as much to obscure their possible relationship to *Vathek and the Episodes* as to display it. *L'Esplendente* does not fit the category of the conte; it is a substantial (75-page) novella of the apprenticeship of a seventeenth-century artist, and needs to be considered together with the *Biographical Memoirs* of imaginary artsts.

One of the most powerful of the *contes* is *Histoire de Darianoc* (published in the first volume of 1992), which is closely related to *Vathek and the Episodes* in its study of a young man's gradual yet inexorable, self-compelled descent into an impressively articulated and visualized series of hells. This major *conte* cannot be isolated but must be seen in the full suite of *contes* related to it; Girard's earlier volume provided only three of them, and one must still look to Parreaux for a fuller listing. (See E. S. Shaffer, 'Milton's Hell: William Beckford's place in the graphic and the literary tradition', in *Milton, the Metaphysicals and Romanticism* (CUP, 1994) for a discussion and translation of some passages into English.) In the new volume the two *contes* Beckford wrote in French also throw light on *Vathek and the Episodes*. *Mazin* represents a tale closer to its sources, the adventures related over 100 pages of a poor young man in Basra and his widowed mother who through a series of unfolding and interlocking tales in which his curiosity and gullibility, and a Beckfordian aesthetic susceptibility, bring him into successive dangers and trials by sorcery. The theme of the magic mountain to which an evil sorcerer lures forty children to their deaths (here Mazin is one of the intended victims) is close to *Vathek*; and the menacing nature of Eblis is fully rooted in folk belief and geography. Some passages, in which architectural settings represent and frame the intense sensuous delight that leads Mazin on, stake out Beckford's special territory as an artist. In the short but powerful tale of *Kebal, roi de Damas*, the love of an innocent brother and sister (Reza and Dilara achieve in their brief moment an intensity akin to Romeo and Juliet) is again a major theme of *Vathek and the Episodes*. All these materials need ordering and annotating, indeed, extended critical comment; Mallarmé is quite right that it is primarily a French context, and one in which Beckford was steeped. In the meantime, Girard's occasional notes are useful in pinpointing the geographical realities of Beckford's exotic places.

It is sad to have to say that the situation is bleaker on this side of the Channel. (Graham is in a Canadian university.) Girard makes a negative assessment of English Beckfordians, who he says have made too little use of the manuscript collection that came to the Bodleian in the 1980's. That too little of it has been published there is no doubt, and we all owe Didier Girard a debt of gratitude for bringing the French-language writings and now also some of the English MSS to book form. The English Beckfordians have at least done their utmost to alter attitudes to Beckford, through their association journal, lectures and events and have produced a good many useful works in recent years—to name but two outstanding examples, the path-breaking work of John Wilton-Ely on the architecture of Fonthill, and the work of Anthony Hobson on Beckford's book collecting. Several of them have been moving forces in the admirable exhibition and catalogue reviewed below.

The main stumbling-block to the overdue reassessment of Beckford is the recent biographers, in particular Timothy Mowl, who has reverted to the bad old days, and morever has done so with relish. Beckford was always 'good copy', and it is perhaps not surprising that a certain kind of writer continues to try to make scandal-sheet headlines with him. Beckford, scion of 'nouveaux riches' in the Jamaican sugar trade, son of a well-known Whig politician who was twice Lord Mayor of London, with aristocratic links through his mother with the Hamilton family, touted as 'England's wealthiest son' (Byron's ever-quoted phrase), ambitious to be raised to the peerage, came into his inheritance at age twenty-one. So much is already a juicy story in the making. That this was capped by a homosexual scandal four years later, in a day when sodomy was a hanging offence, makes it irresistible. But in addition he became famous (and again infamous) for his grand architectural venture, his construction of Fonthill Abbey (having dismantled his father's neo-classic mansion) on the Wiltshire estate he inherited; the public sale in 1823 of the fabled contents, when the closely guarded Fonthill was opened to the public and tickets sold, attracted further notoriety. When this major piece of Romantic Gothic building fell down a few years later, the fictive image of the tower falling around the visionary owner became ensconced in legend;

the fact that its owner had in fact sold the Abbey for a very tidy sum and moved to a comfortable crescent in Bath where he lived to a ripe old age is forgotten. The elements of legend are in place: spoilt child, mad fantasist, spendthrift 'lord', demonic solitary, failed visionary. Beckford became an 'eccentric', at best an 'English eccentric', whose dangerous and dark side could be comfortably accommodated and his oddities trivialized. His career as a writer has only barely survived the prurience, condescension, envy, malice and snobbery roused by these 'facts'.

Mowl, however, is not satisfied with warming up old scandal; he spices up the familiar brew with new inventions of his own. Moreover, he deploys a loose language of insult which past writers, mindful of the circumspection with which some of the material had to be handled in the days before statutes and mores changed, took care to avoid. Mowl is a name-caller: Beckford he calls a 'liar', a 'traitor to his country', a 'barely socialized psychopath', 'madman', 'paedophile', 'forger'. More, he 'corrupted' the 'simple' British taste of his countrymen by importing 'alien French design' and 'international eclecticism' (p. 277). The pretexts for these loaded and defamatory charges are flimsy indeed: Beckford (himself a musician) claimed to have originated a tune that Mozart later used in a well-known aria—well, many people thought Mozart had lifted tunes, for he heard them all about him and transformed them; 'traitor'—well, he at times thought Napoleon would win in Europe (as who did not) and thought about the consequences; 'barely socialized psychopath'— this extraordinary phrase (p. 111) is a comment on a letter of Beckford's to his cousin's wife Louisa reminding her of their shared moment of 'seduction' (Mowl's word); 'paedophile'—he was bisexual, and the two main homosexual affairs we know about were with sixteen-year-old boys, Courtenay and his later companion and agent, Gregorio Franchi (though Mowl gives scant consideration to his love for women, whether his wife Margaret, mother of his two children, who died giving birth to the second; Louisa, with whom his correspondence certainly suggests an affair; or Lady Hamilton, with whom the relationship was a close friendship).'Forger': he rewrote his own letters in later years—well, this was one of his primary means of composition throughout his life (for example, the journal letters to Cozens that he reworked for *Dreams, Waking Thoughts and Incidents*), and he had versions of them written out by an amanuensis, as well as keeping the originals; these drafts were his own manuscripts, his working papers, his raw materials. This is fascinating (hardly reprehensible), and a good edition of his correspondence would reveal a great deal of critical interest about his writerly life.

Mowl's gratuitous mud-slinging finds a kind of explanation late in the book, where he sets out a half-baked theory of homosexual characterology: according to him, 'generally theatrical excess predominates' among gays. At least he stops short of suggesting there is a gene for homosexual bad taste.

Mowl's irresponsible book made a bid to put the biographical study of Beckford back a hundred years, to its beginnings in the first decade of the twentieth century in the unreliable *DNB* entry that in turn depended on a merely anecdotal memoir of 1859 by Cyrus Redding.

Fortunately, the large-scale Exhibition of Beckford at the Bard Graduate Center in New York in 2001 and the Dulwich Gallery in London in 2002 generated a massive catalogue, *William Beckford 1760-1844: An Eye for the Magnificent* (Bard Graduate Center, 2001) which gives an overview of scholarly and curatorial work in the last half century on Beckford's contributions to the development of English painting, silver and furniture design, collecting, landscape gardening and much else (although architecture is unaccountably omitted). This Anglo-American exhibition catalogue, learned and sumptuous, is state-of-the-art in Beckford studies. It gives the lie to Mowl's assertions about the corrupting influence of Beckford's 'French' taste on the nation (already knowledgeably refuted by Andrew Ballantyne's *TLS* review (Sept. 18, 1998)). Mowl's book shows virtually no knowledge of these developments despite earlier publications by most of the contributors (some of which appear in his bibliography); his notion that Beckford 'corrupted English taste' by his foreign importations is simply laughable in the light of them. These new developments have not been carried out by literary scholars, and certainly not by biographers, but by museum curators.

Very significant work has been done on the development of English landscape painting into the leading British art form, in which Alexander Cozens, Beckford's art master, played a leading role as theorist and practitioner, and his son, John Robert Cozens, commissioned by Beckford, executed major paintings and sketchbooks, copied by Turner in the 1790's. As Kim Sloan (building on A. P. Oppé's work on the Cozenses in the 1950's) has shown in her book *Alexander and John Robert Cozens: The Poetry of Landscape* (Yale University Press, 1986), Beckford's commissioning of John Robert, who accompanied him on his second Italian journey, was a crucial intervention in this history. (Mowl refers to him merely as 'Beckford's tame artist' (119).) The influence of his tutor on Beckford's own descriptive style has always been recognized, though not well understood; Sloan (now a curator at the British Museum) examined in detail the nature of Alexander Cozens's writings on art, in particular his attempts, in *The Various Species of Landscape...in Nature*, to analyze pictorial elements and to match them with particular moods of the sublime. Beckford's experiments in prose vision in his early work were steeped in these teachings. This is quite separate from the heuristic 'blot method' Cozens drew from Leonardo, building up a painting from random initial forms, which he wrote up only in 1785, and found to be in advance of his time by much later artists. Typical of Mowl's ill-grounded gibes is his claim that Cozens's 'ugly blot method' ruined Beckford's literary style!

Specialist curators of the Victoria and Albert Museum, which has a number of pieces from the Beckford collections, have led the way on Beckford's collecting. They have also shown that Beckford himself played a role in designing objects he commissioned. Clive Wainwright's fine book *The Romantic Interior: The British Collector at Home 1750–1850* (Yale University Press, 1989) with its chapter on Beckford's design and furnishing of Fonthill, held that Beckford's detailed notes on the provenance of his extensive collections were not wild or fanciful, as had often been alleged, but were for the most part substantially correct as far as the knowledge of his time extended, and would reward further study. Mowl by contrast sneers at Beckford's attributions, while at the same time attacking him for his acute collector's judgement, repeatedly referring to him as a 'dealer'.

Thus the specialists have been quietly unearthing the detailed history of their own disciplines, whether the development of English watercolour painting through Alexander Cozens and Beckford's commissions to John Robert Cozens; Beckford's informed and passionate purchases of first-rate paintings (twenty-eight of them have ended in the National Gallery, as Jeannie Chapel's excellent essay shows); Beckford's contacts, commissions and purchases in Paris (a fine piece of sleuthing by Anne Eschapasse); the history of the invention of 'Gothic' furniture (Wainwright); metalwork and the use of hardstone in designs commissioned by Beckford (Michael Snodin, who with Philip Baker, his V&A colleague, has published a good deal of path-breaking research on Beckford's silver); the beginnings of trade in Japanese red lacquerware of which Beckford was a pioneer collector (Impey and Whitehead). The two major curators of the Exhibition, both British, Philip Hewat-Jaboor and Bet McLeod, have documented for the first time the dispersal of Beckford's furnishings and *objets d'art* in Britain, Europe and the United States through successive sales of the Hamilton family, and Jon Millington has provided a bibliography that represents decades of dedicated work on the part of a leading 'English Beckfordian'. This exhibition and its catalogue, its fifteen contributors of essays and thirty-six entry-writers (some overlapping with the contributors), have provided ample proofs of Beckford's major contributions to the arts in Britain. It is typical of such fundamental research that new biographical information and insight comes to light as a by-product: for example, in order to trace his buying for Beckford and his role in the design of commissioned items, the letters in Portuguese from his agent and companion Gregorio Franchi have at last been translated into English (though still not published in full); this shared professional enthusiasm sheds light on their relationship, about which the partial collection and translation of Beckford's letters to Franchi in *Life at Fonthill* (edited by Boyd Alexander in 1957) can now be seen to have been misleading. Only these detailed specialist studies have begun to give us not only the basis of a just view of his contributions to the arts, but the materials for biography based on fact, not rumour or prejudice or what Beckford himself termed 'ten thousand malevolent insinuations'.

It is now urgent that a proper edition of Beckford's works be produced. Corti has been gradually producing something like an edition of Beckford in French. But while it is eminently readable and helps to fill a void, it is not a full scholarly edition. An edition in English has never existed, not even to the extent of nine volumes being produced by one publisher of good will over a period of time, and it is long overdue that an edition of Beckford in English should be initiated. Ideal would be a bilingual edition, with those texts that Beckford wrote in French in their original form, and those that he wrote in English in their original form, together with translations of both into the other language. Corti has provided much of the necessary translation into French, though the *contes arabes* require translation into English and much more extensive commentary. The translation into English by Frank T. Marzials of the *Episodes* (1912) needs to be checked and if necessary revised or undertaken afresh. Kenneth Graham uses Marzials, while supplying his own translation into English of the Firouzkah variant. Graham is currently working on a further volume, for AMS Press (New York), a fully bilingual edition of *Vathek and the Episodes*, which would make a start. The letters too, a brilliant eighteenth-century correspondence to rank with the best in that epistolary century— letters in French and English and Italian, to correspondents writing in French and English and Portuguese—remain unedited, available only in unreliable partial quotations scattered through a hundred years of inadequate biographies. OUP, whose responsibilities to English literature should make it the obvious publisher, has agreed only to a one-volume selection of the letters. Thus while individual editors and small publishers abroad are inching towards making most of Beckford available in both his languages, nevertheless there is no edition of his works to which anyone seeking this 'lost' writer, a classic in two languages, can turn. Until this glaring omission is put right, no justice can be done to Beckford, as a writer, or as a man.

Comparative Criticism XXV, pp. 267–269. © 2004 Edinburgh University Press
Printed in the United Kingdom

Books and periodicals received

COMPILED BY ANDREA BRADY

Anderson, Amanda, *The Powers of Distance: Cosmopolitanism and the Cultivation of Detachment*. Princeton University Press, 2001

Atik, Anne, *How It Was: A Memoir of Samuel Beckett*. London: Faber and Faber, 2001

Auden, W. H., *Juvenilia: Poems 1922-1928*. Edited by Katherine Bucknell. Princeton University Press, 2003

Beckford, William, *L'Esplendente et Autres Contes Inédits*. Edited by Didier Girard. Paris: José Corti, 2003

Beckford, William, *Vathek et Ses Épisodes*. Edited by Didier Girard. Paris: José Corti, 2003

Beer, Dan, *Michel Foucault: Form and Power*. Legenda. European Humanities Research Centre, University of Oxford, 2002

Beer, John, *Post-Romantic Consciousness, Dickens to Plath*. New York and Basingstoke: Palgrave Macmillan, 2003

Bernstein, J. M., ed. *Classic and Romantic German Aesthetics*. Cambridge Texts in the History of Philosophy. Cambridge University Press, 2003

Broadie, Alexander, ed. *The Cambridge Companion to the Scottish Enlightenment*. Cambridge University Press, 2003

Callaghan, Dympna, *A Feminist Companion to Shakespeare*. Malden, Massachusetts and Oxford: Blackwell, 2001

Champion, Justin, *Republican Learning: John Toland and the Crisis of Christian Culture, 1696-1722*. Manchester and New York: Manchester University Press, 2003

Chapman, Alison and Jane Stabler, eds., *Unfolding the South: Nineteenth-Century British Women Writers and Artists in Italy*. Manchester and New York: Manchester University Press, 2003

Chaudhuri, Amit, *D. H. Lawrence and 'Difference': Postcoloniality and the Poetry of the Present*. With a Foreword by Tom Paulin. Oxford: Clarendon Press, 2003

Chrisman, Laura, *Postcolonial Contraventions: Cultural Readings of Race, Imperialism and Transnationalism*. Manchester and New York: Manchester University Press, 2003

Crofts, Charlotte, *'Anagrams of Desire': Angela Carter's Writing for Radio, Film and Television*. Manchester and New York: Manchester University Press, 2003

Dobson, Michael and Nicola J. Watson, *England's Elizabeth: An Afterlife in Fame and Fantasy*. Oxford University Press, 2002

Eagleton, Terry, *The Idea of Culture*. Blackwell Manifestos. Oxford and Malden, Massachusetts: Blackwell, 2002

Everest, Kelvin, *John Keats*. Writers and Their Work. Tavistock: Northcote House, 2002

Fegan, Melissa, *Literature and the Irish Famine 1845-1919*. Oxford: Clarendon Press, 2002

Fisher, Margaret, *Ezra Pound's Radio Operas: The BBC Experiments, 1931-1933*. Cambridge, Massachusetts and London: MIT Press, 2002

Foakes, R. A., *Shakespeare and Violence*. Cambridge University Press, 2003

France, Peter and William St. Clair, eds., *Mapping Lives: The Uses of Biography*. Oxford University Press for the British Academy, 2002

Gaylin, Ann, *Eavesdropping in the Novel, from Austen to Proust*. Cambridge Studies in Nineteenth Century Literature and Culture. Cambridge University Press, 2002

Glen, Heather, *Charlotte Brontë: The Imagination in History*. Oxford University Press, 2002

Gifford, Zerbanoo, *Thomas Clarkson and the Campaign Against Slavery*. London: Anti-Slavery International, 1996

Guth, Deborah, *George Eliot and Schiller: Intertextuality and Cross-Cultural Discourse*. Warwick Studies in the Humanities. Aldershot: Ashgate, 2003

Hall, Edith, Fiona Macintosh and Oliver Taplin, eds., *Medea in Performance 1500-2000*. Legenda. European Humanities Research Centre, University of Oxford, 2000

Hartman, Geoffrey, *The Longest Shadow: In the Aftermath of the Holocaust*. New York and Basingstoke: Palgrave Macmillan, 2002

Henry, Nancy, *George Eliot and the British Empire*. Cambridge University Press, 2002

Hulme, Peter and Tim Youngs, eds., *The Cambridge Companion to Travel Writing*. Cambridge University Press, 2002

Humble, Nicola, *The Feminine Middlebrow Novel 1920s to 1950s: Class, Domesticity, and Bohemianism*. Oxford University Press, 2001

Jack, Malcolm, *Sintra: A Glorious Eden*. Manchester: Carcanet, in association with The Calouste Gulbenkian Foundation, 2002

Jensen, Margaret M., *The Open Book: Creative Misreading in the Works of Selected Modern Writers*. New York and Basingstoke: Palgrave Macmillan, 2002

Kahlfa, Jean, *The Dialogue between Painting and Poetry*. Livres d'Artistes 1874-1999. Cambridge: Black Apollo, 2001

Kenyon-Jones, Christine, *Kindred Brutes: Animals in Romantic-Period Writing*. Aldershot: Ashgate, 2001

Lapidus, Rina, *Between Snow & Desert Heat: Russian Influences on Hebrew Literature, 1870-1970*. Translated from the Hebrew by Jonathan Chipman. Cincinnati, Ohio: Hebrew Union College Press, 2003

Large, Duncan, *Nietzsche and Proust: A Comparative Study*. Oxford Modern Languages and Literature Monographs. Oxford: Clarendon Press, 2001

Ledbetter, Grace M., *Poetics Before Plato: Interpretation and Authority in Early Greek Theories of Poetry*. Princeton University Press, 2003

Lombardo, Patrizia, *Cities, Words and Images from Poe to Scorsese*. Language, Discourse, Society. New York and Basingstoke: Palgrave Macmillan, 2003

Low, Setha M. and Denise Lawrence-Zúñiga, eds. *The Anthropology of Space and Place: Locating Culture*. Blackwell Readers in Anthropology. Malden, Massachusetts and Oxford: Blackwell, 2003

MacCarthy, Fiona, *Byron: Life and Legend*. London: John Murray, 2002

Mander, Jenny, *Circles of Learning: Narratology and the Eighteenth-Century French Novel*. Oxford: Voltaire Foundation, 1999

Montag, Warren, *Louis Althusser*. Transitions. New York and Basingstoke: Palgrave Macmillan, 2003

Monteieth, Sharon, *Pat Barker*. Writers and Their Work. Tavistock: Northcote House, 2002

Morris, Jan, *Trieste and the Meaning of Nowhere*. London: Faber and Faber, 2001

Nalbantian, Suzanne, *Memory in Literature: From Rousseau to Neuroscience*. Basingstoke: Palgrave Macmillan, 2003

Pocock, J. G. A., *Barbarism and Religion*. Volume 3: The First Decline and Fall. Cambridge University Press, 2003

Pushkin, Alexander, *The Bridegroom, with Count Nulin and The Tale of the Golden Cockerel*. Translated by Antony Wood. London: Angel Books, 2002

Rabaté, Jean-Michel, *The Future of Theory*. Blackwell Manifestos. Oxford and Malden, Massachusetts: Blackwell, 2002

Robson, Catherine, *Men in Wonderland: The Lost Girlhood of the Victorian Gentleman*. Princeton University Press, 2001

Ryan, Michael, *Literary Theory: A Practical Introduction*. Oxford: Blackwell, 1999

Schuster, Shlomit C., *The Philosopher's Autobiography*. With a Foreword by Maurice Friedman. Westport, Connecticut and London: Praeger, 2003

Sebald, W. G., *On the Natural History of Destruction*. Translated from the German by Anthea Bell. London: Hamish Hamilton, 2003

Small, Helen and Trudi Tate, eds., *Literature, Science, Psychoanalysis, 1830-1970: Essays in Honour of Gillian Beer*. Oxford University Press, 2003

Spurling, Hilary, *The Girl from the Fiction Department: A Portrait of Sonia Orwell*. London and New York: Hamish Hamilton, 2002

Taussig, Gurion, *Coleridge and the Idea of Friendship, 1789-1804*. Newark: University of Delaware Press and London: Associated University Presses, 2002

Tomalin, Claire, *Samuel Pepys: The Unequalled Self*. London and New York: Viking Penguin, 2003

Ulea, V., *A Concept of Dramatic Genre and the Comedy of a New Type: Chess, Literature, and Film*. Carbondale and Edwardsville: Southern Illinois University Press, 2002

Wilson, Eric G., *The Spiritual History of Ice: Romanticism, Science, and the Imagination*. New York and Basingstoke: Palgrave Macmillan, 2003

Wood, Jane, *Passion and Pathology in Victorian Fiction*. Oxford University Press, 2001

1. PERIODICALS RECEIVED

The Author 113.4 (Winter 2002)

Books from Finland 33 (1999), 34 (2000), 35 (2001)

The Coleridge Bulletin n.s. 20 (Winter 2002)

Comparative Literature and Culture Bulletin 1 (Sept. 1996)

Journal of Contemporary China 10.26 (February 2001)

Modern Language Review 96.1 (January 2001), 96.2 (April 2001), 96.4 (October 2001), 97.3 (July 2002)

Papers Read Before The English Goethe Society n.s. 71 (2001)

Paragraph: A Journal of Modern Critical Theory 22.2 (July 1999)

The Persephone Quarterly 2 (June 1999), 4 (December 1999)

PMLA 117.6 (November 2002), 118.1 (January 2003)

Stand 38.4 (Autumn 1997), 39.1 (Winter 1997), 39.2 (Spring 1998), 39.3 (Summer 1998), 39.4 (Autumn 1998), 40.1 (Winter 1998), 40.2 (Spring 1999), n.s. 1.2 (June 1999), 2.1 (March 2000)

The Wordsworth Circle 33.3 (Summer 2002)